WILD
SNOW

Guidebooks merely describe the skeleton,
leaving the memory to clothe it with romance.

—Arnold Lunn

WILD SNOW

A HISTORICAL GUIDE
TO NORTH AMERICAN
SKI MOUNTAINEERING

Louis W. Dawson

With 54 Selected Classic Routes, 214 photographs, and 10 maps.

THE AAC PRESS

THE AMERICAN
ALPINE BOOK SERIES
edited by
Jonathan Waterman

◀ Steven Koch rides off the 20,320-foot highpoint of North America,
Denali. *Wade McKoy*

THE AAC PRESS

Published by
The American Alpine Club
710 Tenth Street / Suite 100
Golden, Colorado 80401
(303) 384-0110

The AAC was founded in 1902 and began publishing in 1907. It is a public foundation supported by concerned alpinists. The Press is dedicated to the dissemination of knowledge pertaining to conservation, safety, and the art of mountaineering.

This publication made possible through the support of W.L. Gore & Associates, manufacturers of Gore-Tex® and WindStopper® fabrics and the Premier Sponsor of AAC Press.

Maps by John McMullen, SoloGraphics

ISBN 0-930410-68-8 Manufactured in the U.S.A.

First Edition

Front cover: Art Burroughs throwing breakable crust, Hayden Peak's North Summit. *Michael Kennedy*

Back cover author photo: *Jonathan Waterman*

To Lisa

Louis Dawson

Louis Dawson

Acknowledgments

A book such as this is a community project, and the following community members deserve a strong thanks for their help, support, and contributions to this book and to glisse alpinism:

Anchorage Convention and Visitors Bureau, Bruce Adams, Paul Arthur, Greg Balco, Alan Bard, David Beck, Brian Becker, Fritz Benedict, George Bell, Bill Clark, John Baldwin, Bill Briggs, Mark Bridges, Larry Bruce, Molly Bruce, Rainer Burgdorfer, Peter Chrzanowski, Jo Ann Creore, Russ Criswell, Bil Dunaway, Lisa Dawson, Tomas Dawson, Patricia Dawson, Craig Dostie, Shawn Emery, David Eye, Chris Fellows, Roberts French, Scott Garen, David Goodman, Fletcher Hoyt, Vic Hains, Dave Hale, Susan Hale, Jim Havraneck, Jack Hildebrand, Renny Jackson, Julie Kennedy, Michael Kennedy, Ted Kerasote, Kent Kantowski, Michael Kelsey, North American Telemark Organization, Tim Lane, Brian Litz, Philip LaLena, Chris Landry, Gregg Lowe, Andrew McLean, Kim Miller, John Moynier, Brian Povolny, Marilyn Murphy, Glenn Randall, Doug Robinson, Gay Roesch, David Rothman, Terry Schaefer, Chic Scott, Andy Selters, Basil Service, Steve Shea, Lowell Skoog, Bob Slozen, Hans and Lillian Spieler, Thomas Turiano, Stan Wagon, Jonathan Waterman, Gordon Whitmer, Kendall Williams, Peter Williams, Rick Wyatt, Bela and Mimi Vadasz, Michael Zanger.

More than 100 people and institutions helped with the photographic selection for *Wild Snow*, many for little or no remuneration. Photos not requiring return to an archive or owner will be held for public viewing at the American Mountaineering Center in Golden, Colorado, in the American Alpine Club Ski Mountaineering Collection.

Nor could I have done the skiing described in many chapters of this book without the support of my sponsors: Alpine Underground shell clothing, Ascension Enterprises climbing skins, Yostmark skis, Extreme Energy Nutrition Bar, and Tua skis.

Contents

Map XVI
Author's Note. XIX
Foreword XXI
Preface. XXIII
Introduction XXV

7,000 Years of Backcountry Skiing:
The History of Glisse Alpinism 1

Peaks of Light: California Sierra
and San Gabriel Mountains 25

    Twin Peaks. 34
    Castle Peak 36
    Mount Tallac 38
    Matterhorn Peak 41
    Bloody Mountain 44
    Mount McGee 45
    Mount Tom. 46
    Mount Whitney. 47
    San Antonio Peak. 50

Wet and Scrappy:
Cascade Mountains 57

    Mount Baker 61
    Mount Rainier 63
    Mount Adams. 69
    Mount St. Helens 71
    Mount Hood 74
    Mount Shasta. 78

Ocean Winds: Coast Mountains
of British Columbia. 85

    Mount Munday 90
    Mount Matier. 92
    Mount Garibaldi 93
    Pelion Mountain 95
    Mount Seymour 98

Grizzlies and Big Drops:
Alaska and the Yukon 101

Denali 104
Hatch Peak 110
Flattop Mountain 112
Turnagain Pass 114
Grandview 116
Mount Sanford 117
Mount Logan 120

Infinite Glisse:
Canadian Rocky Mountains 125

Mount Resplendent 132
Snow Dome 134
Mount Gordon 138
Mount Field 140
Youngs Peak 141
Mount Brennan 143

Steep, Rocky and Wild:
Tetons of Wyoming 147

Mount Moran 156
Middle Teton 158
Buck Mountain 159
Static Peak 160

Powder Perfect:
Utah's Wasatch Mountains 163

Mount Olympus 170
Peak 10,420 173
Mount Superior 173
Y Couloir 175
Lone Peak 176
Mount Timpanogos 177

Fourteeners and Snowslides:
Colorado Rockies. 181
    Buffalo Mountain. 193
    Quandary Peak 195
    Castle Peak 196
    Hayden Peak 200
    Mount Sopris. 202
    Mount Elbert 205
    Humboldt Peak 206

Classic by Definition:
Mountains of the Northeast. 211
    Katahdin 218
    Mount Washington. 222
    Mount Marcy. 225
    Mount Greylock 227

Appendix 231
    Directory. 231

Selected Bibliography 235

Index 239

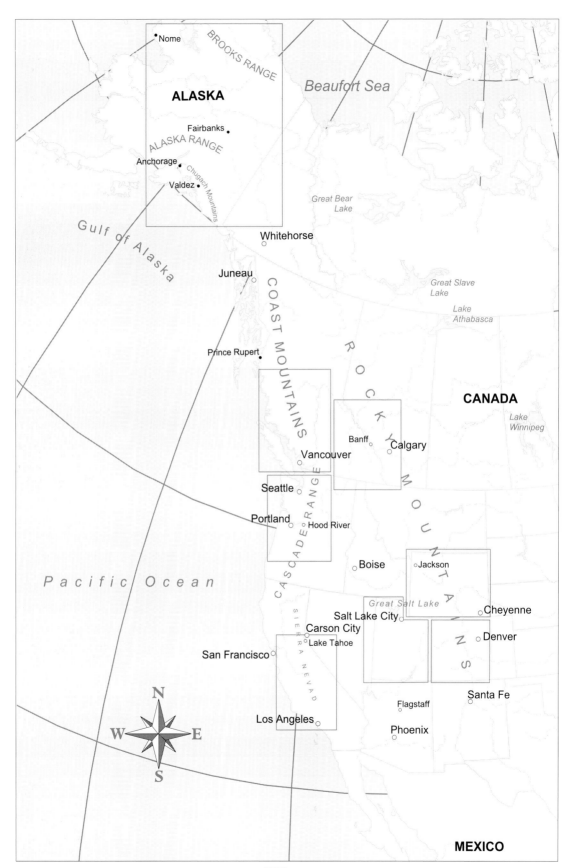

Nome

BROOKS RANGE

Beaufort Sea

ALASKA

Fairbanks

ALASKA RANGE

Anchorage

Chugach Mountains

Valdez

Great Bear Lake

Gulf of Alaska

Whitehorse

Great Slave Lake

Lake Athabasca

Juneau

COAST MOUNTAINS

Prince Rupert

R O C K Y

CANADA

Lake Winnipeg

Banff   Calgary

Vancouver

Seattle

CASCADE RANGE

Portland   Hood River

Boise

Jackson

M O U N T A I N S

Pacific Ocean

Great Salt Lake

Salt Lake City

Cheyenne

SIERRA NEVADA

Carson City

Lake Tahoe

Denver

San Francisco

N

W **E**

S

Flagstaff

Santa Fe

Los Angeles

Phoenix

MEXICO

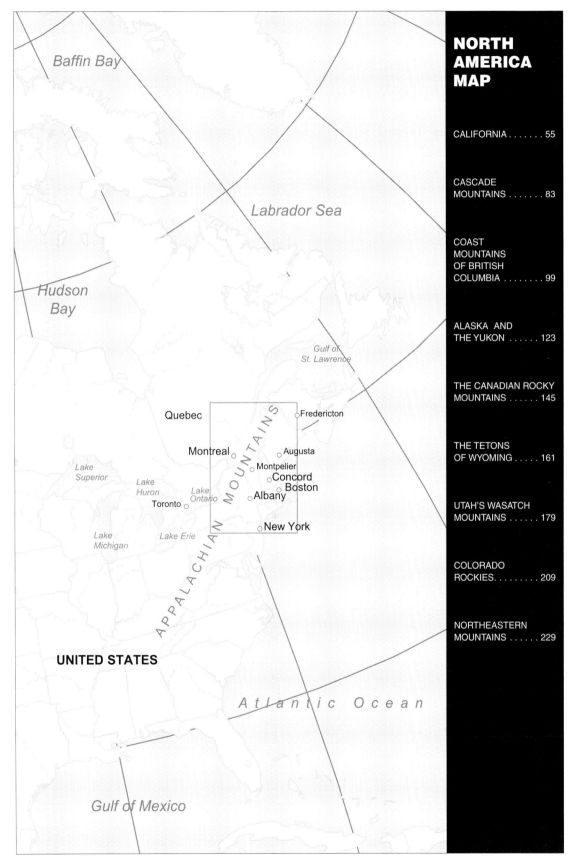

Baffin Bay

Labrador Sea

Hudson
Bay

Gulf of
St. Lawrence

Quebec

Fredericton

Montreal

Augusta

Montpelier

Concord

Boston

Lake
Superior

Lake
Huron

Lake
Ontario

Albany

Toronto

New York

Lake
Michigan

Lake Erie

APPALACHIAN MOUNTAINS

UNITED STATES

Atlantic Ocean

Gulf of Mexico

NORTH AMERICA MAP

CALIFORNIA 55

CASCADE
MOUNTAINS 83

COAST
MOUNTAINS
OF BRITISH
COLUMBIA 99

ALASKA AND
THE YUKON 123

THE CANADIAN ROCKY
MOUNTAINS 145

THE TETONS
OF WYOMING 161

UTAH'S WASATCH
MOUNTAINS 179

COLORADO
ROCKIES. 209

NORTHEASTERN
MOUNTAINS 229

Author's Note

Decades ago everyone used similar gear for ski mountaineering. Then came modern free-heel skiing; then snowboard riding. Now people even make *figle* and Bigfoot descents. Who knows what's next? Yet all these methods have one commonalty: you slide down snow on a steel-edged tool. In this book I use the inclusive term *glisse* to encompass every method of sliding down a mountain using an edged board. This includes, but is not limited to, skis (both free-heel and fixed-heel) and snowboards. Going a step further, I use the term *glisse alpinism* to include the broader activities associated with mountaineering, when a significant goal is to accomplish a descent—preferably from a summit—using glisse methods.

My use of the term glisse is derived from the French verb *glisser*, meaning to slide, the root word for the mountaineer's *glissade* or the musician's *glissando*. When I write the verb *to ski* in this book, unless (as in a historical context) it is clearly applied to the use of two planks, I mean to suggest sliding on skis *or on a snowboard*. When applied to travel over flat ground, or climbing, the verb *to ski* pertains to walking on snow with skis, a split snowboard, or the snowshoes that snowboarders sometimes use for climbing.

Another issue that will arise in this text is the potential for confusion in the naming of Mount McKinley, North America's highest peak. William McKinley was the United States President from 1897 to 1901, until assassinated in office. The mountain was named after him in 1896 (during his presidential campaign) by a prospector, William Dickey. Starting in the late 1960s, a movement arose to rename Mount McKinley with one of the native names for the mountain, Denali, meaning the "High One." The reasons for this vary from a desire to honor native people, to a distaste for politicians. Cultural politics aside, Denali is a beautifully concise name, officially chosen by the Alaska State Board of Geographic Names, and in common use by most mountaineers and Alaskans. In the same vein, the protected land surrounding the mountain was renamed Denali National Park and Preserve in 1980. Thus, I have used *Denali*.

◀ *Louis Dawson*

Foreword

When I was young, climbing and skiing were equally important to me. Both activities are more than just sports: they are ways of coming into intense and beautiful relationships with mountains, and that was what I wanted in my life. During this time I kept four books by my bed, books that I would return to again and again to refresh my dreams. They were Steve Roper's first edition of *The Climber's Guide to Yosemite Valley*, Hervey Voge's *A Climber's Guide to the High Sierra*, Alan Blackshaw's *Mountaineering*, and David Brower's *Manual of Ski Mountaineering*. On many evenings I would pore over the stunning black and white photographs of the pioneers of North American alpinism and the mountains they loved, and I would read the stories of their great feats until I knew them by heart. As my eyes grew heavy I would begin to dream myself into those pictures and stories, and beyond, into the adventures that I hoped I would someday lead.

As I grew, it became more and more clear to me that ski alpinism was the best way to combine my interests and achieve what David Brower has called "mountain blend." I also came to realize that by studying and respecting the history of alpinism, I could better understand where I was and where I was going. In fact, this historical dimension added tremendous fulfillment and enjoyment to my mountaineering, as I began to see that a landscape is more than just topography. After all, that's why we give places names: to associate them with stories that help us to understand our relation to them: Tuckerman Ravine, Pyramid Peak, the Sierra Crest.

When I first met Lou Dawson, we instantly understood each other. We both loved ski mountaineering, and we shared a passion for the history of the magnificent places in which we had chosen to live our lives. To me, Lou is one of the few great all-American ski mountaineers. Not only is his experience both wide and deep, in the sense that he has climbed and skied extensively all over North America, but he also has become the preeminent ski alpinist of his massive home range, the Colorado Rockies.

He has also become one of its greatest champions and chroniclers, as Lou has the gift of describing the routes he has skied (and often pioneered) in a way that respects both the mountains and their history. From the first, it was clear to me that the passion of "mountain blend" was ingrained in him too, and this is evident in the many fine guidebooks he has published, especially his two-volume guide to climbing and skiing Colorado's 54 peaks over fourteen thousand feet—a work only he could have written, as he is still the first and only person to have skied them all.

But in *Wild Snow* Lou does far more than write an outstanding guidebook, although it is that too. In this book Lou integrates his practical knowledge with years of historical study. He combines practical information on many of the greatest North American ski mountaineering routes with an unprecedented overview of the sport's surprisingly rich history on this continent. Whether you are contemplating your first peak or have been pursuing the sport for years, this book will inspire, inform, and educate you about the great achievements of glisse alpinism in the United States and Canada, and some of

◀ *Louis Dawson*

the greatest routes to be found anywhere in the world.

    This book could only have been written by a complete alpinist. Lou has found his route to the "Whole Mountain," which is not only the concrete thing, but the way it exists in the past as well as the present. As a result *Wild Snow,* like the books I treasured as a young man, will no doubt find its way to the bedside shelf of those who realize that the mountains present us not only with challenges, but also with the possibility of a creative way of life in harmony with our world.

—Bela G. Vadasz
Alpine Skills International

Preface

"Skiing is life." For myself and countless other ski mountaineers, those words ring as crisp today as they did when Otto Schniebs first uttered them more than 60 years ago. Schniebs searched out North America's best skiing. His quest often led away from the resorts and up to the mountains of the Appalachians, the Rockies, the Cascades, and others. Since then thousands of skiers have followed Schniebs's strides and turns into the winter wild of North America.

My strides as a ski mountaineer began in 1967, when I left my home in Aspen, Colorado and accompanied outdoor education pioneer Paul Petzoldt on one of his notorious New Year's Day Grand Teton attempts, which were a yearly event. After outfitting in Lander, Wyoming with skis of Schniebs's vintage, 20 pounds of wool, and 30 pounds of pasta, we rode in an unheated bus through a night of hypothermic torture north to the Tetons. Wyoming had sunk into typical midwinter cryogenics; daytime temperatures hovered around forty below zero. Like Siberian refugees, we walked the streets of Jackson in facemasks and expedition parkas.

With skins on our skis and 90-pound frame packs twisting our backs, we slogged up Garnet Canyon. An oldtimer broke trail while we tyros kept a lock-step in a deep trench behind. The cold was intense—as were the blue sky, the wind scoured canyon walls, and the smell of sweat-soaked wool as we labored. We set camp near the lower boulderfield and waited out a storm. One night the mercury plunged to 58-degrees below zero, and our tent filled with steam as we tried to cook soup on a dinky Svea stove. It was like cooking on a candle. We knocked over a billy of execrable gruel, which flowed like sludge under our wimpy sleeping bags. I got a sack of garlic tangled in my bag liner and couldn't get it out until I returned home.

To this day, when I smell garlic it brings back memories of that trip: that coldest of nights, when we wriggled out of our tents and gazed up at the brightest stars I'd ever seen. Or being 16 years old, and worshipping wilderness ski gods like Tom

Otto Schniebs, circa 1938. Known for his natty dress code and visionary skiing, he coined the term "skiing is life."

Warren and Paul Petzoldt. Or the descent after our failed climb, when Warren said, "Go for it Aspen," and I did—only to endure howls as my pack flipped forward and drilled my head into three feet of sugar.

Since my Teton epiphany, backcountry skiing has been the focus of my life. Indeed, to paraphrase Otto Schniebs, I could say it's *been* my life. My wife and I honeymooned on the snows of Mount Hood, and in the Cascade dining room of Timberline Lodge. I've floated on endorphins after climbing 3,000 feet an hour as a 20-year-old animal—then wept in my hospital bed after an avalanche broke my young body. I've made hundreds of special friends in the mountains of winter—and grieved when some died in those same hills we'd loved together. I've helped teens at Outward Bound ease their growing pains, just as mountaineers Dave Farney and Paul Petzoldt helped me during my years of hormone Hades.

Now, during family hut trips and ski days I see my young son getting the same benefits and experiences that have been such a powerful force in my life: beauty, challenge, failure, achievement, friendship, and a sense of history. With this book, my intention is to share such benefits with you.

—*Lou Dawson, 1997*

Lou and Lisa Dawson on Mount Hood, Oregon.
Louis Dawson Collection

Introduction

*Glisse alpinism—
tradition and innovation*

Mountains embody the harsh essence of nature. When a ski or snowboard descent caps a fine climb, the alpinist becomes a joyful, even sublime, part of that wild landscape. No human game is more elegant and joyful than glisse alpinism.

The beauty and intensity of this game is what makes skiing not only a sport, but also a way of life, as Otto Schniebs pointed out long ago. As a result, it raises some complex questions involving definitions and ethics: what exactly is a ski or snowboard descent? How much machinery, such as helicopters, snowmobiles, or ski lifts, can we use and still call what we're doing "alpinism?" How much foot travel? How much rappelling and rope-work?

The question of machinery and technology is an important one, and lies at the heart of what we do as glisse alpinists. Two decades ago, upstart alpinist Reinhold Messner coined the phrase "murder of the impossible." He was speaking of technology and ethics, and how adventure sports such as rock climbing and Himalayan mountaineering are ruined by drilled rock anchors and siege tactics. Messner was also talking about how sports change, and he was warning us that such changes are not always good.

We should heed Messner's advice. One of the wonderful things about backcountry skiing and snowboarding is that it allows us to enjoy mountaineering without causing trail erosion or using destructive practices such as drilling rock anchors. Moreover, the accessibility of North America's mountains allows us to climb and ski without leaving garbage piles such as those found on Mount Everest, and without heavy reliance on mechanical transport.

When we do use machinery we should do so with care and forethought.

Boating into the Skillet Glacier, Mount Moran, Tetons. *Andrew McLean*

"The machine does not isolate man from the great problems of nature but plunges him more deeply into them," wrote French aviator Antoine Saint-Exupery. Yes, machines do have their place in modern mountaineering, especially for trailhead access, transport to remote basecamps and huts, and rescue. Yet if we're using a helicopter, snowmobile, four-wheel-drive, or other engine-powered device, we should beware the difference between true backcountry glisse and a mechanized resort. "To arrive at the top of a steep pitch by lift or helicopter," said the late extreme skier Patrick Vallencant, "is like drinking eau-menthe [a non-alcoholic cocktail]. It's a pleasant drink, but it does not charge you up." Though helicopter access is common in Europe, sentiments such as Vallencant's are prevalent as well. Indeed, at least one extreme star, Bernard Gouvy, died because he encountered ice on a route he had not climbed first, so eschewing machinery can have practical as well as aesthetic ramifications.

There are other ethical questions involved in our sport. One of these is the issue of what actually constitutes a descent. In Europe glisse alpinists often pick a line with minimal snow, stay on snowboard or skis as much as possible, and accomplish what most agree is a glisse descent. Rappelling, downclimbing, and skiing on belay are all acceptable elements of the adventure. At the same time, Europeans admire glisse alpinists who attack a line with little or no ropework and who stay in their bindings the whole way down. North Americans have followed suit, with descents ranging from elegant solo adventures to roped encounters verging on mere (even if extreme) engineering problems. Even so, we tend to admire and strive for long, rope-free, uninterrupted descents. To paraphrase Italian mountaineering pioneer Emilio Comici, "as a single ball of snow would roll, that is the line I would ski."

In this book, the criteria for great ski and snowboard descents are that they begin as high as possible on the peak, preferably from the exact summit, and go all or most of the way down to an obvious finish near the base of the mountain. Further, the line should be continuous, if possible, and have enough snow to make turns for most, if not all, of the drop. Further, I do not cover descents (even if they are original) that began merely by stepping out of a helicopter on the summit. Finally, I discourage glisse alpinism which involves setting up and abandoning a web of ropes, or leaving the mountain with lasting damage, such as bolt-holes and erosion.

Another issue in glisse alpinism is that of the "first descent." A true premier descent, especially of a remote or difficult line, and conforming somewhat to the ideals covered above, is a legitimate claim that epitomizes the exploratory nature of mountaineering.

Mandatory rappel, Pfeiefferhorn, Wasatch Mountains. Too much rope work would detract from a glisse descent. *Andrew McLean*

For most backcountry skiers and snowboarders, knowing the history of a route, who did it first, is inspiring and enhances their appreciation of the adventuresome and creative human spirit. Again, Comici says it best: "The climber who is able to divine the most elegant way, disdaining the easy slopes, then follow that way … that climber is creating a true work of art."

While glisse alpinism has always emphasized summit descents, a current trend is to hit a specific "line," perhaps only several hundred vertical feet out of thousands. In evaluating this kind of achievement, we need to remember what the sport is ultimately about: purity of style and a sense of purpose. Some of these achievements are worthy of note, but others appear to be attention-grabbing feats of athleticism with little connection to the soul of the sport.

Let's take a worst case scenario. Suppose someone climbs part way up a rock and ice filled couloir, turns around, sets up a belay, skis or snowboards a few hundred feet, then rappels back down the remainder. Perhaps the athlete had a good time. Perhaps he or she practiced good mountain craft. Perhaps it was a first descent. Yet for most glisse alpinists, excessive rope work, or skiing only short sections of a mountain, detracts from the expressive quality of the sport, overemphasizing its merely athletic aspect. Whether the mountain is Alaska's Denali or Massachusetts' Greylock, the most complete expression of glisse alpinism involves launching off a summit and linking turns down a mountainside: no ropes, no helicopter, perhaps no witness but a cold sky. That is the art of Comici.

To keep the art of glisse alpinism sublime, we must let the mountains define our encounters with them. Backcountry glisse is not which hut we sleep in, but rather which mountain we climb from the hut. It's not what gear we use, but rather on what mountain we slide. It's not a line forced with ropes, helicopters, or downclimbing, but rather a line that "allows" itself to be. It's not the kind of turns we make, but what memories we make. It's certain the Young Turks will redefine these rules, but activists with vision will see the history of the sport as a star, a fire which gives direction to their own aspirations. If that flame spoke it would say, "I am the beautiful, the difficult—even the impossible. We are both alive: step forward and meet me, face to face."

Defining a selected classic descent

From the ill-fated turns of Koven and Carpé on Denali in 1932, to Toni Matt's legendary schuss in 1939 of Mount Washington's Tuckerman Ravine, to Fritz Stammberger's 1971 descent of North Maroon Peak, we have an important and largely undocumented tradition of ski descents in North America. This tradition has made certain ski descents "classics." Climbs and descents of these routes create some of the most memorable days in a glisse alpinist's life.

A loose definition of a classic ski descent would include all your best memories, and perhaps those of your friends. Dictionary definitions of classic include phrases such as "model of its kind," "famous or well known," and "excellent." Expanding upon those basics, a classic descent as defined for this book has the following qualities:

• Mountaineering spirit

Classic descents are as much climbs as they are downhill runs, and are often located on mountains with rich alpine heritage. Preferably, other routes on the mountain give a feel of being in a place as much a mountaineer's domain as that of a skier or snowboarder.

• History

History is an important measure and had perhaps the greatest role in picking the routes covered here. Nonetheless, many of the featured routes in this book have no directly unusual or glamorous tradition, but rather are located on mountains with an historic background of alpinism, or in a region with a rich social background and local culture.

Colorado Mountain Club skier at Fern Lake, 1922.
Colorado Mountain Club

• Location and access

Classic glisse routes may be located close to civilization or in remote wilderness, though tolerable access plays a role in many a route's status as a classic. A classic is usually climbed then skied, though a minority of routes are accessed in part via aircraft, automobile, ski lift, or other mechanized means. Location also plays a role with snow conditions; most classic ski descents are located in mountain ranges with plenty of skiable snow.

• Safety

While mountaineering always involves physical danger, classic descents are safe enough to achieve a modicum of popularity and repeatability. For example, while Mount Foraker in the Alaska Range has been skied by several routes, all involve a great deal of risk. Indeed, on one potential Foraker descent route you would glide over the bones of other mountaineers previously buried by avalanches in a "valley of death." On the other hand, the Messner Couloir on Denali is frequently skied and is considered reasonably safe, as is Denali's West Buttress route.

• Aesthetics

The only time I've ever heard a mountain called "ugly"—or worse—was during a three day retreat with no food. Yet some peaks are more striking than others, and this plays a role in their rankings as classic glisse descents. Moreover, other aesthetic qualities help rank the routes in this book: sublime summit views, historic gateway towns, consistently good weather, nearby oceans and rivers, interesting topography.

• Quality of climbing

A terrific climb is the foundation of a classic descent. Starting before dawn, the yellow pool of your headlamp seals you in a Zen focus. As your awareness broadens with the day, you climb to the sharp line of the rising sun. Your route might include kicking steps up a swooping, snow-filled couloir; you might scramble up a sculpted arête as fine as the curves of Michelangelo's Pieta; you might spend a few hours on climbing skins ascending a colossal amphitheater.

• Quality of skiing or snowboarding

As David Goodman wrote in his New England guidebook *Classic Backcountry Skiing*, "Quality means variety." While variety is perhaps a given with most routes in this book, since they include interesting approaches and alpine climbing, other factors add spice. Glacier descents offer a spectrum of glisse. You veer below seracs, hop crevasses, and bank off windrows and hummocks—all under the watchful eye of majestic peaks—for glaciers can't exist without full-grown mountains. Descending volcanoes offers thrilling geology, odd topography, and a primal ambiance. Extreme

pitches, especially steep turns with safe runouts, pump jaded glisse alpinists with spurts of adrenaline. Conversely, novice backcountry skiers and riders are amazed by their first run on velvet corn snow, when they find nature has created a perfection only faintly imitated by the finest machine-made groom at the ski resort. Quality can also mean plentiful vertical, and certain routes in this book are classic simply because they let you carve hundreds of linked turns down a mountainside—an experience as close as human beings ever come to perfect mobility on our planet's surface.

• Other classic descents

Plainly, many regions not included in this book boast their share of classics. Wyoming's Beartooth and Wind River mountains have innumerable possibilities, as do Idaho's Sawtooth Mountains and the hills of Canada's Gaspe Peninsula, among others. Even the volcanoes in Mexico might

In 1995, John Montecucco and Julie Faure (shown on route) attempted to ski Sultana Ridge on Mount Foraker. Montecucco fell, broke his ankle, and required a helicopter rescue. *Tyson Bradley*

be North American ski classics. Let this book get you started on your classic journey, then take a voyage of discovery on some "classic" routes of your own.

USING THIS BOOK

Mountain regions

While geopolitical boundaries are most familiar, they serve poorly for dividing up the mountain regions of North America. For example, the Cascade mountain range, which includes classic descents such as Mount Rainier and Mount Adams, extends through at least three states —and two countries. Thus, I have divided the chapters in this book along the lines of geologic regions, with political boundaries mentioned only where appropriate.

"Ascent" ratings

As an inexperienced climber on a *Novice-rated* snow route, you may need an ice ax in hand (experts will be comfortable with ski poles). You must have practiced the ice ax self arrest, and know its method and limitations. A rope and related gear are unnecessary, but you should have enough knowledge to recognize and avoid terrain where you might need such equipment. During seasons with hard snow or ice, all climbers on a Novice route should carry crampons and know how to use them—though they may not be necessary.

For an *Intermediate-rated* snow route you must be expert with ice ax and crampons, and usually carry them. Use of a rope probably won't be necessary, but you should usually carry one and know how to use it. For routes where a rope is probably unnecessary but still carried, some glisse alpinists carry a short coil of seven or eight

millimeter line. Both are adequate for rappels or belays on less-than-vertical terrain. Only experienced snow climbers should climb Intermediate-rated routes. An Intermediate route has more fall potential than a Novice route.

If you take on an *Advanced-rated* climb, you should be expert with varied crampon techniques and the use of an ice ax. If conditions are icy, two hand-tools may be necessary. A rope and climbing hardware may be needed, and should always be carried. Only expert mountaineers will be able to handle an advanced snow route safely and efficiently. Several routes in this book are rated *Extreme*. This rating is reserved for routes with problems such as heavy rockfall danger, mixed climbing (snow, ice, and rock), or formidable route finding.

While many snow climbs in this book are dry by mid-summer, some gradually become ice climbs. Such climbs require more skill and equipment than their rating indicates, and such late summer ice and snow is usually unskiable.

"Glisse" ratings

A *Novice-rated* glisse route is safe for mountaineers who can do a solid stem turn and traverse kick turn. If you can ride a snowboard or ski on moderate ski resort slopes, you have the skill to handle a Novice-rated route. Nearby terrain may be steeper and more dangerous. Thus, if you tackle a Novice route, you must be able to distinguish appropriate terrain from dangerous areas. If you tackle a Novice route as a learning experience, consider traveling with a more experienced friend, or hire a guide.

An *Intermediate-rated* glisse route is serious business for any ability level. To do an Intermediate route safely you

Michael Pokress descending North Maroon Peak, Colorado,1972. One of the first extreme descents done in North America.
Kendall Williams

must have experience with high altitude camping, emergency bivouacs, and avalanche hazard evaluation. Your ski or snowboard skills should be solid intermediate to expert, with experience in poor snow conditions. Some map reading skill is necessary, and you should have a fair degree of mountaineering judgment.

For safe enjoyment of an *Advanced-rated* glisse route, you must have a high degree of skill in all aspects of glisse alpinism, including high-angle snow climbing. Some advanced routes may require belayed rock climbing, especially if you fail to find the best line. Again, if you're new to glisse alpinism, try a few routes with easier ratings before you do an Advanced route; that way you'll get a sense of the rating curve.

For an *Extreme-rated* route you must be highly skilled in extreme skiing or snowboarding, as well as technical climbing. Extreme routes are inherently dangerous because of cliffs and steep snow, possibly exceeding 45 degrees. Nevertheless, the Extreme-rated routes in this guide can be done safely by experienced mountaineers, provided they possess the skill, equipment, and knowledge necessary to tackle the route when the snow and rock are in proper condition. Do not attempt routes rated as Extreme unless you are an experienced glisse alpinist.

Other rating issues

A few routes in this book involve hand-and-foot rock climbing. These are rated with the system of "classes" familiar to rock climbers. This system is highly informative for mountaineers. A simple hike on a trail would be rated 1st Class, a harder hike with steep ground would be rated 2nd Class. Starting with 3rd Class, mountaineers should be aware of fall potential and will encounter hand-and-foot moves; 4th Class involves difficult scrambling, with fall potential—you may need a rope. Technical rock climbing is 5th Class and is the foundation for the Yosemite Decimal System (YDS). This system is open-ended: it starts with 5.0, while 5.14 rates the hardest rock climb existing today. Climbs under 5.5 in difficulty may be possible for even inexperienced climbers, as long as they possess a modicum of fitness. Climbs over 5.5 require specialized balance and hand skills only learned through practice. In this book all 4th and 5th Class climbs are rated advanced or extreme, and the need for rope work is covered in the text, as is the exact YDS rating.

Ratings vary greatly by season. An Intermediate route in spring might be impossibly dangerous in winter. Moreover, rock climbing on wet or snowy routes may be significantly harder than in dry conditions. Thus, most route descriptions include comments about the seasons, and climbing ratings should be considered a variable.

Glacier travel confuses ratings. With good snowcover after a heavy winter, a glacier may be a safe highway to the peaks above. Given a light snowpack or hot weather, the same glacier might be a dangerous maze of thinly bridged cracks. A glacier stripped of snow, with the crevasses fully visible, can again be safe. When possible, such variables are covered in the text.

"Guidebooks"

While this compendium of routes is intended as an overall guide, it is by no means intended as a substitute for detailed local guidebooks and maps available for most areas. Indeed, my sole intent is to complement such materials. Thus, suggestions for local guidebooks are included in the route descriptions and in the bibliography. Please use them.

"Firsts"

If known, the names and dates of those who completed the first ascent or descent are included. Invariably, many descents have gone unrecorded; the author encourages anyone with further information for future editions to contact the publisher.

GENTLE GLISSE ALPINISM

Mountains are priceless resources that give us immeasurable benefit. The increased popularity of climbing North America's peaks, however, is taking its toll: the fragile alpine environment is being damaged by erosion and crowding. As mountaineers, we must reduce the impact of our visits by traveling with care and sensitivity. The following recommendations will help you reduce your impact.

Before your trip, learn about problems for the area you'll be in such as: undue trail erosion, damaged riparian areas, wildlife you should avoid, crowding, limited parking, private land, human waste disposal. Use common sense to mitigate such problems.

Keep your group under six people.

If you camp, plan your itinerary to avoid over-used sites, and avoid camps during times of high use.

Don't use campfires in the backcountry; pack a stove.

Avoid traveling through undisturbed areas. Instead, use designated trails and established paths, or travel over snow.

When climbing or camping do not build structures such as windbreaks, large cairns, rock walls, and fire rings.

Deposit human feces in holes six to eight inches deep, a minimum of 75 paces from water or camp. Burn or pack out your toilet paper. On glaciers, use waste disposal approved by local authorities. Avoid urinating and defecating on or near popular summits.

Consider using clothing and gear colored with earth tones instead of a bright motif. Visual pollution is a valid complaint.

Pack out what you pack in—including organic waste such as orange peels.

Don't feed wildlife.

Leave your pets at home.

Mountaineer during snow seasons to minimize all your impacts.

Be courteous. Wait for climbers below you to move out of rockfall areas. Don't ski above other climbers or skiers. Keep noise to a minimum (except for summit yodels). Be friendly and share information about routes that prevent erosion and rockfall. Share new routes, since they spread use.

Leave undisturbed snow for other glisse alpinists: spoon your tracks, avoid "Zoro" traverses, fill your snowpits and bivouac holes.

Support organizations that help preserve our mountains.

Snowmass Lake, Colorado. By practicing a few simple rules of low-impact travel, the wilderness can be preserved. *George Bell*

7,000 YEARS OF BACKCOUNTRY SKIING:

THE HISTORY OF GLISSE ALPINISM

7,000 Years of Backcountry Skiing: The History of Glisse Alpinism

Bill Briggs gulped from his water bottle, laced his boots, and clicked into his ski bindings. Standing at the apex of Wyoming's precipitous 13,770-foot Grand Teton, he caught his breath and took in the view. To his east the Gross Ventre Mountains rose from the haze like a Tolkien fantasy, while the plains of Idaho faded 200 miles west. Below his feet, snow like a steeple roof dropped thousands of feet to the chasm. Briggs's plan was to slice turns into the abyss—to be the first to ski down the Grand Teton. On that day of June 15, 1971, as his swishing skis arced down to Garnet Canyon, his goal became reality. Briggs's descent of the "Grand," by receiving more publicity than several other similar descents that year, demonstrated that a revolution was occurring in North American glisse alpinism. A new age of difficult, aesthetic glisse from high summits had begun. Yet this new trend should not be thought of as standing alone, for just as the first landing on the moon had to begin with a tentative lift-off at Kitty Hawk, Briggs skied from the summit of a 7,000-year tradition of glisse dreams, failures, and successes.

Backcountry skiing predates known history. The oldest ski extant was dug from a peat bog in Sweden, and carbon dates at 4,500 years old. Even more venerable planks are depicted in cave paintings dating back more than 7,000 years. While the need for gathering food is clearly what inspired those cave dwelling skiers, much of our earliest written ski history resulted from human conflict.

Zenophon, a Greek historian and military leader, briefly mentions skis in a 500 B.C. essay. In 1206, military skiers made legend when they saved the Norwegian monarchy by carrying the infant King Haakonson over the mountains to safety during the Norwegian Civil War. Ten years later, skis helped the Norwegians drive the Swedish army out of their country. Thus Norwegian culture embraced skis, and Norway would be the world's spiritual leader of skiing, both as sport and tool, until Austria's Hannes Schneider won a ski race at Grindelwald 700 years later.

Norwegian soldier, circa 1200. Early military skiing influenced the development of backcountry skiing.

◄ First ski descent of Hayden Peak, Colorado, 1937. *Aspen Historical Society*

Pioneers of glisse

Fun being a basic impulse, the Scandinavians (when they weren't using skis to defend themselves) played with sliding down hills and launching off bumps. They were also equipment innovators. As far back as 1555 A.D., historian Olaus Magnus described how Scandinavian skiers used climbing skins: "when they ascend to a place they may not fall backward, because the hair will rise like spears, or bristles, and by an admirable power of nature hinder them from falling down."

In the mid nineteenth century, young Norwegian farmer and ski jumper Sondre Norheim felt the need for more control of his planks. Norheim attached a twisted willow strap to his toe piece and wrapped it around his heel, and also built a shorter ski with sidecut. Until then, most ski bindings were a simple strap over the boot toe, and the skis unwieldy planks. Norheim's innovations begat a revolution.

With his heels stabilized, Norheim used the split-stride position to cut turns (this position was also used as a shock absorbing landing for competitive jumping, as it still is), and the well known telemark turn was the result, named after Norheim's home county of Telemark. At the same time, Norheim and his friends also refined a turn using a more neutral "parallel" stance. This turn came to be known as the christiania (after the former name of Oslo, Norway), later shortened to "christie" (and other similar spellings). Though recent fascination with the telemark would imply otherwise, Scandinavians have always used both methods to turn skis. The telemark was popular because it was effective for landing jumps and was a powerful tool to force turns from primitive gear. The christie gave the quickest stop and sharpest turn. Both turns were possible with the gear of the day, and both were used where appropriate.

At about the same time as Norheim and his friends were refining their technique, in North America's Sierra Nevada mountains Norwegian immigrant miners (Forty-niners) were developing an entirely different style of skiing. (The Norse influence on North American skiing has a long tradition—Viking explorer Leif Ericsson is reported to have brought the first skis to the New World in 1,000 A.D., although it's unknown if he used them there. The first documented skiing in North America was done by Norwegian immigrants in Beloit Wisconsin, in the early 1840s.) The Sierra Forty-niners used planks mostly for transport, but started a series of maniacal downhill races featuring straight drops down mountains—reaching 80 miles per hour on "longboards" up to 12 feet in length. All skiing those days was technically "backcountry" skiing; the longboarders paid with sweat for every downhill run they made, and it was all done on natural snow.

During this same period, from about 1848 to 1873, other developments were unfolding. First, mountaineering was becoming recreation rather than exploration. The golden age of climbing began in Europe with the first ascent of the Wetterhorn in 1854 and Edward Whymper's 1865 epic on the Matterhorn. In North America, Mount Adams in Washington's Cascades got its first ascent in 1854, and John Muir, in 1873, was the first to ascend the classic Mountaineers Route on California's Mount Whitney. Backcountry skiing, though still not a widespread pleasure sport, was evolving as well. In Colorado, Methodist minister John "Father" Dyer carried the mail over 13,186-foot Mosquito Pass; he slogged on foot in summer—on planks in winter. Reaching Mosquito Pass on skis is still considered a major undertaking in prime

Fridtjof Nansen, wilderness skiing messiah of the late 1800s.

pack-ice as far north as possible, where Nansen and a companion left the warmth of their ship and dashed for the North Pole via skis, dogsled, and kayak. They failed to reach their goal, but came closer than anyone before. Nansen took two years to return from his polar attempt—hunting and fishing to survive while sliding through an unexplored white wilderness.

Nansen saw a spiritual and aesthetic side to his hardships. His book, *By Ski Over Greenland* (or by some translations *On Skis Over Greenland*) inflamed a generation of skiers when he described skiing as "something that develops not only the body but also the soul." One man inspired by Nansen was Austrian eccentric Mathias Zdarsky. In the late 1800s, skiing in the European Alps was stuck at the toddler level. The Norwegian techniques worked for lower-angled terrain and transportation on the flats, but steeper terrain beckoned the adventurous. Zdarsky was not a natural skier; some

avalanche terrain. Even more so than Father Dyer's treks, Snowshoe Thompson's escapades in the Tahoe Sierra were the stuff of legend. In 1856, Thompson started his 20-year stint as a mail hauler by skiing a 118-mile-round-trip run between the towns of Genoe and Placerville in California. It's no surprise that Thompson grew up in Norway, and was only doing what came naturally. Now, all backcountry skiing needed was a messiah.

The prophet of glisse would turn out to be Fridtjof Nansen: Norwegian intellectual, scientist, explorer, and the most visionary wilderness skier in history. In Norseman style, Nansen felt the call of the vast wild. His first target was Greenland in 1888, where he completed a 300-mile epic crossing on skis. Next he sailed north until his specially designed boat, the Fram, stuck like a frozen cork in the Polar ice. This clever ploy allowed the Fram to drift with the

Mathias Zdarsky researched the sport, carved his own skis, and the rest is history.

reports say he'd never skied prior to ordering (or possibly making) a pair of skis. It is known he started skiing with little in the way of preconception, but soon developed a technique that allowed him to descend steep hills in control, using snowplow wedging, stemming, and a single long pole for braking, pushing, and balance. Zdarsky became a self-proclaimed expert, and loudly spouted his wisdom on equipment and technique. Indeed, skiing must have been important to him, because he even railed about dress fashions that might beguile his ever-serious disciples. "Calling attention to the upper part of the female body," he wrote about clothing, "distracts the men from skiing."

It was an associate of Zdarsky's, Austrian army officer Georg Bilgeri, who would refine the technique by eliminating the single dragged stick and emphasizing use of the skis for braking and turning, rather than dragging a stick (Bilgeri no doubt used the christiania technique as well.) Zdarsky and Bilgeri fought bitterly in what one ski historian has termed "the holy war against the big stick." Zdarsky's technique, derisively called "stick riding," was ultimately the loser, and Bilgeri's style went on to become the foundation for modern carved-turn parallel skiing, as well as today's refined free-heel skiing (which takes much of its technique from such parallel skiing).

Not all this evolution was born of technique, as gear was developing concurrently. Shorter skis made Bilgeri's stem technique as effective as the telemark. Metal edges allowed precise carving rather than skidding. Beefy "toe iron" bindings were built. Boots became stiffer. Most technique of the day was a blend of telemark and "arlberg," as Bilgeri's method came to be known. In the steeper Alps, however, stemming and wedging gained favor. Another athlete of the time, Wilhelm Paulke, used a combination of all tech-

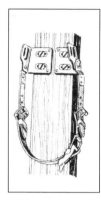

Circa 1940 "toe irons" were remarkably effective, and closely resemble recent free-heel bindings.

niques to accomplish the world's first high alpine ski traverse when he skied across Switzerland's Bernese Oberland in 1897. Then Hannes Schneider, a student of Georg Bilgeri, took the parallel method still further, developing the arlberg technique into an art that, while it didn't kill the telemark turn, certainly demonstrated its limitations. The point of departure was at the 1910 Swiss downhill ski championships. Most of the racers used the telemark, while Schneider used his fall-line stem-christie turn and beat everyone by several seconds.

North American mountain skiers

Technique debates aside, North American skiers now had a full bag of tricks learned from the Europeans. During the winter of 1906-7, Irving Langmuir became the first North American ski mountaineer when he brought an alpinist's attitude and ski skills from Europe to the mountains of New England. Six years later, Dartmouth College mountaineers made the first ski descent of New Hampshire's Mount Washington. Near Salt Lake City, Utah, the informal "Rough Neck Ski Club" made headlines in 1915 with their adventures in the Wasatch Mountains.

The years from 1918 to 1932 were a golden age for climbing and wilderness skiing in North America. In 1918, peakbagging became sport when Herb Clark and Bob and George Marshall pounced on the 46 Adirondack summits then surveyed as higher than 4,000 feet. In 1921, Graeme McGowan made the first ski descent of Colorado's Pikes Peak, and a year later Mount Rainier in Washington got its first winter ascent, in which skis also played an integral part. In 1923, Carl Blaurock and William Ervin were the first to climb all the Colorado 14,000-foot peaks, now fondly known as the "fourteeners" and enjoyed by thousands of climbers and glisse alpinists. The first Winter Olympics were held in 1924 in Chamonix France. While featuring

A fully equipped mountain skier of the 1920s.
Colorado Mountain Club Collection

only Nordic ski events, these first winter games legitimized and built enthusiasm for all forms of skiing. The first recorded skiing in the Pacific Northwest was also done at this time, and the Skyliner's ski club formed in Bend, Oregon. In 1931, Andre Roch, Hjalmar Hvam and Arne Stene made a ski ascent and descent of Oregon's Mount Hood (they did not ski from the summit). Regarding expedition skiing, the consequential event of the decade was Orland Bartholomew's solo 250-mile ski traverse of California's Sierra mountains, via the Muir trail in 1928.

Ski writing reflected the glow of the era: "Your skis quiver with the strain … and you realize to your intense astonishment that you have not fallen. …You are drunk with the wine of speed, and you marvel at the faint heart which so nearly refused the challenge. You glory in the sense of control which you have recaptured over your ski, no longer untamed demons hurrying you through space. …You are playing with gravity. You are master of snow." wrote Arnold Lunn in *Mountains of Youth*, published in 1927.

For almost a half century, up to his death in 1974, Sir Arnold Lunn was the strongest supporter of skiing in the English-speaking world. Starting in 1912 he published more than 16 books about skiing, including a cross-country skiing how-to, and a guidebook for the Bernese Oberland. The Englishman was deeply religious, and always strove for a spiritual component in his mountain writings. Lunn was knighted for his activities in 1952, the only man in history to receive that honor for skiing. He is perhaps best known for inventing the slalom ski race, but he viewed himself as a ski mountaineer.

Canada also provided gritty challenges for the amazing mountaineers of this golden decade. In 1929, Joe Weiss did the first skiing on the vast Columbia Icefield, and a year later Pete Parsons made the first ski descent of remote and classic Mount Resplendent. Ski exploration in the Coast Mountains of Canada began when Phyllis and Don Munday reported their "Ski-climbs in the Coast Range" in the 1930 *Canadian Alpine Journal* (*CAJ*), published by the Alpine Club of Canada. In 1931 the *CAJ* added a section dedicated to skiing, in which Russell Bennett reported on a 300-mile trip that included a magnificent run down Snow Dome on the Columbia Icefield.

North American backcountry skiing was growing, but it was still a fringe sport. Change began with the 1932 Olympic winter games in Lake Placid, New York. The games' location, along with breathless narration by famed ski booster Lowell Thomas, helped popularize North American skiing. Erling Strom also led the first successful expedition to use skis on Denali (he called it Mount McKinley), in that same year, and his subsequent writings did much to legitimize skiing on North America's high peaks.

Mechanized seduction

More than any epiphany of technique or revolution in gear, the invention of machines to carry skiers uphill had the most modern influence on the sport. The first ski train puffed steam in 1924 and hauled enthusiasts into the backcountry above Parley's Canyon in Utah. In 1932, local mechanics in Shawbridge, Quebec, put a Dodge automobile up on blocks, looped a continuous rope over a wheel, and created the first ski tow in North America. Before this the history of North American backcountry skiing had simply been that of skiing. Now a schism was opening.

At first, no-sweat mechanized vertical increased the popularity of all forms of ski-ing: fun seekers could stay with the crowd, or go to the wild from the top of the tow. Nonetheless, savvy skiers of the era could see what was happening. A decade after the first rope tow was strung, northwoods legend Jackrabbit Johannsen would have to explain that:

> Tow hills are but a training ground for the fun that is yours when you set out on your own. You must feel the tug of your muscles as you near the top of a long grade, and know the joy of making your own track down an unbroken expanse of powder snow. *This* is skiing. *This* is adventure.

Even with the advent of mechanized skiing, the gear of the 1930s worked well for everything. Simple bindings held boots that flexed at the sole for easy walking. A cable around the heel ran through two sets of lugs on the sides. Hook the cable under just the front lugs and you had a touring rig for "seal-skin" climbing, cutting telemarks, or swishing down in the long elegant arcs of the early arlberg technique. Use the rear lugs and you could lock your heels down for more control. Skiers all over the continent were using this simple and effective gear for backcountry adventures. For example, in 1932, the first ski exploration of the Wapta Icefield in Canada was done by Alexander McCoubrey and several companions. A few years later Andre Roch led the first descent of Colorado's Hayden Peak, photographers Bob and Ira Spring were using skis extensively in the Cascades, and Walter Mosaur was exploring California on his planks.

Visionary backcountry ski activity of the 1930s also occurred in Sun Valley, Idaho. In 1936, an Austrian count Felix Schaffgotsh was hired by railroad magnate Averell Harriman to search the continent for European-style skiing. The count ended up in a valley near Ketchum, Idaho, where the treeless slopes reminded him of his homeland ski terrain. Although the present state

Pioneer ski mountaineer Andre Roch in 1938. He came to North America as a consultant, to map out mechanized ski resorts. *Aspen Historical Society*

of the Sun Valley resort implies that Count Felix was looking for mechanized skiing, he was actually searching for the good touring terrain preferred for that era's style of skiing. At the time, rope tows were considered an adjunct to a pair of seal skins. With the Count's blessing, Harriman quickly completed North America's first dedicated luxury ski lodge, along with the world's first chair lift. To top that, a year later Harriman built several backcountry huts. Pioneer Lodge still stands. During this period, other huts and lodges were being constructed around the country (such as the San Antonio Hut in southern California), but the Sun Valley lodges were the most well financed, and perhaps the most popular.

Sun Valley Lodge was completed in December of 1936, and the ski instructors arrived soon after. Among Harriman's chosen group of bronzed gods was a feisty skier named Andy Hennig, who came to the U.S. in 1938 from Kitzbuhl, Austria. With companions Florian Haemmerle and Victor Gottschalk, Hennig spent the next decades skiing hundreds of alpine ski descents and tours in the mountains around Sun Valley, including almost every high summit of the Sawtooth Mountains. Indeed, the only skier of the time who equaled Hennig's drive and accomplishment was Otto Steiner, who pounded the Mineral King area of California's Sierra Nevada.

Sadly for backcountry skiing, pioneers such as Steiner and Hennig portended lesser things: they crested a wave of experts who skied backcountry in North America to explore and develop land for ski resorts.

Ski patrols started out as volunteer groups, but evolved into paid professionals who spent much of their time herding skiers away from the backcountry. *John Moynier Collection*

It was no coincidence that the same year Andre Roch was skiing backcountry in Aspen, the first chairlift in the world was being built at Sun Valley, and the Winter Olympics were featuring "downhill" events for the first time. The small schism between backcountry and resort skiing had widened to a bergschrund. Now people who had never backcountry skied were riding lifts, spending money, and would soon be herded like sheep by ski patrollers.

In 1939, after breaking the same leg two years in a row, Hjalmar Hvam began selling the first safety release binding. His "Safe-Ski" used a cable, thus allowing both touring and alpine modes: arguably the safest, lightest, and most versatile binding system yet invented. But it foretold the future of downhill gear, which was to become more specialized, and subsequently less effective for touring. Boots became stiffer, and bindings began to attach these boots down in ways you couldn't modify for walking on skis.

Nonetheless, though the media's and much of the public's enthusiasm was turning to ski resorts and designated ski hills, North America's backcountry trudgers kept at it. In 1938, North Star Mountain in the Cascades got its first ski descent. The Wasatch Mountain Club's lodge in Utah

was a popular destination for both adventure skiers and those wanting a more civilized experience. Meanwhile, in Europe, improved ski gear and the latest techniques allowed Andre Tournier to make what was perhaps the world's first "extreme" ski descent on the Argentiere glacier. But by 1941, World War II realities such as gas rationing had brought recreational skiing to a virtual halt worldwide. Still, the war was to be a milestone in ski development, for an effective army needs ski troops, and like Norway 150 years before, North America was to have its skiing soldiers.

War years

On November 15, 1941, the United States created the 87th Mountain Regiment to specialize in mountain warfare. The nascent alpine infantry began training at Fort Lewis, Washington. "We climb to conquer," was the new regiment's motto, and their training was designed to make the slogan into reality. While at Fort Lewis, the new troops did a (then rare) winter ascent of Mount Rainier. They also rounded off their Northwest stint with an orbit of Mount Rainier (much on skis), and several trips into the Olympic Mountains.

In 1942 the 87th moved to Camp Hale high in the Colorado Rockies, where the better mountaineers in the division did a number of ski treks and winter ascents (see Colorado chapter for details). The 87th soon became the 10th Mountain Division, and the men of the "10th" went on to fight in Italy, where they scaled cliffs for surprise attacks during the battle of Belvedere, and then spearheaded the decisive Po Valley offensive. While the 10th Mountain Division never used skis for actual combat, they did use their white camouflage planks for important patrols in Italy.

The men of the 10th developed a strong camaraderie, and many of them gained or at least reinforced a great love for skiing and mountains. Even so, a veteran wag stated that the one thing he learned in the army, "was to never ski uphill on skis again." Perhaps that's why so many 10th vets were involved in the postwar ski resort boom, during which many of North America's ski lifts were built. At least 2,000 Division veterans became postwar ski instructors, and hundreds went into ski area management and development. Yet resorts aside, many more 10th veterans did like to ski uphill, and were important figures in the development of the United States' mountaineering tradition, both in skiing and climbing. A few such vets were Wyoming mountaineering pioneer Paul Petzoldt, Colorado hut developer Fritz Benedict, and Idaho

ski alpinist Andy Hennig. As historian Morten Lund wrote of the 10th: "The effect on U.S. skiing was little short of miraculous." The same could be said for North American mountaineering.

Moreover, the well publicized saga of the 10th Mountain "ski troops" contributed greatly to the acceptance of ski mountaineering by North America's general population. Magazines carried innumerable articles about the troops, and their experiences became part of the common vernacular. For example, a joke about their mountain training was widely circulated: A soldier is on maneuvers atop 13,209-foot Homestake Peak; he picks up the radio voice of a pilot landing in Denver. "Am at 11,000 feet, coming in for a landing, gliding gliding gliding," says the pilot. Keying his mike, the trooper cracks over the airways, "This is Private so-

Soldiers training above Camp Hale, obscured by smog on the valley floor. Homestake Peak is at far left, Mount Holy Cross is the pointed peak just left of center. *Colorado Ski Museum*

and-so of the mountain troops, am at 13,000 feet, walking walking walking."

World War II and events leading up to it had other important effects on North American backcountry skiing. Ski technique over the continent improved when some of the best skiers in the world escaped Germany by moving to North America, where many found work as ski instructors. Industry perfected products such as nylon fabric and ropes, material soon to become standards of modern mountaineering. What's more, until the late 1960s, would-be alpinists could walk into almost any "army-navy" store and completely outfit themselves for a ski trip, including mounting a pair of the white wooden skis originally issued to the 10th Mountain Division. If you paid more than $5 for such skis you'd paid too much; the same planks are now collector's items going for over $300.

Postwar renaissance

After World War II ended in 1945, resort skiing and backcountry skiing began a postwar renaissance marked by construction of European-like shelters and lodges. Near Aspen, Colorado, skiers fixed up an old dam tender's cabin now known as the Tagert Hut, still one of Colorado's best huts for alpine backcountry skiing. A year later, in 1947, the Alpine Club of Canada built the Wheeler Hut on Rogers Pass. The same year, Sun Valley Idaho's indomitable Averell Harriman hired a promoter for spring and summer skiing in the Idaho backcountry, using his local lodges which had been closed during the war. Three backcountry ski huts were also completed soon after this in the Wasatch Mountains of Utah.

Most importantly, like reborn crusaders chasing the grail, postwar skiers sought new lands and new challenges. Ski

technique had evolved to a powerful form of Schneider's arlberg, the gear was effective, and priorities in a new order after the austerity of conflict. It was time to play. In 1948, Mount Rainier got its first ski descent, and Sun Valley, Idaho's Andy Hennig authored the *Sun Valley Ski Guide*, North America's first true backcountry ski guidebook. Three years later, American Bil Dunaway joined famed French guide Lionel Terray for a bedrock event in the history of extreme skiing: the first ski descent of Mount Blanc in France, the highest peak in western Europe.

Gear improvements delayed by war came at a scorching pace. Most importantly, in 1950 Howard Head invented the composite ski which leads by direct genealogy to today's superb backcountry skis and snowboards. The new ski technology allowed a more powerful technique with tight continuous fall line turns known as *wedlin*. Using *wedlin* and variants, backcountry skiers of the 1950s negotiated steep couloirs with ease, made elegant runs through tight trees, and effortlessly picked their way down intricate glacier descents.

While other equipment innovations would eventually help backcountry skiers, many (if not most) improvements in the late 1940s and 1950s caused problems since design efforts were oriented toward fixed-heel resort skiing. For example, the same year Head's skis came out, Cubco of New Jersey started selling the first commercial step-in binding. Unlike cable bindings, the only touring you could do with a Cubco was to shuffle around like a wounded duck. Boots got stiffer with the invention of plastic boots by Bob Lange. Terms such as "Lange bang" and "foot vise" entered the vernacular of limping aprés-skiers. Ski touring in the new boots had become next to impossible.

Savvy backcountry skiers got around such gear limitations by using state-of-the-art skis combined with the cable bindings and leather boots of a few years past. For example, in 1957, Head skis, cable bindings and flexible boots were used by Bill Briggs, Sterling Neil and Roberts French in Canada's Bugaboo mountains to complete the first modern style alpine ski traverse in North America.

New goals and new terrain

The Bugaboo traverse marked the start of a new era. No doubt inspired by what Briggs had done, in 1960 Austrian émigré and guide Hans Gmoser led a group of Canadians along the Continental Divide from Kickinghorse to Jasper. A year later, Briggs and others made a modern-style ski descent of Mount Rainier via the Ingraham Glacier. Another classic, Buck Mountain in Wyoming's Tetons, had its first descent that same year. Meanwhile, reports of amazing extreme descents were filtering in from Europe. A compact Tyrolean chimney sweep named Heini

Holzer was skiing down routes most people regarded as difficult climbs. In France, fervent self-promoter Sylvain Saudan proclaimed himself the "skier of the impossible" after his stunning descent of the Spenser Couloir near Chamonix. North Americans took notice. In 1964 American Fritz Stammberger skied from 24,000 feet on Cho Oyu in the Himalayas—the world's highest ski descent at the time. Back in North America, Wyoming's Mount Moran got its first descent in 1968, via the stunning and classic Skillet Glacier route. All over North America, the ski was fast becoming a tool of modern alpinism.

Improved access to the mountains also began to drive the evolution of backcountry skiing. The pioneer ski mountaineers of the 1950s and early 1960s were tough, but not everyone was a Bill Briggs. While most backcountry skiers saw the value in a degree of discomfort and hardship, they had their limits. Of any single access event, the 1961 opening of Canada's

In Canada, the opening of the all-season Icefields Parkway in 1961 was an access milestone for North American ski mountaineers. Athabasca Glacier in foreground, North Face of Mount Athabasca to left, Mount Andromeda to right. *American Alpine Club Collection*

paved and redesigned Icefields Parkway stands out as the event that created much of Canadian glisse alpinism as we know it today. Farther south, skiers reached the high ground via highways in the Washington Cascades and Colorado Rockies. Meanwhile, Hans Gmoser recognized another form of access as the key to backcountry glisse: he started the helicopter skiing industry in 1965.

Unlike today's fenced boundaries and coddled public, yesterday's ski lifts and backcountry skiers blended seamlessly, and many a 1950s skier considered the climbing above the top ski lift to be the cap on a fine day. The rift between resort and backcountry, however, was ever widening, and the final break came with the 1949 invention of slope grooming and the 1951 patent on artificial snow making. From those moments

American Bil Dunaway and French guide Lionel Terray—with metal edged wood skis—preparing to descend Mont Blanc, France. Their 1951 descent sired modern extreme skiing. *Bil Dunaway Collection*

on, for most skiers on North American resort slopes, the wild snow of the back-country would seem as far away as the pocked surface of a lunar crater.

While North American ski areas ignored the needs of backcountry skiers, the continent's mountain huts gradually became another solution to the access equation. Skiers still had to spend a day getting to a hut; but at least they could do it with some-thing less than the 90-pound pack required for a high camp. The first "modern" huts had been put up in 1904: the Appalachian Mountain Club built the Carter Notch Hut in New Hampshire, and imported Swiss guides built the Hermit Hut in Glacier National Park. Subsequent hut building had been sporadic for 60 years, then the early 1960s saw the start of a "hut boom." Most of the Alfred Braun huts in Colorado were

Bill Briggs, a transition figure in several facets of North American ski mountaineering, holding composite Head skis used on his 1957 ski traverse in Canada's Bugaboo Mountains. *Bob French*

The demise of natural snow began in 1949 with the invention of the Bradly Packer Grader. *Colorado Ski Museum*

Yuichorio Miura schussed a few hundred feet down Mount Everest then took the most amazing ski fall ever recorded on film.

The crew of Fridtjof Nansen's polar expedition taking a break from their ice bound ship.

built during this period, as were many of Canada's finest, including the Balfour, Fairy Meadow, and Great Cairn huts.

Extreme skiers and distance artists

The current era began with the most famous clown act in ski mountaineering history. In 1970, Japanese promoter Yuichorio Miura climbed to the 26,201 foot South Col on Mount Everest. Sucking oxygen like a beached trout, he clicked into his skis and made a straight schuss toward basecamp 4,000 feet below. Never attempting a turn, Miura deployed a parachute to slow down. The chute fluttered like a tattered flag in the thin air, and Miura took the harshest ski fall ever recorded on film, eventually stopping just shy of a certain-death bergschrund. Miura's movie, "The Man Who Skied [sic] Down Everest," has been the butt of cruel jokes ever since, but awareness of what you could do *outside* the ski resorts took a giant leap forward. Later that year the Japanese redeemed themselves when Tsuyoshi Ueki made the first complete ski descent of Denali, the highest summit in North America.

The next year, 1971, was truly the birthday of North American mountain skiing. To kick things off, the now heavily sponsored Sylvain Saudan amazed Oregon's locals when he skied down Mount Hood from the summit. Several months later Bill Briggs made his visionary first descent of the Wyoming's Grand Teton. Two weeks later, with sublime creativity, Fritz Stammberger cramponed to the summit of Colorado's 14,014-foot North Maroon Peak, turned around, and stunned Colorado skiers by blithely skiing back down a cliff-banded face that's taken scores of lives on the peaks still nicknamed the "Deadly Bells." Unlike Briggs, Stammberger received little publicity.

Meanwhile, while skiing the steeps was sexy and thus touted by the media, another movement was afoot. Exploring the wilderness on skis, not to make turns but to cover distance, appealed to a traditional breed of adventurer with roots in the days of Norway's Nansen and Canada's Mundays. In 1967, Canadian hardmen Don Gardner, Neil Liske, Charlie Locke and Chic Scott skied the Great Divide Traverse, 190 miles from Jasper to Lake Louise. A few years later, Jim Ward, Trish Nice and five others trudged from Denver to Aspen in Colorado. In 1970, Doug Robinson and Peanut McCoy brought "ski trekking" to the Sierra when they made the first repeat of Bartholomew's 1928 Muir Trail traverse. Two years later in Alaska, Jed Williamson, Wayne Merry, Ned Gillette and Jack Miller made a 32-day

Ned Gillette and Jed Williamson traversing Alaska's Brooks Range, 1972. Expedition skiing still evokes the experience of early Nordic explorers. *Jack Miller*

traverse of the wild Brooks Range. Gillette went on to ski through the St. Elias Mountains, then made a ski circumnavigation of Denali. In the 1970s John Isaacs, Mark Udall and Randall Udall skied a three-week traverse of Wyoming's Wind River mountains. Several ski traverses were made in Canada's Coast Mountains during this period, and skiers even made treks across remote wilds such as arctic Baffin Island.

All this new activity was driven by, and sometimes drove, the evolution of modern backcountry ski equipment. Since the first cable bindings, early European heavy duty bindings worked both for free-heel walking and fixed-heel downhill. For example, the original Silvretta binding used a cable combined with a primitive hinge at the toe, while regular cable bindings of the time allowed heel-lift when the cable was released from lugs at the sides. These systems evolved into the classic "alpine touring" or "AT" bindings in use today, which allow a free heel for walking and a latched-down heel for skiing. Most glisse alpinism in the Alps required such gear, since the terrain was steep and the tradition of arlberg technique so strong. North Americans followed suit. Skiers such as Briggs and Stammberger used modified or full-on alpine gear for steep terrain. Other aggressive skiers used the alpine touring bindings of the day, even if they were fraught with problems such as excessive weight, lack of durability, and doubtful safety release.

With such problems in mind, a number of backcountry skiers of the 1970s, in particular those pursuing routes that mixed flat touring with steeper skiing, eschewed alpine touring gear and favored the flimsy boots and skis of imported Nordic ski equipment. When pressed into such heavy service the frail skis splintered and the boots ripped from bindings; skiing downhill on such gear remained an occult art mastered only by

select acolytes. Then, in 1972, Fischer Ski Company imported the Europa, a lightweight skinny ski with sidecut, aluminum edges, and solid construction. The new skis were still harder to ski downhill on than alpine equipment, but average skiers could begin to link enough turns to feel like they were doing something besides falling. A "telemark revival" began in earnest, and North Americans

The author on Fischer Europa skis in 1972. This light, metal edged touring ski was pressed into service as a mountaineering ski. *Louis Dawson Collection*

once again had ski gear that covered distance as well (or better) than the multipurpose skis of the old days, while they could still be forced into downhill performance.

While equipment fetishism dates back to Norheim, North American "free-heel" skiers of the 1970s took gear obsession to

Telemark skiers of the 1970s used exaggerated hand positions to try and keep their balance on flimsy boots and skis.
David Barnes

new heights. A small group of exceptional athletes mastered downhill skiing on "skinnys," and despite the availability of ever lighter and safer latched-heel alpine touring gear, they claimed their way was better. "Free your heel—free your mind" they'd say between telemarks. To prove their point, free-heelers claimed a number of "Nordic" descents of extreme routes. The epitome of this was Rick Wyatt's 1982 descent of the Grand Teton using low-top boots and skinny skis with aluminum edges. Wyatt's feat was indeed an amazing athletic accomplishment, but how important it was to ski mountaineering remains to be seen, since the peak had already been skied several times.

The same year Wyatt skied the "Grand" on his toothpicks, brothers Brad and Randall Udall used Nordic racing skis to skate the Muir Trail down the spine of California's Sierra: 230 miles in a week.

Randall Udall skied light by building snow shelters across the Sierras, the Wind Rivers, and Baffin Island. *Randall Udall Collection*

Downhill antics aside, the Udalls showed that when applied to a ski traverse with rolling terrain, Nordic skis ruled.

It should be noted that debate about telemark versus parallel skiing was nothing new: in the December 1932 Colorado Mountain Club newsletter, articles entitled "Condemnation of the Telemark" and "Defense of the Telemark" made detailed cases for both techniques. (By 1993 most reasons for this equipment fetish became moot; both heavy-duty Nordic and alpine touring gear reached equal weights, and today's skiers choose gear based on style rather than necessity.)

The 1970s also brought the advent of modern publications about ski mountaineering. Guidebooks written for Utah's Wasatch and California's Sierra opened skiers' eyes to the infinite American wilderness. A modern how-to book for the sport, Lito Tejada-Flores's *Wilderness Skiing*, emphasized the use of skins over wax, and included information about extreme skiing. *Powder Magazine*'s first issue was published in December of 1972 and covered skiing with an emphasis on natural snow, as it does to this day. The wilderness ski technique book of the 1970s, Steve Barnett's *Cross Country Downhill*, gave telemark tyros a modern look at Norheim's vintage free-heel tradition.

Meanwhile the impossible was still becoming possible. In 1973, California ski racer and climber Rick Sylvester one-upped Miura's Everest stunt by skiing off El Capitan in Yosemite Valley, then parachuting 3,000 vertical feet to the valley floor, thus locking his career as a stunt skier. On a less factitious note, that same year Aspen carpenter and former ski racer Chris Landry made the most technical descent of the 1970s when he skied the East Face of Colorado's Pyramid Peak—a feat yet to be repeated. Landry's contribution was covered by a landmark article in *Sports Illustrated* magazine—the first time the mainstream North American press covered such skiing.

While Landry and a few other artists (such as alpinist Steve Shea in the Tetons) were making lonesome technical ski descents in North America, a group of inspiring European extremists were heavily covered by the ski media. Led by flamboy-

Steve Barnett's 1970s how-to book, *Cross Country Downhill*, helped popularize North American backcountry skiing. *David Barnes*

Chris Landry's visionary extreme skiing in the 1970s helped set the tone for modern ski mountaineering. *Michael Kennedy*

ant French star Patrick Vallencant, Jean-Marc Boivin and other alpinists played one-upmanship for sponsorships and media coups. Boivin, bolder than even Vallencant, showed just how far the limits could go when he descended the Matterhorn's East Face in 1980, linking a discontinuous line with jumps and precision skiing on slopes steeper than 60 degrees. At a Telluride Film Festival in the 1980s, audiences were stunned by footage of Boivin's desperate skiing. "My hands broke a sweat as I watched Boivin," remembers a Film Fest participant, "He'd make a turn, then slide for 40 feet with his skis shaking and uphill hand dragging on the snow, finally gaining enough control to make another 'turn.' It was an awesome display, and made us realize just what could be done using skis as a tool of alpinism."

The European extremists led the development of ski alpinism. Moreover, they went beyond mere achievement and dipped into the spirituality Nansen had written of a century before. Vallencant describes his experiences thus: "When I concentrate so, the world disappears. …To ski a very steep slope is completely beautiful; it is pure, hard, vertical, luminous in a dimension that, by its nature, is foreign to us, yet I become a part of this cosmic dimension."

Other than a small cadre, North Americans did not pursue the limits of the sport as did Europeans such as Vallencant. Many good skiers lacked the mountaineering background necessary to tackle climbs and descents such as Pyramid Peak, while others with the requisite climbing skills were often distracted by free-heel skiing as a challenge in of itself. To fill the gap, the North American ski media focused on a small but accessible group of western skiers who jumped off cliffs, promoting their stunts as "extreme" skiing. A 1981 *Powder Magazine* article entitled "Ski to Die" epito-

mized the American approach. Picturing a few minor cliff jumps and people skiing straight down slopes with safe run-outs at the bottom, the article included photo captions urging such advice as "if it's too narrow to turn in and too steep to check, you can always just TUCK IT!" Try that on Mount Rainier or the Grand Teton.

Indeed, to seasoned ski mountaineers the cliff jumpers of the 1980s seemed more a clown act akin to Miura on Everest—especially when one gentleman made the first ski descent of Niagara Falls. Yet these skiing thespians knew their scripts. Many were actually superb technicians, fine athletes who created their telegenic persona for the simple expediency of making a living. Simply put, while traditional extreme skiing was about control on impossible slopes, media-inspired extreme skiing was about taking any terrain and skiing it on the edge of control, an activity better described as "acrobatics" than "skiing." A California star named Glen Plake was the epitome of these extremists. Out-skiing his peers during a film audition, he raked his hair into a sky-scraping mohawk, glissed fast and crazy, and his pockets jingled. Ski mountaineers were flabbergasted with the circus, and "cliff jumper" became a term of derision among the North American skiers who were climbing and skiing extreme routes similar to those being done in Europe. One disgusted glisse alpinist went so far as to shave a stripe down the middle of his scalp: an "anti-mohawk" in protest of what skiers like Plake had done to the concept of "extreme skiing."

Fortunately, media extreme skiers appeared who were as much mountaineers as skiers, such as Scott Schmidt and Doug Coombs. Also, critics didn't know Glen Plake spent time in Europe, knew real extreme skiing, and realized his own limitations. "The word *extreme* got overused", said Plake in a *Powder Magazine*

Doug Coombs—a popular media "extreme skier" and an accomplished mountaineer—on the Otter Body route on the Grand Teton, Wyoming, exhibiting the "moving billboard effect" of a sponsored skier. *Andrew McLean*

article 10 years after the ski-to-die article appeared, "Some guy jumps off a cliff and calls himself an extreme skier—he's not even close."

If anything, the late 1980s were a time of funerals and books—and much growth in the popularity of backcountry skiing. Briggs, Landry and Saudan are still alive, but Vallencant and Boivin died doing extreme sports (though not skiing). In 1980, the first North American extreme skier to die while skiing met his end on Mount Wedge, in Canada's Coast Mountains. Gerhart Singler was skiing the route with three companions. He stopped to take a photo, lost his footing, and slid to his death. Sadly, Singler had stopped to shoot his friend skiing with a dog in his arms, so the pet could make it down safely. In 1987, legendary eastern ski pioneer Jackrabbit Johannsen died at 111 years old. "I have been after adventure, always having a wonderful time. That's the reason I'm still alive," he'd said after breaking the century mark. In the end, Jackrabbit would stand gripping his ski poles in the back yard of his rest home, no doubt imagining the wind in his face and a perfectly waxed pair of skis gliding effortlessly over his beloved northeastern wild.

State of the art

The 1990s also began with mourning. Pierre Beghin, who'd done the first ski descent of Mount Foraker in Alaska, met his end while climbing on Annapurna. In North America, the dubious sport of cliff jumping reached a tragic extreme when Paul Ruff died trying a record drop of 160 feet. Yet the vitality of North American ski mountaineering had gained the momentum of a bullet train. The magnificent Sierra Nevada got a new guidebook, *Backcountry Skiing the High Sierra*. Also in California, the continent's first dedicated magazine of ski mountaineering, *Couloir*, began North American distribution. In Colorado, this author finished skiing all 54 of the state's 14,000-foot peaks in 1991, a 13-year project ranging from sublime corn snow bowls to terrifying avalanches. As an inspiration to ski mountaineers the world over, Mount Everest was skied in good style from just below the summit in 1992 by prolific extreme skier Pierre Tardivel. (Everest was skied from the summit in 1996 by Hans Kammerlander, but he climbed down a significant part of the route due to lack of snow.) In 1994, the finest backcountry ski guidebook yet published hit the shelves when Chic Scott's *Summits & Icefields* was released, detailing the vast glisse of the Canadian Rocky Mountains.

In the realm of recent North American glisse descents, Tyson Bradley and John Montecucco's 1994 ski descent of the Wickersham Wall on the North Peak of Denali stands as an inspirational feat. And North America's ultimate prize was claimed in 1995 when Ptor Spricenieks and Troy Jungen made a clean ski descent of the North Face of Mount Robson in Canada.

For the future, backcountry skiers and snowboarders have rediscovered the joys of access. Hut and lodge skiing is much more popular than roughing it with a heavy pack. Parking lots are filled with glisse alpinists' rides at access spots such as Teton Pass in the United States and Rogers Pass in Canada. Moreover, the ski resort industry (whose numbers have been flat for years) has taken notice. From Taos, New Mexico, to Whistler, British Columbia, resorts court disenchanted customers with "off-piste" and "extreme" runs that mimic the backcountry —albeit with a convenient ski patrol, minimal avalanche danger, and nearby bar stools as underpinning for brag sessions.

The 60-degree North Face of Mount Robson, Canadian Rockies, was skied in 1995—one of the hardest and most sought-after descents completed in North America.
Carl Skoog

In the hustle of modern life, we need more than ever balms to ease our souls

During his arctic ski adventures a century ago Fridtjof Nansen wrote:

> Is life a vale of tears? Is it such a deplorable fate to dash off like the wind … over the boundless expanse of ice … in the fresh, crackling frost, while the snow-shoes glide over the smooth surface so you scarcely know you are touching the earth? This is more, indeed, than one has any right to expect of life; it is a fairy tale from another world, from a life to come.

In the hustle of modern life, we need more than ever balms to ease our souls: those that dry the tears in Nansen's vale. Ski mountaineering is one such salve, and if past history is any indication, today's glisse alpinists will continue to embellish the rich tradition recorded in these pages, adding their own contributions as they escape the travail of civilization and return to lands of wild snow.

Subzero wonderland of Bighole Mountains, Idaho. Tetons in rear. *Jonathan Waterman*

PEAKS OF LIGHT:

CALIFORNIA SIERRA AND SAN GABRIEL MOUNTAINS

Peaks of Light: California Sierra and San Gabriel Mountains

California's mountain spine is one of North America's best places to backcountry ski and snowboard. You can tick descents off 14,000-foot peaks, enjoy the comfort of backcountry cabins or camp in friendly wilderness, or spend days on high routes that mimic a "low level flight over some of the most spectacular country on earth," as guide Allan Bard wrote. The Sierra's peaks range from the elegant granite arêtes of Mount Whitney, to the huge mounds of "east-side" giants such as Mount Tom. Perhaps the best thing about the Sierra Nevada, which means "snowy range" in Spanish, is its snowpack. It's a deep, avalanche-stable mass, and makes Rocky Mountain skiers weep with envy as they quake in fear of their own often precarious snow. What's more, come spring, that dense Sierra "cement" becomes some of the best corn snow on the planet.

Skiing in the Golden state began when Norwegian prospectors during the gold rush of 1849 introduced "Norwegian snowshoes," as skis were known at the time. The "Forty-niners" were stuck in high mining camps for the winter. When the legendary Sierra snow piled rooftop deep, bringing much of normal life to a halt, the most appropriate activity was obvious.

The center for mine district skiing was the town of La Porte. Located 60 miles northwest of Lake Tahoe, La Porte was a hodgepodge of hotels and bars with a plenitude of bored miners when snow shut down the prospecting. Starting about 1860, organized ski races were held in the La Porte area. These were not slalom races, but rather high-speed brouhahas with hundreds of spectators, mass starts, and speeds over 80 mph—precursors to modern speed skiing events. The racers rode huge planks, known as "long-boards," that sometimes reached 12 feet in length. La Porte racing was an honest backcountry endeavor; the participants climbed for every vertical foot they skied, and much of the sliding was done on unprepared snow.

The La Porte skiers organized North America's first ski club in 1867, which they named the Alturas Snow-Shoe Club. They had their first big race the same year: a wild cannonball run held on a 1,230-foot course. With hubris typical of downhill racers even today, the club placed an ad in the newspaper advertising their charter: "This is to let the world and the balance of creation know that the members of the Alturas Snow-Shoe club do hereby agree and bind themselves to furnish a man to compete with anybody that's 'ON IT' in the snowshoe line for any sum of money from $1,000 to $100,000."

While some miners were schussing, other Forty-niners shuffled through the mountains on skis. One such hardman was John "Snowshoe" Thompson, who immigrated from Norway in 1837, when he was 10 years old. In 1851 Thompson succumbed to the call of gold and followed the Forty-niners. Once in California he found a likely tree, chopped it down, carved a pair or skis, and thus hacked his place into ski history.

In January of 1856, Thompson skied the first Sierra high traverse when he trudged

The legendary Snowshoe Thompson, who carried mail through the Tahoe Sierra in the 1800s. *Western Ski Sport Museum*

The nineteenth-century "longboarders" of the Sierra mining district schussed at over 80 mph. *Western Ski Sport Museum*

90 miles from Placerville to Genoa, then turned around and skied back to Placerville in three days. For 20 years after that, Thompson carried mail through the Sierra backcountry, using skis whenever conditions warranted. For years he was the only winter communication between the Sierra mining district and the rest of the world.

Thompson received much publicity in the tabloids of the day. His extensive fame swelled his head, and he humiliated himself by challenging the downhill specialists of the Alturas Snow-Shoe Club—who roundly trounced the backcountry master in a race with no turns, obstacles, or climbing. From then on the "longboarders" ridiculed him.

Thompson disdainfully challenged the longboarders to a race "from the top to the bottom of the highest and heaviest timbered mountain we can find." The race was never held, but the whole affair showed skiing had already branched into distinct disciplines: downhill racing and backcountry travel.

Years later, when Thompson's skis went on display in Carson City in 1874, La Porte's local newspaper couldn't resist a dig: "Wonder if these are the same shoes that he brought to La Porte some years ago. If we remember rightly he went home with a large sized bug in his ear."

It wasn't until after World War I, during the Roaring Twenties, that skiing became widespread in California. During this period, "work skiers" made their living checking the Sierra snowpack. One such skier, Orland Bartholomew, made (in the winter of 1928–29) an amazing three-month solo traverse of the 250-mile Muir Trail. This Odyssean tour included partial or complete ski descents of 14,018-foot Mount Tyndall, 14,092-foot Mount Langley, and 14,495-foot Mount Whitney (see following selected routes).

Orland Bartholomew made an epic ski of the 250 mile Muir Trail in the winter of 1928-29.

Bartholomew recorded his adventure in the 1930 *Sierra Club Bulletin*, the official publication of the now well known Sierra Club. Founded in 1892 by John Muir and a group of California academicians, the Club began as an outing group; the *Bulletin* covered early ski alpinism in great detail. One of the first ski articles, in 1903, told how to make "skies" [sic] 12-feet long.

In 1930, the Sierra Club president appointed a winter sports study committee, which soon evolved into a Winter Sports Section. That same year, a prescient *Bulletin* author would write that: "Spring skiing in the Sierra is practically unknown, but many European skiers believe that California affords ideal conditions for this type of skiing ... the writer confidently believes that within a very few years ... ski-mountaineering will have thousands of devotees."

It was to be more than just a few years before there were thousands, but backcountry skiing's hundreds of disciples were skilled and committed. Within 10 years alpine pioneers such as David Brower, Dr. Walter Mosauer, Bestor Robinson, Lewis Clark, Joel Hildebrand and pioneer climber Norman Clyde recorded their thoughts on ski alpinism for the pages of the *Sierra Club Bulletin*, and no doubt informing and inspiring those who were to come. In 1933, for example, Lewis Clark wrote of a 55-mile ski across Yosemite Park, and published an extensive illustrated review of California skiing in the *Bulletin* of the Appalachian Mountain Club. This no doubt spread the word about the fine touring available in California.

In 1934, the Sierra Club built a ski hostel near Donner Summit in the Tahoe Sierra. Known as the Clair Tappaan Lodge, this was intended as the first in a series of huts on a ski route connecting Donner Summit and Yosemite National Park. The route was known as the "Donner Skiway," and

could have been one of the finest hut systems in North America. Two other huts were built, but politics and World War II intruded, and the Skiway was never completed.

By now, development of ski resorts was becoming somewhat common. At least a few backcountry skiers were being lured away from the backcountry by seductive packed trails and warm lodges. David Brower, well known for his leadership of the Sierra Club, felt called upon to defend ski mountaineering in the 1938 *Sierra Club Bulletin*:

> Everyone becomes aware, once in a while, of certain basic truths pertaining to practice [resort] slopes: (a) quest for the perfect christy is futile; (b) filling other persons' sitzmarks is monotonous; (c) it is less fun to fall on packed snow than on powder; (d) it is frightening when skis go too fast; (e) it is terrifying to be mistaken for a slalom gate. ...Now and then it's essential to have a change—to strike off on a ski-tour, or better still, to try ski-mountaineering.

A great influence on early California ski mountaineering was Otto Steiner, an expert skier from Germany. Steiner was also one of those backcountry skiers seduced by the ski resort *gemütlichkeit*. He fell in love with an area of the high Sierra known as Mineral King, now contained in the southern end of Sequoia National Park. During several decades of intense activity, Steiner skied hundreds of peaks in the area, and in 1937 did a high crossing of the Sierras from Lodgepole (now inside Sequoia National Park) to Mount Whitney and back to his newfound skier's paradise, Mineral King, all in a speedy 10 days. This was the time various European skiers, such as Andre Roch in Aspen, were backcountry skiing to research land for development as ski resorts. Steiner was to follow suit; devoting his life to exploring Mineral King and promoting it as the perfect place for ski lifts. By 1965 famed media producer Walt Disney had gotten involved, and building on Steiner's work, made an ambitious proposal to develop Mineral King as a ski resort. Unfortunately, both Steiner and Disney failed to acknowledge the nascent environmental movement and went loggerheads with the Sierra Club. In a protracted court battle, the environmentalists hit Disney's proposal like a slab avalanche mowing a forest. The proposed resort was nixed in 1969, and three decades of Steiner's life work were buried forever. To his last days, Steiner derisively called the environmentalists "flower sniffers."

Steiner was from the old school: those who felt resort skiing and backcountry could blend and work together. He'd failed to see many California backcountry skiers had become environmentalists who considered any new ski resort an abomination. Indeed, while Steiner was doing his work leading to the Mineral King fight, the most active ski mountaineers in the Sierra were those of the opposition: the ski group of the Sierra Club, often led by David Brower. In the late 1930s and 1940s, Brower and his cohorts made ski ascents and descents on scores of High Sierra peaks, including aggressive descents off Matterhorn Peak, Mount Lyell, Mount Clark and Mount Starr King. Brower and his crew would ski as high as possible, do a sometimes technical snow climb to the summit, then ski from the loftiest point they could. "Not very long ago," wrote Brower, "the attainment of the summit was the climax of the climber's day. Now there are two climaxes. Hail to the schuss!" Brower summed up his vast experience when he wrote an early and remarkably complete ski mountaineering how-to book, the *Manual of Ski Mountaineering*. The book was published in 1942 and used as a training manual for the U.S. Army ski troops.

While common wisdom holds that Steiner pioneered much of Sierra back-country skiing, it's possible the range's most prolific early skier was a trapper named Shorty Lovelace. From about 1920 to 1940, Shorty spent most of every winter trapping and hunting in the high Sierra, mostly in a region that's now the southern area of Kings Canyon National Park. He was an alcoholic, and the only way he found to avoid drinking himself to death was to live in the mountains away from temptation. Shorty's work included thousands of miles on home-made skis while running his trap lines in the Mineral King area and beyond. Most likely he skied every canyon below the modern-day high routes, and in crossing from canyon to canyon climbed the high ridges. Indeed, he probably skied most of the terrain Otto Steiner explored. Shorty was 5'4" tall, and built several dozen cabins that were exactly 5'5" tall—true precursors to modern ski huts, if you had the right physical characteristics. "If we're going to have a father of California backcountry skiing I think Shorty deserves it," says Sierra high-route pioneer and guide Dave Beck.

An important event of this era was the construction, in 1940, of the Ostrander ski touring hut in Yosemite National Park. This beautiful stone cabin, replete with a live-in ranger-cum-caretaker, was haven for several generations of California backcountry skiers. Sadly, in 1994 the hut closed. This came about because of bureaucratic bumbling and misguided environmental regulations. "By 1994 six departments of the [National Park Service] bureaucracy were involved in the turf at Ostrander, and nothing, down to food scraps in the sink or dishwater, was considered too insignificant to regulate," wrote Howard Weamer in *The Perfect Art*, his book about the hut. The Ostrander outhouse was deemed unacceptable by the 'crats, and rather than allowing simple fixes such as a removable holding tank or an approved septic system, the red tape grew like a jungle vine. It turned out that the legal wilderness boundary was drawn to include the hut, and the outhouse was classified as a toxic waste site! As of this writing the hut is tenuously open.

In the late 1950s and early 1960s, a small cadre of Californians brought modern ski mountaineering to the Sierra. Eccentric Hans George, founder of the small ski area that preceded Mammoth Mountain, did many ski descents in the high peaks, most of which are lost to history. In 1956, George teamed up with a young ski racer named Paul Arthur, and the pair made the first ski descent of Mount Tom's grand Elderberry Canyon. Arthur went on to make the first descent of Mount Whitney, California's highest (see following routes).

Other influential skiers of the 1960s and 1970s were writer and guide Doug

Robinson, and Carl "Peanut" McCoy (the son of Dave McCoy, founder of Mammoth ski area). In 1970, Robinson and McCoy repeated Bartholomew's 1928 Muir Trail traverse, and brought a modern attitude to the game. While Bartholomew had skied out of the mountains several times for resupply, Robinson and McCoy skied a higher line and used food caches so they could stay in the mountains for longer periods. Robinson had experimented in the late 1960s and early 1970s with backcountry skiing, and he was somewhat the leader of a group of Sierra skiers informally known as the "Armadillos." A Taoistic spirit marked many of the California skiers, culminating when some adopted a philosophy holding that the hype surrounding Yosemite Valley mountaineering was best avoided by not reporting first ascents—or descents. Indeed, one Yosemite climber, when developing routes in his own "secret"

Shorty Lovelace—the most prolific early Sierra skier—hand crafted his skis for winters trapping and hunting.
Sequoia Natural History Association

Orland Bartholomew at Muir Pass during his 1928-29 Muir Trail traverse. His route was not repeated until 1970.

area, is reported to have said (in a not so Taoist way), that he'd kill anyone who wrote a guidebook. Sadly, because of this attitude a part of California's inspiring mountaineering history has been lost.

Stunts, stealth and Taoism aside, another backcountry enthusiast, Rick Sylvester, and his peers did much note-worthy ski mountaineering in the 1970s, including early descents of the Central Couloir on Castle Peak and routes on such High Sierra giants as Mount Tom. In 1972, some of the most extreme glisse of the time was done in the U-Notch and V-Notch Couloirs on the Palisades, by firewood cutter and extraordinary skier Bruce Fessenden. In 1974, photographer Galen Rowell put together a 16-day ski traverse of the White Mountains, a Sierra sub-range to the east of Bishop; he and his *compadres* also skied 14,246-foot White Mountain Peak during

their trip. In 1980, Rowell joined up with Yosemite climber Kim Schmidtz and Squaw Valley wildman Carl Gustofsen to make the first ski descent of enormous Mount Williamson, at 14,375 feet the second highest of California's "fourteeners." Another active glisse alpinist of the time was filmmaker Eric Perlman, who skied down the East Face of Yosemite's mono-lithic Half Dome in 1980 with Bob Bellman, then teamed up with Bruce Fessenden and skied the stupendous central couloir off Mount Williamson in 1982; they christened their Williamson route "Chute the Works." Perhaps the most well known extreme ski-ing of the time happened when Chris Landry visited from Colorado in 1981, and stunned the locals when he skied down the Mendel Couloir on Mount Mendel in the high Sierra, an ice filled gash previously known only as an ice climb. Landry's descent

Carl "Peanut" McCoy at far left with the "Armadillos," early 1970s. Eschewing climbing skins, Doug Robinson (at far right) wrote that "No Armadillo would put the skin of a fellow mammal on the bottom of his skis ... that's not nice." *Jan Tiura*

included changing to crampons so he could downclimb a patch of steep blue ice; a witness to the event says it was one of the scariest things he'd ever watched.

Recent ski mountaineering history of the Sierra includes numerous traverses and high-routes. In 1971, David Thompson did a fairly high-altitude solo rendition of Steiner's Sierra Crossing. Then in 1975, David Beck, Bob Couly, and Nick Hartzell did a modern *haute* version of the route, staying with the high ridges and thus maintaining uncorrupted alpine atmosphere. This has since become known as "The Sierra High Route" and is repeated yearly by numerous parties. Bill Nicolai and Pam Kelley did a long version of the Muir Trail traverse in 1978, spending 55 days skiing from Carson Pass to Whitney Portal. In 1983, Allan Bard, Tom Carter and Chris Cox made a mountaineering version of the Muir Traverse, staying as high as possible while climbing and skiing steep terrain on the Sierra Crest. They called their route the "Redline Traverse."

While Californians were perhaps remiss in recording their recent history, they were busy leading North America in back-

A modern glisse alpinist ponders the U-notch and V-Notch Couloirs, first skied in 1972 by Bruce Fessenden. *Craig Dostie*

country ski publishing. *Summit Magazine*, North America's first mountaineering periodical, started publication in 1955 in the town of Bishop on the east side of the Sierra. *Summit* focused on climbing, but still published the occasional ski article. In 1971 California also produced North America's second ski mountaineering guidebook, H.J. Burhenne's *Sierra Spring Ski Touring*. (The first was Andy Hennig's 1948 *Sun Valley Ski Guide*.) Burhenne had hut skied in the Alps, but wrote that in California "the conditions are better … the weather more reliable … and there are practically no crevasses to fall into."

California's backcountry locals remained somewhat tight lipped throughout the 1980s and early 1990s. A guidebook covering high crossings of the Sierra was authored by Dave Beck in 1980, but it included few ski descents. Then, in 1992, mountaineering guide John Moynier authored the Sierra's modern glisse alpinism guidebook, *Backcountry Skiing the High Sierra*. The secrets were out of the bag—and some of the finest descents on the continent are easy to find and enjoy. Moynier reports that presently Davey McCoy, Scott Schmidt, Glen Plake, and others may be aspiring to a new level of glisse alpinism in the Sierra. For example, Plake recently made a fine ski descent of Clyde's Gully on Split Mountain, one of California's "fourteeners." No doubt other descents have been made; will the locals declare these a Golden State secret? One would hope they will share their treasures, to give us our legends—but wealth has a way of being hoarded.

California's mountains are divided into three regions in this chapter. The "Tahoe Sierra" includes the mountains in the greater Lake Tahoe area. The "High Sierra" includes the Sierra south to Mount Whitney. (The Cascade mountains extend into northern California, and are covered in their own

chapter.) The San Gabriel Mountains rise to the north and northeast of the city of Los Angeles (and are connected to the San Bernardino Mountains farther to the east).

TAHOE SIERRA

Populous and accessible, the lands around Lake Tahoe provide a range of opportunity. You can hike to Twin Peaks after gaining part of your vertical at the Alpine Meadows ski area. Or stay away from resort crowds and venture to the backcountry from Donner Pass on Interstate 80.

Guidebook author John Moynier defied the covert California attitude and detailed the secrets of Sierra glisse alpinism. *John Moynier Collection*

Twin Peaks—North Face

Twin Peaks is an elegant summit located just behind the Alpine Meadows ski area next to Lake Tahoe. While backcountry purists may find the resort too close for comfort, they can rest with the knowledge of the legal wilderness boundary passing through Twin Peaks' summit, thus insuring much of the land near the peak will remain as backcountry. The first skiing on Twin Peaks is lost in history, and no doubt occurred more than 40 years ago.

Lake Tahoe and Twin Peaks (at center of horizon). *Craig Dostie*

Drive Interstate 80 to the Lake Tahoe region. Turn off the Interstate at the exit for Highway 89, and head south about 15 miles to Ward Creek Road (past the turnoffs for Squaw Valley and Alpine Meadows ski areas). Turn west on the Ward Creek Road, and drive 2 miles to parking at the Twin Peaks Trail. Parking may be limited, and by using a car shuttle you may be able to start your trip farther up the road.

From parking, ski up Ward Creek to the basin below Twin Peaks. Swing south, gain Twin Peaks' East Ridge, and take the ridge to the summit. With stable snow conditions, an Advanced-rated snow climb takes the Main Chute from Ward Creek to the summit. For the easiest descent, drop west from the summit into the Granite Chief Wilderness via a broad snowface, then climb back to the summit or any of several saddles, and descend Ward Creek back to parking. For more challenging skiing or riding, take the Main Chute from the summit (rated Advanced/Extreme).

When Alpine Meadows ski area opens its boundary to backcountry skiing, the ridge tour from the ski area to Twin Peaks is a classic. Arrange a car pickup at Ward Creek, or traverse back to the ski lifts after you ski Twin Peaks. Such a tour involves several miles of traversing from the ski area, and may take the better part of a day.

Start: 6,640 feet (varies with exact parking)
Summit: 8,878 feet
Vertical gain: 2,238 feet
Round trip distance and time: 8 miles, 7 hours
Ascent: Intermediate
Glisse: Advanced
Maps: USGS 7.5 minute, Homewood; Alpine Meadows Ski Area trail map
Guidebook: Alpenglow Ski Shop brochure, Lake Tahoe
Weather: Copious snowfall is the rule here, but the area is usually graced with periodic sunshine, especially in spring. Use television and commercial radio for reports. The ski resort snow report can also give you a good idea of prevailing conditions (see Directory). The Tahoe and High Sierra have somewhat similar weather patterns, though the east side of the higher range may be drier due to the moisture shadow effect. Prevailing westerly winds move regular storms across the Sierra. To the benefit of recreationists, such storms are staggered with periods of good weather which can last for several days

Kern Barta descends Twin Peaks—the mountain offers a full repast of glisse. *Grant Barta*

(or weeks) during a normal winter. Huge weather events, known as *pineapple storms*, may happen when a high lingers over the Pacific Northwest—such storms can make both road and ski travel impossible. Most importantly, snowfall in the Sierra is copious and of the dense maritime variety, which is often less avalanche prone than continental snow. The price mountaineers pay for such safer snow is a condition called "Sierra cement," a sticky brew that demands flawless ski technique, good wax, and the right pair of skis. Luckily, for skiers worshipping at the Sierra altar, in spring the cement soon hardens into perfect corn snow.

Red Tape: The route to Twin Peaks from Alpine Meadows ski area is subject to closure by the Alpine Meadows ski patrol. Obey such restrictions. If you don't like someone else making your decisions, climb the peak from the base. Be aware of private property in Ward Creek.

Castle Peak—Central Couloir

Castle Peak rises four miles north of Donner Pass, in an area that's been a traditional backcountry ski destination for many decades. The first ascent and descent of Castle are lost in antiquity. In 1935, Joel Hildebrand wrote of skiing on the peak in the *Sierra Club Bulletin* in 1935; it's unknown how high the skiers launched from. No matter, make a little of your own history. Castle is a rocky ridge rising to the north of Interstate 80 and the Boreal ski area. The peak boasts many ski routes: a mellow West Ridge, an East Ridge with a rock scramble to the summit, a beautiful North Face, and the south facing Central Couloir covered here.

Drive Interstate 80 to the west slope of Donner Pass, and turn off at the exit for the Boreal ski area (signs indicate "Castle Peak Area"). Take a left and park at the well signed "Snowpark." (For parking you need a "Snowpark Permit," which you can purchase at local mountaineering shops and commercial establishments close to trailheads.) From Snowpark, walk back to the underpass under I-80, and continue to road's end a few hundred feet farther. (There may be parking here for several cars.) An obvious and well-traveled trail leads up toward the peak, eventually deviating to the Sierra Club's Peter Grubb Hut (located on the far side of the peak's West Ridge). Leave the main trail where appropriate, and climb up the Central Couloir. If the couloir is not in condition, descend the peak's West Flank.

Start: 7,100 feet
Summit: 9,103 feet
Vertical gain: 2,003 feet
Round trip distance and time: 6 miles, 6 hours
Ascent: Advanced
Glisse: Advanced
Map: USGS 7.5 minute, Norden
Guidebook: Alpenglow Ski Shop brochure, Lake Tahoe
Weather: See preceding Twin Peaks section
Red Tape: Purchase a Snowpark Permit for parking, available at local retailers.

Castle Peak from the south, showing Central Couloir and the highway. *Louis Dawson*

Mount Tallac—Northeast Face

Towering above Lake Tahoe, Mount Tallac is the area's signature mountain. Sprouting from the south shore of Lake Tahoe, Tallac catches each sunset like the pallet of a master painter. Little is known of the peak's mountaineering history. The easier ski lines no doubt received their first turns in the 1940s, while the steep Cross Couloir's probable first ascent was done in 1960 by Paul Arthur and Wally Ballinger. The peak's name means "large mountain" in a Native American tongue.

Lake Tahoe and Mount Tallac (to left), the area's signature peak. *Craig Dostie*

In the Lake Tahoe area, drive Highway 89 south from Interstate 80. After a long drive around the west shore of the lake, you'll come to the town of Camp Richardson. From the south, you can drive to Camp Richardson via Highway 50. From Richardson, drive Highway 89 west (double back if you came from the north) 2 miles to Spring Creek Road. Follow the road to public trailhead parking in a residential area.

From the trailhead, hike southwest and cross a brushy field, then climb an obvious shoulder to the peak's long North Ridge. Take the ridge to the summit. For glisse descents you have several options: a broad slope, obvious on the way up, drops to the north of the ascent shoulder, while a steeper option plunges north from the summit. If you like extreme descents, the well known Cross Couloir drops northeast from the summit (super-steep, rated Extreme). For a "daily double," glisse the huge bowls on the south side, then climb back up for the northerly runs.

Start: 6,400 feet

Summit: 9,735 feet

Vertical gain: 3,335 feet

Round trip distance and time: 6 hours

Riding Mount Tallac. *Grant Barta*

Camp in Deadman Canyon, during David Beck's aggressive new Sierra High Route in 1975. *David Beck Collection*

Ascent: Intermediate
Glisse: Advanced
Map: USGS 7.5 minute, Emerald Bay
Guidebook: None.
Weather: See preceding Twin Peaks section
Red Tape: Park with care in the midst of private property. Tallac is popular, so consider skiing it on weekdays.

HIGH SIERRA

The High Sierra is a place of wonder and delight for all lovers of mountains; a place of worship, of growing, of learning. Indeed, as many have found, traveling to the world's so called "great ranges," with their objective hazards, altitude problems and political nightmares, can make a "friendly" range like the Sierra seem like Nirvana. As for skiing, the Sierra's stable snowpack, virtually infinite array of skiable peaks, and fine weather all combine to make this one of the best ski mountaineering ranges on the planet.

Mountaineering in the High Sierra began in 1864 when surveyor and fanatical explorer Clarence King crossed Kings-Kern Divide and climbed Mount Tyndall, in an effort to reach the "high portion of the Sierra." Soon after King, naturalist John Muir made his first trip into the range. Muir's life was an epoch of exploration and inspiration. He wrote extensively of the range, campaigned for preservation, and founded the Sierra Club. In 1868, he penned the oft-quoted words which so distill the Sierra essence: "it still seems above all others the Range of Light, the most divinely beautiful of all the mountain-chains."

Aside from secular sunrises, Muir found deep spirituality in the Sierra. His "light" was that of divinity. "In my first hour of freedom from that terrible shadow, the sunlight in which I was laving seemed all in all," Muir wrote after he faced death on a solo climb, and was rescued by an otherworldly presence. To bask in the light so dear to Muir, grab your glisse tools of choice, and head for the High Sierra.

Matterhorn Peak—East Couloir

Matterhorn Peak is the highest arête on a jagged section of the Sierra Crest known as the "Sawtooth Ridge." The peak is known for its fine alpine mountaineering, including all manner of ski terrain, from mellow to extreme. Matterhorn resembles its European namesake (though on a much smaller scale). The classic ski line on the peak is the East Couloir, a steep gully dropping from a point about 200 vertical feet below the summit.

The peak was first climbed in 1899 by a group including James Hutchinson, a future Sierra Club president. Soon after the first ascent, Sierra Club ski groups began using the peak as a playground. Participants on such outings no doubt skied from high in the steep east couloir (Paul Arthur reports skiing the couloir many times from the exact crest, starting in 1963, but he "never found the summit in skiable condition.") It's doubtful any of the early skiers made summit ski descents, since the rocky summit "horn" is impossible to ski on all but the best snow years, and even then it's extremely steep and improbable.

While not on skis or a snowboard, 1960s bard Jack Kerouac found the essence of glisse during his own Matterhorn

Matterhorn Peak from the east, with the glisse route down the main couloir. *John Moynier Collection*

Starting an extreme descent on a ridge adjacent to Matterhorn Peak. *Grant Barta*

descent, when he learned to blend with gravity and wrote about it in his book *Dharma Bums*:

> Then suddenly everything was just like jazz. ...I looked up and saw Japhy running down the mountain in huge twenty-foot leaps, running, leaping, landing with great drive of his booted heels, bouncing five feet or so, running, then taking another long crazy yelling yodelaying sail down the side of the world. ...And with a yodel of my own I suddenly got up and began running down the mountain after him doing exactly the same.

Matterhorn Peak: on the east side of the Sierra Nevada, drive Highway 395 to the town of Bridgeport. From Bridgeport, drive a well signed road 13 miles to parking at Twin Lakes. Hike the Horse Creek trail, or with snowcover simply ski straight up the drainage. At about 2 miles you'll reach the best camping spot (8,300 feet). Camping above here may expose you to rockfall and avalanches. From the camp spot, continue up Horse Creek a short distance, then take the first main feeder creek on your right. Climb the route of the creek, which leads you to a view of Matterhorn Peak (it looks like its namesake), then to the East Couloir. Climb the couloir, leave your skis or board at the ridge, then scramble to the summit. Descend your ascent route. The steep part of the couloir is about 45°.

Start: 7,100 feet
Summit: 12,279 feet
Vertical gain: 5,179 feet
Round trip distance and time: 10 miles, overnight or long day
Ascent: Advanced
Glisse: Extreme from highpoint of couloir
Maps: USGS 7.5 minute, Matterhorn Peak, Dunderberg Peak, Buckeye Ridge
Guidebook: *Backcountry Skiing In the High Sierra*, John Moynier
Weather: Mid-to-late winter and spring are the best seasons for skiing on Matterhorn Peak. For general information, see preceding Twin Peaks section.
Red Tape: Register for wilderness travel at the Forest Service station near Bridgeport

Bloody Mountain— Bloody Couloir

Bloody Mountain, with its intimidating Bloody Couloir, greets you when you drive into the town of Mammoth Lakes. The history of Bloody is lost in a sea of Mammoth locals who regard this as the local testpiece for extreme skiing. Most certainly, as soon as the Mammoth Mountain ski area attracted skiers such as Dave McCoy and Hans George, the peak got skied, and probably the couloir.

Bloody Mountain main couloir drops from right summit, while other options abound. *John Moynier Collection*

Bloody Mountain's approach is simple: Use a four-wheel-drive high clearance auto, and drive the Sherwin Creek Road south from the town of Mammoth Lakes. Turn left on the Laurel Lakes Road, and drive to snowline. Travel on foot up the remainder of the road, and continue to the base of the couloir. For the best climbing route, stay left of two rock towers splitting the couloir—the standard descent route. It's narrow and over 45° steep. For easier skiing, other routes drop down various aspects from the summit.

Start: 8,800 feet (varies with snow closure of road)

Summit: 12,544 feet

Vertical gain: 3,744 feet

Round trip distance and time: approximately 6 miles, 7 hours

Ascent: Advanced

Glisse: Extreme

Map: USGS 7.5 minute map, Bloody Mountain

Guidebook: *Backcountry Skiing in the High Sierra*, John Moynier

Weather: See preceding Twin Peaks section

Red Tape: None

Mount McGee—East Gully

Mount McGee is an accessible peak located just west of Highway 395 on the Sierra east side. During the winter of 1952-53, when record snows closed access to the Mammoth Mountain ski resort, Mammoth's owner Dave McCoy installed a rope tow on the flanks of Mount McGee. No doubt many early climbs and descents of McGee were made by ski instructors such as Hans George who worked at the stopgap ski area. The earliest documented descent was made by Peanut McCoy in 1972.

Mount McGee from the east, as seen from the highway. *John Moynier Collection*

For Mount McGee, drive Highway 395 north from Bishop or south from Reno, Nevada to Lake Crowley. Park near the highway and lake shore, and climb any of several obvious routes up the peak. A long gully on the Northeast Face is popular.

Start: 6,900 feet
Summit: 10,871 feet
Vertical gain: 3,971 feet
Round trip distance and time: 5 miles, 6 hours
Ascent: Intermediate
Glisse: Advanced
Map: USGS 7.5 minute, Convict Lake
Guidebook: *Backcountry Skiing in the High Sierra*, John Moynier
Weather: See Twin Peaks above
Red Tape: None

Mount Tom—Elderberry Canyon

If you're driving to the town of Bishop on the east side of the Sierra, scrub the bugs off your windshield, keep your eyes to the zenith, and lock a firm hand on your steering wheel. There it'll be, rising in front of you like a white siren: a mountain of abysmal drops, massive vertical, and moderate yet lively terrain the greatest ski resorts in the world can only dream of grooming. In the words of guidebook author John Moynier, it's "the finest peak descent in the Sierra," Mount Tom.

Mount Tom viewed from the east. This gigantic monolith is a must-do for any glisse alpinist. *John Moynier Collection*

For Mount Tom, drive Highway 395 from Bishop about 10 miles north, then turn left (west) on the Pine Creek Road and drive 2 miles to the small town of Rovanna. From Rovanna, follow a dirt road to the lower flanks of Mount Tom (6,300 feet), then follow a trail into Elderberry Canyon. Climb the canyon to the large cirque at its head. To reach the summit, climb the headwall to the North Ridge, and take the ridge to the summit. Most people start their glisse descents from below the headwall. To descend from the summit, follow the ridge down to the headwall, then glisse one of several steep couloirs down into Elderberry Canyon.

Start: 6,300 feet

Summit: 13,652 feet

Vertical gain: 7,352 feet to summit

Round trip distance and time: 16 miles, 12 hours

Ascent: Advanced (to summit)

Glisse: Advanced to Extreme from summit

Maps: USGS 7.5 minute, Mount Tom, Mount Morgan

Guidebook: *Backcountry Skiing in the High Sierra*, John Moynier

First ski descent: Paul Arthur and Hans George, 1956

Weather: Late winter or spring are the best times for this route. See Twin Peaks above.

Red Tape: None

Mount Whitney— Mountaineers Route

Whitney is not necessarily a great ski peak—it just happens to be tall—kind of like Mount Everest, says backcountry guru Doug Robinson. Indeed, Mount Whitney, at 14,494 feet is the highest peak in the continental United States, and while it doesn't have the skiing of Mount Tom or Mount Williamson, several excellent glisse routes grace Whitney.

When snow coats the peak to its summit (which it rarely does), variations on Whitney's northeast side hiking route make the easiest ski routes. Orland Bartholomew, during his heroic Muir Trail traverse in 1928, "skied" part of this route. Eugene Rose, in *High Odyssey*, describes how Bartholomew jury-rigged a toboggan from his skis and starting at 12,600 feet "leaned forward, grasped the bindings, and set off straight down the chute, praying he had selected an unbroken gully. ...Miraculously, he was uninjured ... the casualties were his pride, frayed nerves,

and two pairs of trousers which had frozen during the impromptu descent."

Whitney was first completely climbed on skis by a Dr. F. Zwickey in 1929; but it's highly unlikely he skied from the summit. The first documented summit ski descent of Whitney was made in 1956 by Paul Arthur and Larry Yout, again by sticking close to the standard hiking route. The pair were diehard skiers who'd learned skiing with an aggressive Boy Scout troop on San Gorgonio Peak in Southern California. No doubt viewing the 16-year-old Arthur as no threat to his goals, pioneer skier Hans George told Arthur of his plan to ski from the summit of Mount Whitney. George should have kept his mouth shut. Arthur grabbed his friend Larry Yout and the pair skied from the summit on Washington's birthday; thus becoming the first to ski from the highest peak in the conterminous United States.

While not the first summit descent, the most direct route off Whitney was first skied in 1983 by guides Allan Bard and Tom Carter, during their Redline ski traverse of

Skiing the lower section of the Mountaineers Route, Mount Whitney. *Craig Dostie*

Paul Arthur (who was first to ski Mount Whitney with Larry Yout in 1956) during a Sierra ski crossing in the 1960s.
Paul Arthur Collection

the Sierra Crest. The route they chose, the broad ice mantle of the peak's North Face, is usually a serious ice climb. The pair took advantage of good snowcover and made the descent without incident. Bard described it as "steep, dangerous, and scary."

The most classic ski route on Whitney is the Mountaineers Route, a broad couloir on the northeast side first climbed in 1873 by Sierra Club founder John Muir. To avoid all the people climbing Whitney via the easy hiking route, Muir scrambled up the broad snowy couloir above Iceberg Lake on the northeast side of the peak. He would later write in disgust that "soft, succulent people should go the mule way." The first ski descent of Muir's "Mountaineers Route" was done in 1974 by photographer Galen Rowell. By self admission an "average" skier, Rowell made the descent by using a pair of short *figle* skis and "hopping" down the couloir.

Mount Whitney: enjoy a scenic drive on Highway 395 to the town of Lone Pine, then drive 12 miles west on the Whitney Portal Road to the Whitney Portal trailhead. Follow the beaten trail up Lone Pine Creek to Iceberg Lake. The Mountaineers Route couloir rises above the lake. Climb the couloir, then reach the summit by continuing up the steep northerly face. For your descent, downclimb the steep section below the summit, and ski or snowboard from the top of the couloir.

Start: Whitney Portal, 8,367 feet

Summit: 14,494 feet

Vertical gain: 6,127 feet

Round trip distance and time: 16 miles, overnight

Ascent: Intermediate

Glisse: Advanced

Maps: USGS 7.5 minute: Mount Whitney, Mount Langley

Guidebook: The Mountaineers Route is not covered in any existing guidebooks. For the approach and information on other routes see *Sierra Classics* by Moynier and Fiddler.

First ascent of route: John Muir, 1873

First ski descent of route: Galen Rowell, 1974

First ski descent of peak: Paul Arthur and Larry Yout, 1956

Weather: April and May are good months for skiing this route. See Twin Peaks above for a general weather description.

Red Tape: Registration is required, do so at the Forest Service office in Lone Pine (see Directory). Mountaineering permits are limited in summer months, so go early.

Mount Whitney, 14,494 feet, the highest peak in the contiguous United States. The Mountaineers Route follows the couloir right of summit. *John Moynier Collection*

SAN GABRIEL MOUNTAINS

San Antonio Peak—
Southeast Bowl

S outhern California and backcountry skiing would seem a strange
pair. Indeed, the San Gabriel and San
Bernardino Mountains rising up from the
Los Angles basin are most often hot and
dry, but winter always provides a skiable
coating of snow.

In 1932, several Pomona college students and University of California ski coach
and biologist Dr. Walter Mosauer had mastered the arlberg technique and were tired of
"Scandinavian skiing" (the media of the day
was hot on ski jumping and Nordic racing).
Mosauer and his crew made many backcountry trips in the area, including the first

descent of the San Bernardino Mountain's
highest peak: Mount San Gorgonio (11,510
feet). In 1933, Mosaur was appointed chair-
man of a southern California section of the
Sierra Club Winter Sports Committee. In
1934, he published an early how-to book
called *On Ski over the Mountains*. By 1935,
Mosaur and his fellow skiers had established a Sierra Club sub-group known as the
"Ski Mountaineers Section."

The Ski Mountaineers Section took
their planks to southern California mountains such as Ontario Peak, Telegraph Peak,
Blue Ridge, not to mention Mount San Gorgonio. Mosaur made the first ski descent of
San Antonio Peak (Baldy), an obvious ski
alpinist's destination rising close to the city
of Los Angeles. In Mosauer's words from
the *Sierra Club Bulletin*:

Baldy Bowl on San Antonio (Baldy) Peak, just a few miles away from millions of people. *Craig Dostie*

My first major ski tour in Southern California took me to Baldy's summit in what was considered the first ski ascent to the rounded summit, from which a glorious view encompasses the purple immensity of the Mojave desert and, far beyond, the snowy Sierra ... to the west the ocean and Catalina Island, and to the east the bulky massifs of mounts San Gorgonio and San Jacinto.

In 1936, Walter Mosauer and his group of Sierra Club skiers decided that the best way to take advantage of the short (but often excellent) southern California ski season was to build a hut, and they did so at the base of San Antonio Peak's southern bowl. Their San Antonio Ski Hut burned to the ground that same year. Fortunately, the hardy mountaineers who built it saw fit to try again, and in 1937 they rebuilt the now classic structure. From the outside it remains as it was built, though numerous improvements have been made to the interior, from insulation to decorative pictures and historical notes. Mosauer died tragically from plant poisoning while in his thirties,

The San Antonio Ski Hut is pioneer skier Walter Mosauer's lasting legacy. Baldy Bowl in background. *Craig Dostie*

and another southern California skier's cabin, known as the Keller Peak Hut, was built in his memory. Among ski mountaineers the Keller Peak Hut has never achieved the status of the San Antonio Hut, where Mosauer's legacy is a history of skiing and snowboarding both prolific and creative; every cranny and couloir of San Antonio Peak (aka, "Mount Baldy") has been marked by the kiss of glisse.

The joy of glisse in Baldy Bowl. *Craig Dostie*

For the classic tour of San Antonio Peak, stay at the San Antonio Ski Hut (see Directory). Reach the hut as follows: In the Los Angeles basin, drive Interstate 10 to the vicinity of the town of Upland, and take the Mountain Avenue Exit. Drive north on Mountain Avenue for about 6 miles to a switchback right, where Mountain Avenue then merges with Euclid Avenue. Continue on Euclid, which winds up past a reservoir (often dry), then take a right on the Mount Baldy Road. Follow the steep Mount Baldy Road 10 miles as it winds along the San Antonio Creek drainage past Mount Baldy Village, then through a steep section of hairpins and switchbacks to the trailhead. At the end the grade mellows out and the road becomes divided as you pass Snowcrest Lodge. In another ¾ mile there is a crossing cut into the boulevard. Turn left here. Though unmarked, this is Forest Road and also the trailhead. Parking is obvious.

Total distance from I-10 to the trailhead is approximately 25 miles. If you end up at the Mount Baldy Ski Resort you've driven about a mile past the trailhead.

From parking, hike up Forest Road approximately ¾ mile. At about ½ mile, the road comes to an overlook of San Antonio Falls, and switches back to the right. Follow this another ¼ mile, until the road bends left, and you can see down to Mount Baldy Road, about 400 vertical feet below. The trail angles up a scree slope on your left. If you get to a second, distinct bend to the left, you've gone too far. Once you're on the trail (it's well beaten and easy to follow) continue hiking 1¾ miles to the base of the bowl, and the San Antonio Hut.

The safest route to the top of the bowl is to hike left along the base of the bowl and switchback up through the trees at the far left of the bowl. Once above the trees, follow the rim of the bowl to the top. Descend your ascent route, or one of the many short couloirs splitting the rim of the bowl.

Start: Trailhead 6,000 feet, Hut 8,300 feet

Summit: 10,063

Vertical gain: 4,063 feet

Round trip distance and time: 4 miles from trailhead, long day (1 mile from hut)

Ascent: Novice

Glisse: Intermediate- Advanced

Map: USGS 7.5 minute, Mount San Antonio

Guidebook: None

First ski descent of peak: Walter Mosauer and companions, 1932

Weather: Compared to the Sierra, the climate of the San Gabriel Mountains can only be called tropical. At times, midwinter temperatures rise and melt most of the snow, or reduce the snowpack to desperate ice. Warm winds known as the Santa Anna can melt several feet of snow in as many hours. Early spring may see a coat of perfect corn snow at the 10,000-foot level, but slush and dirt patches will block your path. On all but the best years, plan on starting your trip on foot, and bring your most versatile skis. The southern California snowpack is not particularly avalanche prone, but people have died in slides created by quick and massive snowfalls from maritime storms.

Generally, if you can resist skiing or climbing avalanche paths until 48 hours after a storm, conditions will be relatively safe. Ski during any season you can find snow.

Red Tape: While no registration is required for mountaineering in this area, reservations are required for the San Antonio Hut. Contact the Angeles chapter of the Sierra Club for booking (see Directory).

Riding Donner Summit, Tahoe Sierra, California. *Grant Barta*

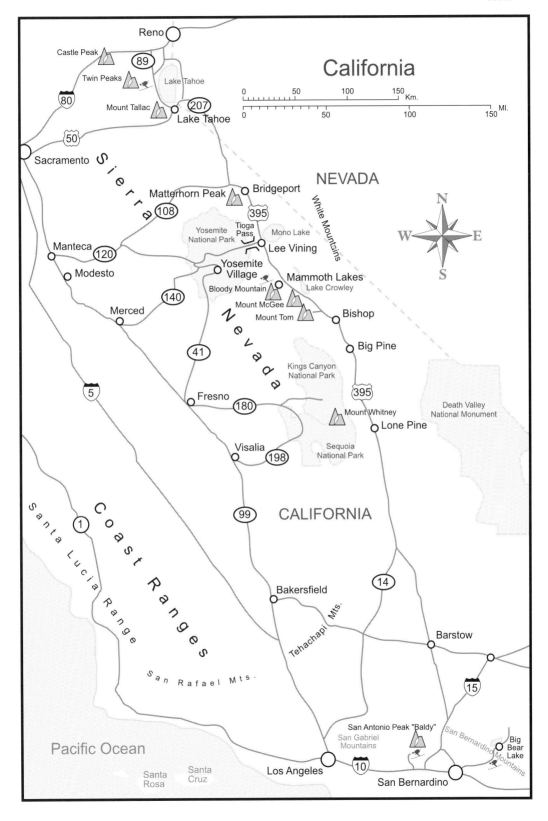

California

WET AND SCRAPPY:
CASCADE MOUNTAINS

Wet and Scrappy: Cascade Mountains

Fire-spewing mountains, 100-foot snowpacks, secret yeti, primal forest and oceans, jagged glacier peaks that cut the sky as shining teeth—the Cascade Mountains are the demanding grail of United States mountaineering. You can find mountains with better weather than the Cascades; you can find mountains with better access; but you can't find better mountains.

The Cascades are a coastal range extending north from California through western Oregon and Washington and into British Columbia. Scores of volcanic peaks stud the region like raisins on a cake, and a half dozen such fire-breathers stand above their surroundings as mammoth deities of ice and snow. Mount Shasta towers 8,000 feet above its foothills. Mount Rainier juts 10,000 feet and is easily the largest mountain in the conterminous United States.

For glisse alpinists such vertical is the stuff of dreams: runs of more than 5,000 vertical feet are common in the Cascades, and at the right time and place you could ski twice that in one shot! What's more, each fiery monolith has a unique personality, a long history, snow lasting into summer, and perfect slopes for carving turns.

What the volcanoes offer in fun they equal in challenge. Acclimated to the coddled climes of sea level, your lungs flop like wet rags while gulping air at 14,000 feet. You can start a descent on perfect snow, and by the time you rubber-leg your last

turn everything from ice to trap crust have extracted their price. Moreover, the terrain often makes a dramatic change from mellow to extreme near the volcanic summits. Thus, while skiing from the apex of Cascade peaks is the supreme experience, conditions and skills may dictate doing otherwise.

An important Northwest contribution to mountaineering is the region's clubs. The first club still extant was formed in 1894, when 105 climbers signed in at the summit of Mount Hood to become charter members of the Mazamas Mountain Club. The Mountaineers, another great Northwest club, was born 12 years later. Both clubs presently boast thousands of members, and have played an astounding role in the development of North American mountaineering. The Mazamas are known for their early skiing and continuing enjoyment of Mount Hood, while the Mountaineers Books is a leading publisher of mountaineering literature, including numerous backcountry guidebooks.

The center for mountaineering development in the Cascades is Mount Rainier, the huge volcano rising to the southeast of Seattle, Washington. The first ascent of Rainier was made in 1870, but skiing was not introduced to the Northwest until the early 1900s by Scandinavian immigrants—several decades after skiing began in other parts of North America. Nonetheless, development of the sport was rapid. By 1911, cars were driving to Paradise, the access portal on the south side of Rainier. Paradise became a mountaineering center, and was no less so for skiing.

One intrepid slider of the Paradise area, W.J. Maxwell, wrote glowingly of

◀ Ski mountaineering above the undercast on the northwest side of Mount Hood, one of the signature Northwest volcanoes. *Louis Dawson*

An early outing on Mount Baker. Northwest clubs were important in the development of mountaineering, and also engendered a conservatism only recently dissipated. *American Alpine Club Collection*

the "wild ecstasy of speed" to be had on the 3,600-foot ski run from Steamboat Prow to the Storbo mining camp, and his fascination with the peak's ski potential was clearly shared by many other early enthusiasts.

The greatest figure in Cascade mountaineering is Fred Beckey, who almost single-handedly put the range "on-the-map" by making exploratory ascents and writing about them over a career spanning a half a century. A talker and a doer, Beckey is known for his bulldog motivation; he's credited with more first mountaineering ascents than any man in history. Though he never focused on skiing, Beckey's endless alpine quest resulted in first glisse descents of several Cascade peaks: his ski of North Star Mountain in 1938 is perhaps the first high route done on skis in the Cascades, and several years later he was the first to ski

Eldorado Peak and Ruth Mountain. In 1953, he made the first ski descent of Silver Star Mountain, a popular backcountry run on the east side of the Cascades, recently diminished by helicopter skiing.

Northwestern mountaineers have a history of conservatism—a justifiable bias considering Cascade weather, glaciers, and heinous approaches. This reactionary attitude influenced ski mountaineering in the region, and doing summit ski descents on steep terrain has been derisively termed "stunt skiing" by at least one crusty Nor'wester. Lowell Skoog, a modern pioneer of Cascade backcountry skiing, wrote that, "Jens Kieler and my older brother Gordy skied the North Face of Mount Shuksan back in the early 1980s. They both found the experience scary and decided it wasn't what skiing was about (for them).

I was influenced by this, and to this day have never been enthusiastic about extreme skiing. If it is so steep that descending on foot is safer or easier, I take my skis off."

If the locals wouldn't crank the steeps, it was up to outsiders. Bill Briggs and Sylvain Saudan made notable descents in the 1960s and 1970s. Chris Landry, North America's most accomplished ski mountaineer at the time, came in 1980 and wowed conservative northwest mountaineers when he skied down Liberty Ridge on Mount Rainier—a precipitous route still regarded as a major climbing accomplishment, let alone a ski descent.

Even if they dodged the steeps, the Northwest locals found other challenges. A North Cascade high route, the 35-mile Ptarmigan Traverse from Cascade Pass to Downy Creek, had been a popular summer traverse for years. Steve Barnett and Bill Nicolai failed on the Ptarmigan in 1977, and Barnett returned the next year with two

Three Sisters, Oregon. Another classic destination for Northwest glisse. *Craig Dostie*

companions. "Cascadian" weather trapped the trio, food ran low, and they escaped via a legendary bushwhack. Meanwhile, Brian Sullivan, Dan Stage and Dick Easter had seen a Barnett slide show about the Ptarmigan, and in 1981 were the first to complete it as a snow and ski route. Luck gave them reasonable weather.

Since the early Ptarmigan ski explorations, Northwest mountaineers have created a number of spectacular ski traverses that include optional (and sometimes mandatory) peak descents. A few of the best are "Inspiration High Route" to Primus Peak (Brian Sullivan and Greg Jacobsen, 1984),

Brothers Carl (left) and Lowell Skoog have been prolific Northwest ski mountaineers. *Lowell Skoog*

On the Fuhrer Finger, Mount Rainier's steepest digit. *Carl Skoog*

"The Backbone" from Little Devil Peak to Eldorado Peak (Carl and Lowell Skoog, 1990), and "Thunder High Route" from Fisher Peak to Eldorado Peak across the headwaters of Thunder Creek (Jens Kuljurgis, Dan Nordstrom, Lowell Skoog, 1987). A method known as "blitz skiing" is the best tactic for beating the weather on these routes. "You wait in town for a weather break, continuously rearranging vacation schedules and banking extra work hours," wrote Skoog. "When the weather breaks you head for the mountains, packing as many peaks and ski runs into the trip as possible before collapsing in your car at the end of the traverse."

The region's most popular traverses, with the best odds for success, are farther north in British Columbia, in Garibaldi Park. This area is not technically the Cascade Mountains, but rather a gray area in the transition of the Cascades to the Canadian Coast Mountains. The weather here might be slightly better than in the regions holding other traverses, and in some cases access is easier due to the use of ski lifts to gain initial vertical. In the region of Garibaldi Park, the Spearhead Traverse connects Blackcomb Mountain and Whistler ski areas, and is often done with two nights out, though it can be blitz skied in a day. "The Spearhead is done by many parties each year. ... It's the closest thing we have in the greater northwest to a European style haute route," wrote Skoog. Another popular trip in Garibaldi is the Névé Traverse, covered under Mount Garibaldi in the Coast Mountains chapter.

Presently, locals have picked up the Cascade ski descent torch. In 1993 brothers Don and Pete Pattison, along with Mike Hattrup, did the first ski descent of the steepest digit on Mount Rainier when they descended the Fuhrer Finger Couloir. One of the Northwest's most technical descents, the Summit Couloir on the south side of Mount Shuksan, was made in 1995 by Brian Povolny, an orthodontist by trade and a devoted backcountry skier. "Caution should have made me trade my skis for downward kick-stepping," wrote Povolny, with a nod to Northwest conservatism. "Instead I fasten my bindings. Edged up to the brink, I visualize the landing after leaping from the cornice … then I'm off into the yellow couloir … down a steep gully, down a huge glacier, down miles of ridges and forest, down trails and roads, all the way down to the car, which waits in the darkness of the woods, below the shining tower."

Mount Baker—Easton Glacier

Another of the Northwest's ski and mountaineering centers, Mount Baker was first climbed in 1868 by English alpinist Edmund T. Coleman, along with David Ogilvey and one other climber. In those days the peak was sequestered in the Cascade outback, and the explorers had to canoe 80 miles through "desperate coun-try" before they even thought about climbing. Present road access is much improved.

Capped by glaciers, with a number of low-angled slopes holding thick snow into early summer, Baker is a natural ski mountain. The first ski descent was made in 1930 by Ed Loness and Robert Sperlin. In 1932, Darroch Crookes, Don Henry, and Benton Thompson did a ski traverse of the peak. Lift-served Mount Baker Ski Area was opened in 1953 on the northern reaches of the peak. The resort has always accommodated backcountry skiers, but because of their short hours and seasonal closures, it is of little use for serious ski mountaineering. After the lifts close, summer skiers walk up the ski runs to reach the Sholes Glacier. The most aesthetic tours are the Boulder Glacier on the southeast side of the peak and the Easton Glacier to the south of the summit. Because of good access and less hazardous glacier travel, the latter route is the classic descent of Mount Baker.

Mount Baker, Easton Glacier. *Carl Skoog*

Mount Baker: drive Interstate 5 to Highway 20 (North Cascades Highway). At 22 miles from I-5, turn left on the Baker Lake Road. Drive the Baker Lake Road north 12 miles and turn left on Road 12 (the Loomis-Nooksack Road). Stay on Road 12 for 3.5 miles, where you take a turn right on the Schreibers Meadow Road (#13) and drive several miles to snowline or 5 miles to road's end. Look for signs indicating the Schreibers Meadow and Sulphur Creek Trailhead, and follow trail markers ½ mile to Schreibers Meadow. Head through the meadow, then ski north toward the Mount Baker summit. You'll gain the glacier at about 4,000 feet, at its steep snout. Roped travel is advised here, though crevasse danger is minimal. Crampons and ice axes may be useful for frozen morning snow. In late season, hike the summer trail which ascends a westerly lateral moraine, and intersects the glacier at about 5,500 feet. Ski (or crampon) up the glacier. Head toward Sherman Crater, which may be steaming. Continue just left of Sherman Crater and to the left of Sherman Peak, then climb the last 1,000 feet to Baker's summit. Descend your ascent route.

The area is heavily used by snowmobiles. This results in packed trails and good road access, but Schreibers Meadow may be crowded with machines. The upper reaches of the peak are contained in legal wilderness, where internal combustion, at least of the petroleum variety, is not allowed.

Start: 3,200 feet (varies with snowline)
Summit: 10,778 feet

The smoking Sherman Crater is a landmark on the Easton Glacier route.
Jonathan Waterman

Vertical gain: 7,578 feet

Round trip distance and time: 11 miles; long day-trip, or high camp overnight

Ascent: Advanced, may require roped glacier work

Glisse: Advanced

Maps: Green Trails (commercial map series available from local shops) #13 and #45; USFS Mount Baker National Forest (see Directory)

Guidebooks: *Backcountry Skiing Washington's Cascades*, Rainer Burgdorfer; *Exploring the Coast Mountains on Skis*, John Baldwin

First ascent: Edmund T. Coleman, David Ogilvey, and one other, 1868

First ski descent of peak: Ed Loness and Robert Sperlin, 1930

Weather: As with most Cascade volcanoes, spring and early summer are the best times to ski Mount Baker. The weather here is as wet as anywhere in the Cascades. For example, Mount Rainier has been known to accumulate more than 90 feet of snow in a winter. Mid-winter rain is common, and clouds smother the region for weeks, sometimes months, on end. Apocalyptic cyclones may also drop 10 feet of dense snow in several days. NOAA weather radio, commercial radio, and television all provide weather reports. Generalities about hideous Cascade weather only cover part of the picture. Vast areas of "rain shadow" exist on the eastern reaches, with climate similar to the North American continental ranges. Thus, it's possible to escape the worst weather by going farther inland. While planning a Cascade glisse vacation can be a risky business (storms last long and clear spells are short), if you spend any length of time in the range you'll probably see enough good weather to accomplish something. For visitors, the best months are May, June, and July, when you'll find good sunshine.

Red Tape: While Mount Baker is heavily used, such use is presently unregulated. The summit is in legal wilderness, with the boundary roughly following the 3,400-foot contour.

Mount Rainier–Emmons Glacier

Seattle, Washington's glacier-crowned monarch, Mount Rainier is the Northwest's defining mountain. It begs to be climbed—and for a century has been the siren call for countless skiers. The huge volcanic cone rises 10,000 feet above its kneeling foothills. It holds more glacial ice than any other peak in the contiguous United States: 26 named glaciers and innumerable permanent icefields. Huge ice rivers such as the Tahoma, Carbon and Emmons flush their loads down to nourish primal forest.

In the early days Rainier was hard to access. After a high-reaching attempt led by Lieutenant A. V. Kautz in 1857, the brush-beaten fly-eaten climbers returned "hardly recognizable." One nearly died of exhaustion, and two spent several months in hospital. Kautz pulled through the healthiest, only suffering a legendary bout of hemorrhoids caused by dehydration.

The peak was first climbed in 1870 by Hazard Stevens and Philemon Van Trump. The two horsepacked to Rainier's base with famed British alpinist Edmund Coleman, who had much to do with motivating the trip. In the dark forest on the approach, Coleman was separated from his companions because his heavy pack was loaded with what he considered essential mountaineering gear. He returned to a lower camp, while Stevens and Trump ignored the dire warnings and funereal chants of their Yakima Indian guide and climbed to the summit. The pioneers bivouacked in a

Before roads accessed Mount Rainier, early mountaineers horsepacked into the huge volcano. *American Alpine Club Collection*

steam cave within the summit crater, enduring an exhausting night while being drenched by warm steam and scoured by gusts of freezing wind—a fate familiar to the many mountaineers who have since sought similar shelter.

Stevens's and Trump's climb was a 250-mile round trip from the town of Olympia. Yet inexorable progress soon brought roads to the mountain, and by 1911 the first automobile reached the gateway area known as Paradise, high on the mountain's south side near the toe of the Nisqually Glacier. With such convenient access, Mount Rainier soon became the center for Northwest mountaineering and a focus for climbers from all over North America. Commercial alpine guiding on the

peak's glaciers began in 1903, and was probably the first of its kind in the United States. Because the various guide services have been run under different names and owners, the present concession cannot make the claim as "the longest running service." Exum Guides in Wyoming has operated since 1931. Presently, the Rainier Mountaineering guide service operates from Paradise. Thousands of people climb the peak each year, and it's frequently snowboarded and skied.

Early skiing on Mount Rainier was done in 1922 by a trio of French ski mountaineers who made the first winter ascent. They used skis up and down the Muir Snowfield. The 1922 climb was covered by a media frenzy, and no doubt introduced the locals to what skiing had to offer. One of the winter party, Jean Landry, wrote that "no one seemed to have discovered, as they had in the Alps, that mountains are even more beautiful in winter."

A few years after the winter ascent, skiers starting from the Paradise area created such trips as a traverse over Camp Muir, and in 1927 several ski descents of the Emmons Glacier from the 12,000-foot level. In 1935 the National Alpine Ski Championships were held on Rainier, and it was during this era the infamous Silver Skis races were held from Camp Muir down to Paradise. These wild events included runs dropping 4,550 vertical feet down the Muir Snowfield, and bear a startling similarity to ski mountaineering races presently held in Europe; the participants climbed, the snow

was natural, and gates a nuisance. Apparently, turns were unpopular as well. The events were canceled in 1940 after several racers schussed to death.

The first ski descent of Mount Rainier was made on July 18, 1948, when Kermit Bengston, Dave Roberts, Cliff Schmeidtke and Charles E. Welsh ski climbed to near the summit. Roberts continued to the summit on skis, while the rest of the group used crampons. Roberts reported that he definitely skied down from the crater rim, while everyone else in the group skied from high on the summit dome and down the Emmons Glacier. The tricky part is that the exact summit of Rainier is a bump on the crater rim known as the Columbia Crest, across the crater from where Roberts skied. In terms of ski descents, the crater rim on

1928 skiers on the upper Emmons Glacier, Mount Rainier. *University of Washington, and The Mountaineers*

volcanic peaks may be considered the summit, and thus Roberts can lay rightful claim to the first ski descent of Rainier.

A well known early descent of Rainier was made in 1961 by Wyoming guide and pioneer extreme skier Bill Briggs, along with Rainier Guides Jim and Lou Whittaker, film-maker Roger Brown, and four others. The plan was to film a ski descent, and Briggs was making his last hurrah before possibly crippling hip surgery. In pain and eating pep pills like a homeward bound trucker, Briggs blasted to the summit and made what is at least the first ski descent via the Ingraham Glacier, and possibly the first true drop from the exact summit at Columbia Crest.

Mount Rainier with Chris Landry's 1980 Liberty Ridge descent at center; he called it a "classic." *American Alpine Club Collection*

In the annals of extreme North American descents, Rainier's Liberty Ridge plays a central role. In 1980, this cliff-studded icy rampart on the mountain's north side was something most Northwest mountaineers thought long and hard about climbing—much less skiing. The first ascent party climbed it in winter when "all the rotten rock would be in shadow and remain frozen," wrote Arnie Campbell of his 1935 climb. By 1968, climbers had realized the route was well coated with snow in early spring, and conventional wisdom viewed the climb as a classic snow (and sometimes ice) route rather then an ice and rock scramble.

By 1979, at least one person was thinking of skiing Liberty Ridge. After years of practice in his home mountains around Aspen, Colorado, carpenter, climber and former ski racer Chris Landry had molded his mountaineering and ski skills into a seamless blend. Landry knew Aspen publisher Bil Dunaway, who'd skied and guided on Rainier and made several notable first ski descents in the early days. Dunaway agreed with Landry's assessment of Liberty Ridge as a possible ski descent. After his 1978 ski of Pyramid Peak in Colorado (see

Colorado chapter), Landry was able to get a small amount of sponsorship, and aimed his planks toward Rainier.

In spring of 1980, Landry and California alpinist Doug Robinson made the long approach to the base of Liberty Ridge. After 10 days of approach slogging and storm sitting they made it up the climb. Robinson picked his way down on crampons, and later wrote, "the powder is coming in rhythmic waves, too small to be an avalanche. Soon I can see a figure behind them, pumping turns as it comes into view, skis flashing in the air between edge sets that are scraping off this cascading powder. ... For a split second the skis are aimed straight down the ice face. He brings them around with his edges sliding eight or ten feet to brake before launching into the next turn."

Landry completed his descent in fine style. "It's a classic," he would later tell a Seattle newspaper, "definitely the finest descent I've ever done and well worth the two years of preparation." The mountain was not yet finished with Landry and Robinson, however, and their epic departure included dodging terrifying avalanches falling from the North Face on an Alaskan scale (probably triggered by concurrent Mount St. Helens volcanic events).

At least one person has repeated Landry's feat, but because of the long approach and variable conditions, Liberty Ridge has not become the classic Landry envisioned. Another route, the Emmons Glacier, has the history and popularity to qualify.

You can reach Rainier's Emmons Glacier two ways. When snowcover is still good in early summer or late spring, you can start at White River campground, do a backpack approach, and climb Emmons Glacier from snowline. A more interesting (and perhaps better for skiing) method is to start from Paradise and hit the Emmons at its middle. This route starts 1,000 feet higher than the route from White River, and is more direct. From Interstate 5 or Interstate 82 in northwest Washington, drive any of several state highways to the Longmire entrance on the south side of Mount Rainier National Park, and continue to the ranger station at Paradise. Inquire at the ranger station about overnight parking and prevailing conditions. Leaving Paradise, head up the slopes above the parking lot, and climb steeper terrain to Panorama Point (6,950 feet). Vary your route here according to avalanche conditions and snowcover. From Panorama Point, take a northerly tack up the ridge and pass to the left of Anvil Rock (9,580 feet). Head for the notch at the head of the snowfield, and you'll walk into Camp Muir, a collection of huts and wind-scoured terrain on a rocky rib below Gibraltar Rock. Total distance from Paradise to Camp Muir is 4½ miles.

From Camp Muir, head up the Cowlitz Glacier to Cadaver Gap, a breach through a rocky ridge that leads to the Emmons Glacier. You'll see several alternatives for your summit route up the Emmons Glacier. For skiing, it's often best to take a climbing

Mount Rainier from the east, Emmons Glacier to left, Liberty Ridge in convoluted rocky area to right. *Brian Litz*

traverse north until you can find your way through a crevassed area. Above Disappointment Cleaver the angle eases, and you can usually stay on skis up the broad slopes of the upper glacier. For a ski descent, you'll probably feel good if you click in anywhere on the summit crater rim. To reach the exact summit bump (Columbia crest, 14,410 feet), slog across the crater. On both the Cowlitz and Emmons glaciers, you'll need to swing around or cross crevasse areas. Travel roped, and descend your ascent route.

Start: Paradise Ranger Station, 5,450 feet

Summit: Columbia Crest, 14,410 feet

Vertical gain: 8,950 feet

Round trip distance and time: 14 miles; high camp in Camp Muir vicinity

Ascent: Advanced (includes roped glacier travel)

Glisse: Advanced

Maps: USGS 7.5 minute, Mount Rainier East, Mount Rainier West

Guidebooks: *Backcountry Skiing in Washington's Cascades*, Rainer Burgdorfer; *Cascade Alpine Guide Volume 1*, Fred Beckey

First ascent: Hazard Stevens and Philemon Van Trump, 1870

First ski descent: Dave Roberts, 1948

Weather: Mount Rainier can dish up weather as severe as Denali. Carry plenty of food in case you get snowed in at Camp Muir. Bring wands, and mark your routes well so you can return in a whiteout. Get your weather reports from the Paradise ranger station, weather radio, and television. For general information on Cascade weather, see Mount Baker above.

Red Tape: Registration and a fee are required. Be sure you're parked in overnight parking.

This ski mountaineer left a dry parking lot at Paradise, and returned a few days later to find his ride buried in a white wilderness.
Louis Dawson

Mount Adams—Suksdorf Ridge & Southwest Chute

Ski descent artist Brian Povolny says "If you fly from the south into Washington, you'll view almost the entire Cascades. In spring, the most stunning ski descent you'll see in the whole range are the southwest chutes on Mount Adams."

Indeed, even if you're a skiing atheist, and you manage to carve turns down this amazing line, you might be convinced that, yes, there is a God—and yes, the Supreme Being must be a skier.

Mount Adams was first climbed in 1854 via the South Ridge. The first ski descent was made in July of 1932 by University of California ski coach and professor Walter Mosauer, along with three other skiers. Mosauer and his friends had mastered the arlberg technique, and after applying it to the mountains of Southern California, they'd taken a ski trip to the

Northwest and enjoyed descents on Rainier, Hood and many other slopes. "A last adventure before going back to sunny Southern California," wrote Mosauer, "I organized a little party: Dr. Strizek, a renowned ski-mountaineer, and Hans-Otto Giese and Hans Grage, both winners of many ski races, climbed Mount Adams with me … from our camp at Cold Spring in 7 hours and 20 minutes. We had continuous skiing on the descent from the summit to about 6,000 feet … an altitude difference of more than 6,000 feet in mid-July!"

But Mosaur could not claim the first glisse on Adams. In 1867 Samuel Brooks had skimmed down the peak on a tin plate.

Another of the Northwest's huge volcanoes, Mount Adams rises like a titanic shoulder 6,000 vertical feet above its surrounding hills. The peak has several active glaciers, but the ski route described below avoids glacier travel—an unusual and pleasant variation from the tedious rope-work often needed on other routes in this chapter.

Mount Adams from the south, immense Southwest Chute angles from the summit to the left. *American Alpine Club Collection*

Mount Adams: on the southern Washington State border, drive Interstate 84 to the town of Hood River. Drive north from Hood River across the Columbia River to Bingen, and take Highway 141 north to the town of Trout Lake. Stop at the ranger station. Next, drive 3 miles north on Road N90 to the junction of Road N81. Continue driving on N81 to snowclosure, or ideally 7.5 miles to parking at Timberline camp. If the road to Timberline Camp is closed by snow, you'll definitely need to make this a two-day trip, or use a snowmobile.

Once at Timberline Camp you have two choices for routes. With firm snow and low avalanche hazard, you can simply climb up the ski route. Follow the route of the pack trail about a mile northwest from Timberline Camp, then swing north to follow the lower slopes, and finally the couloir, to the summit ridge.

Your other choice, and usually a better one (since it's hard to know what avalanche conditions are like 6,000 feet above you) is to take the southerly Suksdorf Ridge to the summit, then ski the Southwest Couloir if snow conditions cooperate. To do so, start from Timberline Camp and travel north. The terrain gradually steepens and gradually becomes a ridge. Continue up the broad ridge another ½ mile to the Lunch Counter, a low-angled part of the ridge at 9,000 feet.

Slog up this Sysiphian ridge 1½ miles to a false summit called Pikers Peak, then "pike" your way up the last lead-leg vertical and plant your flag. Ski the ridge, or, for the descent of the gods, drop down the Southwest Couloir between Avalanche Glacier and the South Ridge, watch your altimeter, and traverse a mile back to Timberline Camp from about 6,000 feet.

Whatever your exact route, remember what Rainer Burgdorfer wrote: "The only obstacle to complete enjoyment of this tour is exhaustion. ... After climbing to the summit few skiers will be at the top of their form." Start your climb in the morning dark. With legs of iron, do the route in one day—otherwise use a high camp.

Start: Timberline Camp, 6,300 feet

Summit: 12,310 feet

Vertical gain: 6,010 feet

Round trip distance and time: 9 miles; possible in one day, high camp recommended

Ascent: Intermediate

Glisse: Advanced

Maps: USGS 7.5 minute, Mount Adams West, Mount Adams East

Guidebooks: *Cascade Alpine Guide Volume 1,* Fred Beckey; *Backcountry Skiing in Washington's Cascades*, Rainer Burgdorfer

First ascent: A.G. Aiken, E.J. Allen, A.J. Burge, and B.F. Shaw, via the South Ridge, 1854.

First ski descent: Hans-Otto Giese, Hans Grage, Otto Strizek, Walter Mosauer, Sandy Lyons, July 16, 1932

Weather: Being an inland peak, Adams may be slightly drier than other monoliths closer to the coast. Nonetheless, this is the Cascades so be ready for anything. Use local television and commercial radio for weather reports. For general information on Cascade weather see Mount Baker above.

Red Tape: Mount Adams' south side is located on public land in the Mount Adams Wilderness, inside the Gifford Pinchot National Forest. Register by filling out a permit form at the trailhead or ranger station (see Directory).

Mount St. Helens–South Side

In 1961, Fred Beckey wrote that "this beautifully symmetrical peak with its dazzling and unblemished mantle of snow and ice has often been called the Fujiyama of America." Little did Beckey know how soon his observation would become specious. As an active volcano Mount St. Helens fumed for 19 years, then on March 27, 1980, an ominous boom was followed by a minor eruption. A few weeks later the eruptions ceased, but portentous earthquakes continued and the north side of the peak began cracking and moving in the area around the Boot, a formation then familiar to Northwest climbers. Locals prepared for a larger volcanic eruption—but no one was ready for the hellfire soon to follow.

At 8:32 A.M. on May 18, another earthquake shook the mountain. Stunned observers saw the North Flank liquefy then fall in a stupendous avalanche which removed 1,300 vertical feet from the summit. Simultaneously, a lateral gas explosion with

Ski signaturing the ash covered snow of Mount St. Helens.
Louis Dawson

the force of an atomic bomb devastated 235 square miles of land north of Mount St. Helens. Sixty-one people and thousands of animals died. Like the coming of the apocalypse, rivers plugged with steaming lahar, and day turned to night as towns were blanketed with smothering ash—the Mesozoic had revisited twentieth-century America.

Five more eruptions punctuated the remainder of 1980, and a series of quieter eruptions have occurred since then. A lava dome continues to grow in the crater. Experts estimate that at present activity rates, Mount St. Helens will spurt to its former height in just several hundred years.

In 1982 the Mount St. Helens Volcanic Monument was created to encompass the peak and surrounding lands. While St. Helens was not opened to the public for several years, skiers made several bandit climbs and descents soon after the mountain calmed down. One group of outlaws carried

Mount St. Helens before its 1980 decapitation. The lake pictured here is now filled with mud and ash.
American Alpine Club Collection

The mountain-sized lava dome inside the St. Helens crater. *Louis Dawson*

sheets to throw over their heads so they could hide from aircraft. These early explorers gingerly approached the decapitated peak to find a land of wonder—a fantasy of mountains growing within mountains, snow the color of soot, and a feeling of lonely insignificance in the face of ominous power. Ski mountaineering on St. Helens is still a unique experience. Making steps in "black snow" created by a layer of ash, you arrive at the crater rim. Belayed by a rope in case the edge crumbles, you crawl to the crest and stare in awe at the primal lava dome growing from the crater floor. You are dwarfed by the scale, and the crater seems to expand—to swallow you—as you realize that any moment, wham, you could join an ash cloud for a climb to the stratosphere. With such thoughts in mind, after taking a breath of sulfurous steam gusting from the crater, more than one skier has jumped on their sticks for a fast getaway.

Mount St. Helens was first climbed in 1853 by newspaper editor Thomas J. Dryer and companions. In prescient words, Dryer wrote that the peak was "seeming to lift its head … struggling to be released from its compressed position." The mountain's first ski descent is lost in history, but no doubt occurred at least a half century ago.

Most people glisse Mount St. Helens from the south, though orbits of the peak are common, and rumor holds that bandit sojourns into the active crater are a regular occurrence. Trailheads and road closures vary greatly by season—and by events such as mud slides and washouts. In summer, climbers must obtain permits; before you tackle any skiing on Mount St. Helens you should stop and inquire at the National Volcanic Monument Visitor Center near the town of Castle Rock (see Directory), preferably the day before your climb so you can get an early start the next morning. To reach the visitor center, drive Interstate 5 south from Tacoma, Washington (80 miles), or north from Portland, Oregon (45 miles), turn off the highway at obvious signs, and drive 5 miles east to the visitor center on Highway 503.

Mount St. Helens's most efficient south side routes start from the Ptarmigan Trailhead, also known as Climber's Bivouac. To reach the trailhead from the visitor center, drive back to Interstate 5, head south for about 30 miles, and turn off at Woodland. Drive east from Woodland on Highway 503 (which becomes Forest Road 90). At approximately 27 miles from I-5, stop at Cougar (at Yale Lake) and register. Continue another mile from Yale Park, and turn left on Forest Road 8100.

Drive Road 8100 for 15 miles through a variety of interesting terrains, and take a left on Forest Road 830, just past a mudflow area (where the road is often closed—you checked at the visitor center, yes?). Continue on Road 830 for several miles to the Ptarmigan Trailhead. In winter continue past Cougar and drive Forest Road 83 to the Swift Creek Trailhead, and climb from there. The higher trailhead is usually opened around Memorial Day.

After parking at the trailhead, follow the well marked Ptarmigan Trail through forest to timberline. The summer trail continues up a marked route to the crater rim, but skiers can vary their line according to snowcover. The ash and volcanic rubble in this area make for tedious hiking, so look for snowcover and stick with it. Use a rope belay to approach the crumbling crater rim, and you'll get a heart twisting view into the apocalyptic crater with its primal lava dome. During your descent, be ready for the Northwest's varied snow conditions.

Start: Ptarmigan Trailhead, 3,700 feet (start varies with snow closure)

Summit: Crater Rim, 7,060 feet

Vertical gain: 3,360 feet

Round trip distance and time: 6 miles, 8 hours

Ascent: Intermediate, ropework required for crater viewing

Glisse: Intermediate

The eerie moonscape of the south side, Mount St. Helens. *Louis Dawson*

Map: the United States Forest Service produces an excellent map entitled *Mount St. Helens National Volcanic Monument*, available from the visitors center, or by mail order from same (see Directory)

Guidebooks: Mountaineers Books publishes a handy eponymous pocket guide for the Monument; *The Cascade Alpine Guide, Volume 1*, by Fred Beckey, has detailed information

First ascent/descent: Early settlers of the 1800s might have been the first to climb the mountain. The first documented ascent was by Thomas Dryer in 1853. Fred Beckey made an early ski in 1961, which may have been the first.

Weather: The skiing on Mount St. Helens, as with other Cascadian volcanoes, is best during spring and early summer, after the winter storm cycles have ceased. The weather on this peak is as wet as anywhere else in the Cascades. Use NOAA weather radio, television and commercial radio stations for weather reports. For general information on Cascade weather, see Mount Baker above.

Red Tape: Climbing registration is required, check at the visitor center (see above and Directory).

Mount Hood—Palmer Glacier

As the city of Seattle, Washington claims Mount Rainier as its own, so does Portland, Oregon claim Mount Hood. While not the colossal mass of Rainier, Hood holds its own as a mountain, and pulls climbers and skiers with its own special vitality. It gets climbed and skied by thousands of people each year and has led the history of Oregon mountaineering.

As is the case with many Cascade peaks, Victorian-era climbs on Hood are a morass of hyperbole and verbiage. The first to claim honor was writer-cum-alpinist Thomas Dryer. In 1853 Dryer had made what's probably the first ascent of Mount St. Helens, and in 1854 he set his sights on Mount Hood. The climb began on horseback in the city of Portland, and by Dryer's account it was an epic of Homeric proportions. One of Dryer's companions dropped out because of blood oozing from his skin. Slopes were measured at over 70° on a low-angled ridge, and each man started the climb via a different route. Though Dryer recorded picayune observations such as losing his hat while riding, he failed to detail his route.

Moreover, his description of the summit jibes with an area lower down on the mountain. Thus, while climbing as high as he did was a notable achievement at the time, Dryer is not credited with the first ascent.

After Dryer was published, a wannabe named Belden spoke up and claimed he'd been the first. Belden substantiated his legend by finding the summit to be 19,400 feet, and corroborating the nasty experience of blood spurting from the eyes, skin, and ears. In 1857 the first fully documented climb was made by James G. Deardorff and five others. Deardorff's written account started a war with Thomas Dryer, who used his bully pulpit as a newspaperman to trash Deardorff with such sanctimonious retorts as, "These panting aspirants, ... must learn the elementary principles that constitute gentleman." Deardorff got the last laugh, though. One of Deardorff's companions on the documented first ascent, Henry Pittock, worked for Dryer and ended up owning the newspaper, while Dryer spent his last days as a bureaucrat in Hawaii.

Skiing on Mount Hood has a noble tradition. Pioneers of the late 1800s enjoyed sliding through Hood's lower reaches on hand-hewn planks. The Mazamas Mountain Club organized much of the early glisse, including an expedition in 1903. By 1914 the Mazamas headed up for snowy fun every winter, traveling by train and stage to a lodge on the lower slopes of the peak. By 1931 ski races were being held on the Eliot Glacier, and ski industry consultant Andre Roch, along with Arne Sten and safety binding inventor Hjalmar Hvam, skied from outside Portland to Hood and back in under nine hours via Eliot Glacier. The men reached the summit, but it's doubtful they skied from the apex. In 1951, Ray Conkling and Bill Oberteuffer started at Timberline Lodge and made the first high orbit of the peak on skis.

A singular event in the history of skiing on Mount Hood was the completion of Timberline Lodge, high on the mountain's western reach. This crafted example of Cascadian architecture was built as a government work project during the depression recovery years, and was dedicated in 1937 by President Franklin D. Roosevelt. Timberline Lodge was an instant hit for winter sport fanatics, and skiing on the slopes above the lodge, both with lifts and without, continues as a popular pastime.

In the spring of 1971, extreme skier Sylvain Saudan showed up at Timberline Lodge to make the first summit descent of Mount Hood. The compact Frenchman had been making a name for himself as "the skier of the impossible," and he left little to chance. Keeping a low profile so his (mostly imaginary) competitors wouldn't ace him, Saudan stoically waited out the weather for several weeks. On March 1, he and his entourage (including French extreme pioneer Anselm Baud) were dropped by helicopter on the summit. After waiting on top for the afternoon shadow to cool the snow, Saudan launched down the Wy'east Couloir, then cut south

to the Newton Clark Glacier. The star even had a snowcat arranged for a pickup at the bottom of the route.

Saudan put too much energy into the project. Three years later Brian Raasch, a local 18-year-old, repeated the route in much better style: he simply climbed up and skied down. Since then Mount Hood has been skied many times from the summit, down any number of lines. The Cooper Spur route to the northeast is one of the most direct and longest: with good spring snowcover you can ski 6,000 vertical feet to the Cloud Cap Inn. Eliot Glacier has been skied as well, and is recommended by extreme skiers. Saudan's route has the appeal of being the first, and has interesting route finding. Those routes aside, the simplest and most popular ski route takes the often crowded climbing line from Timberline Lodge up the Palmer Glacier and Hogback Couloirs.

President Franklin D. Roosevelt dedicated Timberline Lodge in 1937, and the hand-crafted building became central to Oregon skiing. *Timberline Lodge Collection*

Timberline Lodge and the west side of Mount Hood. The Hogback is the small curved feature in the center, below the summit cliffs.
Timberline Lodge Collection

Mount Hood from the north. Cooper Spur route is on left. *Bill Stevenson*

Mount Hood's Palmer Glacier route starts at Timberline Lodge. From the city of Port-land, Oregon, drive east to Gresham, then follow Highway 26 for about 50 miles to Timberline Lodge and Mount Hood.

If you can afford it, stay at Timberline Lodge. Regular rooms are expensive; dormitory style rooms are more affordable (see Directory.) Campgrounds and budget lodging are available around the town of Government Camp, about 45 minutes from Timberline.

An early morning walk up the ski area above the lodge, or a snowcat ride (arrange at lodge desk) gets you to the top of the Palmer chair lift at the 8,600-foot elevation. From here, continue up the Palmer Glacier (roped glacier travel may be necessary) to the "Hogback," a ridge of snow below the short summit couloirs known as the Hogback Couloirs. Climb the Hogback, then continue up either of the two couloirs to the summit. From the summit you can ski one of the Hogback Couloirs if they looked okay during your climb (maximum angle 50°). To descend a slightly easier (but still extreme) route, ski north from the summit to a small false summit, then continue a few hundred feet far-ther north to a point just above Mazama Face. If you're on ice, forgo your skis and use crampons until you find skiable snow. Ice in the Northwest is *ice*, not hard snow. Ski the Mazama Face, traverse back to the Hogback, and ski down Palmer Glacier.

Once on the mid reaches of the mountain, a classic mistake is to follow the fall line from Crater Rock. You think you're headed for the Palmer chair lift and lunch at Timberline Lodge. Sadly, a true fall line route takes you down into the endless moraines of the White River drainage. Read your compass and map at Crater Rock, and the Ram's Head Bar will be yours.

During any skiing on Mount Hood you may need a rope for glacier travel. Skiers may not need to rope up as often as foot travelers. Nevertheless, if you get off route you may find yourself in dangerous crevasse fields. So carry a lightweight rope, harnesses, ice ax, crampons, and ascenders.

Start: Timberline Lodge, 6,000 feet

Summit: 11,235 feet

Vertical gain: 5,235 feet

Round trip distance and time: About 6 miles, 8 hours

Ascent: Advanced

Glisse: Extreme from summit, Advanced from Hogback

Maps: USGS 7.5 minute, Mount Hood South, Mount Hood North; USFS Mount Hood Wilderness

Guidebook: *Mount Hood, A Complete History*, Jack Grauer

First ascent: Henry Pittock, L.J. Powell, William Buckley, W. Chittenden, James Deardorff, 1857

First ski descent of peak: Sylvain Saudan, 1971

Weather: A dormant volcano, Mount Hood rises from the plains like a mystic sentinel, glowering over more than 20,000 square miles of forest, river, ocean and desert. Any mountain so exposed and so close to the ocean will have rabid weather. Hood is no exception. During a "good winter" on the mountain, the snow will accumulate up to 75 feet deep in certain areas. However, a sparse winter's snowpack will still yield magnificent spring skiing. Snow comes packaged with horrid storms. During one winter on Hood, high winds blew out a window in a snowcat being used for a rescue; the driver froze and had to be evacuated. As with much of the Cascades, sometime in May or June a slightly better weather pattern may begin. Storms still roll in, but less often. This is the time when ski mountaineers will find the best travel. All talk of good weather aside, any local can tell you Mount Hood makes its own bad weather—at any time of year, at any moment. For general information on Cascade weather, see Mount Baker above.

Red Tape: You should register for mountaineering on Mount Hood. This is best done by ducking into the registration booth at the Wy'east Day Lodge across the parking lot from Timberline Lodge. Here you'll find excellent oblique aerial photos of all sides of Mount Hood, and a weather radio. If your plans do not include a stop at Timberline Lodge you can register at the Forest service offices in Government Camp or Hood River. You'll also need a "Snow Park" parking permit to park at Timberline. This is available locally.

Mount Shasta–Avalanche Gulch

Care to worship ephemeral beings at a glowing quartz altar in view of North America's most stupendous volcanic peak? Visit Mount Shasta, and you can do so—the mountain is considered by scores of metaphysical sects to be the spiritual center of North America. Or does your passion takes a secular turn, and you'd like to ski such a mountain? With a deep coastal snowpack, the largest glacier in California, and 6,000 vertical feet of perfect ski terrain, Shasta is, simply, the best ski mountain in North America.

First topped in 1854 by Captain E.D. Pierce, Mount Shasta is technically an easy mountain to climb and ski, though Cascade weather may mock the term "easy." When John Muir climbed the peak 20 years after

The Avalanche Gulch route follows the features to the left of the summit. *Louis Dawson*

the first ascent, he nearly died in a snow-storm. Muir barely survived an open gear-less bivouac by lying for 12 hours over steam vents at the summit. At least one climber has been literally blown off the mountain to his death, while others have been lost when storms turn the vast peak into a white tomb. The mountain is named for the Shasta Indians who believed the peak stood at the dawn of Creation, a soli-tary pinnacle in an ancient sea. When the sea dried, or if you prefer, the volcanic eruptions ended, Shasta stood as a vibrant monument 10,000 feet above the surround-ing land as "lonely as God and white as a winter moon," as early nineteenth century poet Joaquin Miller wrote.

The most interesting modern legend concerning Mount Shasta is that of the Lemurians. In 1931 a mystical order known as the Rosicrucians published a book de-scribing Mount Shasta as the former edge of Lemuria, the lands now covered by the Pacific Ocean. The Lemurians were an advanced race, and escaped the flooding of their continent by burrowing into Mount Shasta. The idea is that Lemurians still live inside Shasta, holding secrets of technology which make modern science look like Stone Age bone chipping. Every so often, locals in the Mount Shasta area encounter strange individuals wearing robes and sandals.

It's unknown if Lemurians ski or ride snowboards; but for North Americans slid-ing on Shasta is a noble tradition. First ascensionist Pierce and his buddies might have done the earliest glissade in North America during their descent. Pierce must have had the ancient Shastan seas in mind when he described his crew's novel tech-nique for navigation: "We sat ourselves down on our unmentionables, feet foremost, to regulate speed, and [used] our walking sticks for rudders. Off we sped ... the like I never saw before. Some unshipped their rudders before reaching the quarter hour (there was no such thing as stopping), some broached to and went stern foremost, making wry faces, while others got up too much steam and went end over end; while others found themselves athwart ship, and making 160 revolutions per minute."

At least 30 climbing routes gird Shasta, many of which are fine glisse routes. With so many options this is indeed a mountain to savor; stay for a few days and do more than one descent. On the southeast side of the mountain, the Clear Creek route offers a vast slope of perfect angle. For a steeper challenge the snowfield between the Hotlum and Wintun Glaciers is a plunge you'll remember the rest of your life. On the opposite side of the peak, Diller Canyon offers what's been called "the best ski route in North America." Diller was first skied in 1968 by Gorden Thomas, Phil Holecek and another. Filmmaker Eric Perlman skied it in 1978, and wrote in *Skiing Magazine*: "I will never forget that descent: the trampoline feel of firm spring snow, the blinding play of sun on spray, and, ricocheting off the canyon wall the ruckus of hissing steel and howling laughter … as I powered huge, white arcs across the empty slopes."

The Sierra Club built a ski and mountaineering hostel in 1922 on Shasta's south slope. Throughout the next decades many ski descents were made from part way up the mountain—some from close to the summit. The first documented summit descent was made in December, 1947, by Andes mountaineering pioneer Fletcher Hoyt and four others. One of Hoyt's companions was Leonard Yaekle, a Swedish "down mountain skier." Hoyt says that Yaekle didn't know about turning, but "went straight down the mountain! I wasn't used to that myself, but I gave it a try. … When I got down to Helen Lake I knew I was going to live—that's the last time I tried that!"

Mount Shasta "the best ski mountain in North America." *Craig Dostie*

The route Hoyt and his friends shot was Avalanche Gulch, a southerly defile dropping like a giant toboggan run from Shasta's summit cap down more than 6,000 vertical feet of perfect ski terrain. Back in the 1930s, Avalanche Gulch and Mount Shasta got a lot of publicity as a ski center. Newspaper mogul Randolph Hearst had a summer home in the shadow of the peak, and no doubt influenced his winter sports writer, Oliver Kehrlein, to propose the "longest and continuously steepest ski run in the world," dropping 12,900 feet and almost a vertical mile down Avalanche Gulch to the bottom of the mountain. Kehrlein's Schuss, as the run became known, "was one of the great publicity stunts of the early days," says Shasta newspaperman Orr Apperson. "No one ever skied the whole thing back then, but it attracted skiers from all over." Oliver Kehrlein was also a pioneer skier of the era, secretary of the Sierra Club's first winter sports committee, and known for his exploration of Shasta and sister volcano Mount Lassen.

In 1956, highway access to Shasta's south side was completed. A huge bowl just east of Avalanche Gulch was chosen for a lift-served ski area, and Fletcher Hoyt was hired to camp in the area and report on conditions prior to building the lifts. Hoyt came back with a gloomy report: they'd lose up to 75 percent of their ski days to fog and high wind, and the avalanche danger was obvious. The investors snubbed Hoyt and by 1959 the lifts were built. Nineteen years later an avalanche scoured anything made by man out of the bowl, and the owners ran with their tails tucked. The area is known as "Old Ski Bowl," and is a popular backcountry ski run, as is Avalanche Gulch (the next drainage to the west), the most accessible and direct ski route to and from the summit.

In northern California, drive Interstate 5 to the town of Mount Shasta, then drive the Everitt Memorial Highway 11 miles to parking at Bunny Flat (7,000 feet). Head up the well-used route to the Sierra Club Hut (a.k.a. the Shasta Alpine Lodge), then begin the climbing by ascending the "Middle Moraines" to avoid avalanche on either side of Avalanche Gulch. At 9,500 feet the gulch widens and leads to Helen Lake (10,443 feet, usually snow-covered). Continue northeast up the gulch, and climb to the east of rocky Red Banks. After you've topped Red Banks, you'll find out why the next obstacle is called Misery Hill, as you lift legs of lead another 1,200 vertical feet to the summit. Descend your ascent route, with variations you eyed on the way up.

Start: Bunny Flat, 7,000 feet

Summit: 14,162 feet

Vertical gain: 7,162 feet

Round trip distance and time: 11 miles; long day or high camp

Ascent: Intermediate

Glisse: Advanced (possibly extreme if snow is icy at Red Banks)

Map: Wilderness Press Mount Shasta topographic

Guidebooks: *Mount Shasta Climber's Review*, published by Fifth Season (see Directory); *The Mount Shasta Book*, Zanger and Selters (includes USGS map)

First ascent of peak: Captain E.D. Pierce, 1884

First ski descent of peak: Fletcher Hoyt and companions, 1947

Weather: Mount Shasta snatches every horrific storm the Pacific Ocean can throw. Look in the *Guinness Book of Records* for the most snowfall from one storm, and there you'll find Mount Shasta: 189 inches in six days. Prepare for the worst, and don't force your route into a storm. The best months for skiing most routes are May, June and July. The Avalanche Gulch route may be crowded in June and July, if so consider the Clear Creek route, Hotlum/Wintun, or others. For weather reports, use local radio and television and call the area's superb weather and climbing phone recording (see Directory). When using weather reports, remember the mountain makes its own climate. Thus, slightly unsettled weather at lower elevations can mean a cataclysm higher on the mountain. For general information on Cascade weather, see Mount Baker above.

Red Tape: Registration is mandatory for overnights. For day trips you can self-register at the trailheads. For overnights register at the Ranger District office in the town of Mount Shasta (see Directory).

The vertical relief is so great on Mount Shasta you feel like you're looking down from a jet airliner. *Michael Kennedy*

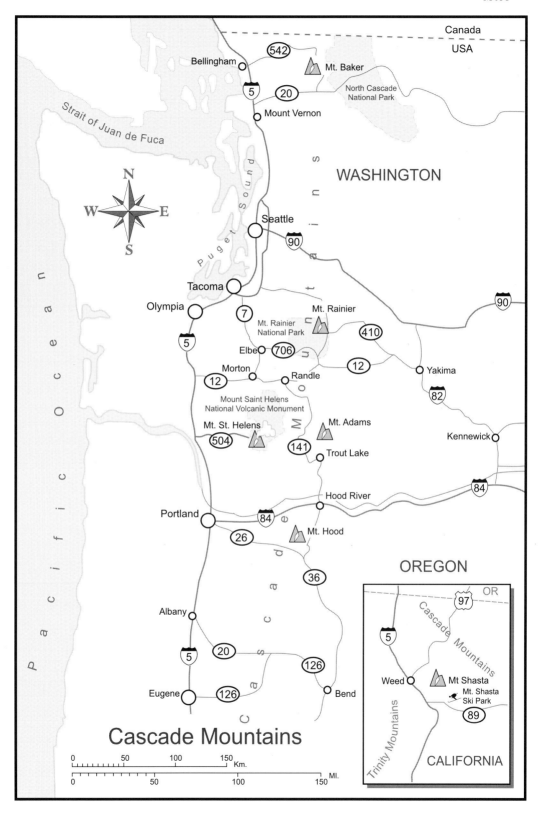

Cascade Mountains

OCEAN WINDS:
COAST MOUNTAINS OF
BRITISH COLUMBIA

Ocean Winds:
Coast Mountains of British Columbia

The Coast Mountains of Canada are a continuation of North America's Sierra and Cascade Mountains. Extending north from Vancouver 450 miles to the Alaska-Canada border and beyond (see Alaska and the Yukon chapter), the Coast Mountains can be roughly divided into three lateral regions: The coastal area consists of low rugged peaks split by inlets and fjords. Beyond this, the spine of the range rises to high glaciated summits surrounded by large icefields. The third region is the inland areas in the rain shadow of the spine. For visiting glisse alpinists, the latter offers the most reliable recreation, while the spine is where you'll get the most glaciated alpine ambiance.

Early skiing in the Coast Mountains was sporadic and uneventful. No towns existed in the area until the 1800s, and even the local mountains near the city of Vancouver were not climbed until the 1900s. Skis were first tried near the coast about 1910, but didn't prove useful. In the 1920s alpinists began exploring the vast icefields and glaciers near the spine of the range.

A married couple, Don and Phyllis "Phyl" Munday, were the most prolific early explorers of the Coast Mountains, first as climbers, then as ski mountaineers. From the 1920s to 1949 the pair created an amazing legacy of geographic exploration. They reported countless ski and climbing trips, including dozens of first ascents and descents, and participated heavily in Alpine Club of Canada (ACC) outings and business.

Indeed, the Mundays were the most successful husband and wife team in the history of North American mountaineering. "She and I formed a climbing unit something more than the sum of our worth apart," was how Don Munday put it. What's more, it was Phyllis Munday who provided the vision, piercing intelligence, and general enthusiasm that drove the couple to their heights of achievement.

Phyllis Munday was born on September 24, 1924, in Sri Lanka, where her English parents managed tea production for Lipton. The family lived part-time in England as well, and "Phyl" emigrated to Canada with her parents when she was seven years old. The family finally settled in the west Kootenay region of British Columbia, near a rugged backcountry of deep-cut rivers and steep hills. Straight away Phyl led the outdoor life. Her parents gave her a rifle with which she kept the family well supplied with game meat. She spent much of her backcountry time on horseback, and loved balance walking on logs crossing the Kootenay ravines. Her father wanted Phyl to take up tennis, but she wanted to be an outdoors-woman and mountaineer.

Starting as a youth, Phyl was a life-long member of the Girl Guides, the female version of the Boy Scouts. With the Guides she made numerous mountain rambles and backcountry camping trips, further fostering her enduring love for outdoor activities. Her favorite was the hike up Grouse Mountain near Vancouver, which was considered quite a climb for a young girl.

Phyl worked at a military hospital during the last part of World War I. It

Don Munday. *Whyte Museum of the Canadian Rockies*

was there that she met a wounded veteran named Don Munday. In 1920 they married. The shared passion of the Munday partnership was immediately obvious—they honeymooned at the foot of Mount Robson; in marital bliss they climbed Lynx Mountain and made a first ascent on Mount Resplendent. Being so close to noble Robson and not climbing it was no doubt the source of some angst for Phyl. She spent the next four years trying to climb the peak, and in 1924 reached the summit with famed guide Conrad Kain. In doing so she became the first woman to make the ascent.

Mountain exploration became the Mundays' focus. While on Robson they'd caught an enticing glimpse of the Cariboo Mountains, and the next year they became the third party to visit that remote area. The couple were becoming honed alpinists. On one climb in the Cariboos they did 10,000 vertical feet in 17 hours—a respectable pace to say the least! The Mundays continued to live near Canada's west coast, and with their penchant for exploration, their attention focused on the virtually unexplored western mountains.

Coast Mountains pioneer Phyl Munday (circa 1958). Along with her husband Don, she inaugurated ski mountaineering in the region. *Whyte Museum of the Canadian Rockies*

Phyl Munday secured the couple's alpine fate during a rest break in 1925 on a small mountain on Vancouver Island. They were enjoying the view when the clouds broke to the north, and rising at the limits of their vision was a huge craggy peak that had yet to be climbed—or even penned on a map. "Phyl's eyes shone as she handed me the binoculars and pointed to a tall mountain," wrote Don Munday, "it was the far-off finger of destiny beckoning. It was a marker along the trail of adventure, a torch to set the imagination on fire." The looming monolith was the then-unnamed Mount Waddington, the highest peak in provincial Canada, and one of the most rugged glaciated peaks in North America. Waddington, nicknamed "Mystery Mountain," became the focus of the Munday mountaineering career. For 12 years the couple probed the rugged lands around the peak, making almost one major expedition a year, and totaling 15 months of harsh exploratory mountaineering. As for Mystery Mountain, the Mundays got up the peak's northwest summit twice, but they never reached the main summit spire (which is guarded by technical rock).

This was a golden age; a time of naiveté that perhaps helped explorers such as the Mundays endure amazing hardships. Their primitive gear was effective but incredibly heavy, and you didn't hop a helicopter to the glacier in those days. What's more, without a gas stove the couple had to use firewood for cooking. This severely limited their ability to camp on glaciers close to the peaks. Without the luxury of such high camps, they'd drive themselves to hallucinatory exhaustion on 30-hour summit pushes. Many trips started with a lengthy journey by boat—some including time pushing the oars of a small rowboat. They used horses for several trips, but more often Don and Phyl were their own pack animals, relaying huge loads for days through heavy underbrush.

Phyl's athletic ability became legend. She'd bear as heavy a pack as Don. As the lightest member of the group, she was usually the first to test shaky snowbridges over crevasses. Photos of Phyl Munday show a lean, hardened woman, but one with the smiling eyes and feral glow any seasoned mountaineer has seen on countless companions. Any athlete would have suffered under the brutal pounding Phyl endured. In her case, every night she wrapped her knees in cold wet towels to relieve arthritic swelling. "A bit of a nuisance," was her only comment.

Grizzly bears were a constant source of concern for the Mundays. While photographing a grizzly during one of many close encounters, the couple were startled to find a sow and two cubs behind them. Yelling and throwing his hat Don tried to ward off the female's subsequent charge—in doing so he tangled in the bushes at the top of a cliff. After that it was one matriarch against the other when Phyl stood above her helpless husband and brandished her ice ax at the bear. The grizzly gave a bellow and turned—bowing to the superior female.

By the late 1920s, recreational skiing had been introduced to the Vancouver, B.C., area, and the sport was a popular way to enjoy local mountains such as Hollyburn, Seymour and Grouse. At the same time, local mountaineers were skeptical of skis as a tool of alpinism. One "influential" local climber went so far as to offer a cash reward for the first person to do a ski climb of the Camel, a local pinnacle that's too craggy to hold snow. Such incentives were unnecessary to entice the Mundays, who found skiing was an obvious choice for winter recreation. Don and Phyl partook in Vancouver's ski scene and became competent practitioners.

The Waddington area the Munday's chose to make their life's work is a maze of huge glaciers, icefields, and permanent snow— perfect terrain for glisse alpinism. With confidence in their new tools, in 1930 they set their sights on their eponymous Mount Munday, a sublime peak near "Mystery Mountain." With special wax cooked up by Don, and with their ski skills perfected, the couple made the first ascent. Don Munday later wrote: "The four following days were mostly wet. They served to add to our satisfaction at having brought skis with us and so having won our mountain." As the pair descended Mount Munday, Don watched as his wife "struggled to steer her ski through a trail-less thicket." "Were they worth it?" he asked. "Every bit of it!" she answered without pause.

It's generally agreed that the birth of ski alpinism in the Coast Mountains occurred when Don Munday reported in the 1930 *Canadian Alpine Journal* that "three seasons in the Mount Waddington section of the Coast Range fully convinced us skis were the logical equipment" for effective mountaineering. This 15 page illustrated article was titled "Ski-Climbs in the Coast Range," and its publication was a seed event in North American glisse alpinism. Here were two pioneer mountaineers knocking off previously unexplored summits, and claiming skis made it possible. One had to listen.

After the Mundays primed the pump, the Coast Mountains gained a long and venerable tradition of ski alpinism. During the 1940s, better gear drove a trend to more winter activity (the Mundays had often traveled in summer, due in part to equipment that would have compromised winter mountaineering). At this time, much of the more accessible Coast Mountain terrain was explored by Vancouver ski alpinists, who spent vacation days on Mount Seymour, Sky Pilot, Roderick, and Golden Ears, not to mention Garibaldi Provincial Park (see below). One amusing incident of this period occurred when a group of youngsters,

including Fred Beckey, made a ski traverse from Mount Waddington to the Tiedeman Glacier, then returned and did the second ascent of Mount Waddington. "Our teen-age success was shocking news to the Canadians," wrote Beckey in his autobiography.

Coast Mountain ski alpinism stagnated in the late 1950s and early 1960s, as it did in much of North America. Many alpinists shifted their focus to more technical climbs, while others were seduced by mechanized skiing. In the late 1960s, however, a vigorous timber industry bloomed in western Canada and logging roads probed the remote valleys. This, together with a new climber's guide to the range helped renew interest in exploration. Naturally, skis were the tool of choice.

Along with roads, the logging companies brought bush pilots and their aircraft. No three-week Munday horsepacking trips required; just hop in your car or hire a plane, motor to a remote trailhead or basecamp, and explore. The British Columbia Mountaineering Club (BCMC), a small but active group based in Vancouver, led such work. In 1967, the BCMC's first official ski trip used a bush plane to reach a remote area in the Lillooet Range. Subsequent BCMC trips made many contributions to Coast Mountain ski exploration.

The 1960s also brought the high-and-light ski traverse to the Coast Mountains, when Bert Port and three other University of British Columbia Varsity Outdoor Club (VOC) members made a nine-day traverse of the Spearhead Range. Known as the Spearhead Traverse, this popular route crosses two glaciers to connect the ski resorts of Blackcomb Mountain and Whistler Mountain.

In the 1970s, alpinist John Clarke began an amazing stint of Coast Mountains exploration. In May of 1972, he made a 10-day solo ski traverse of a remote area north from Mount Tinniswood (northwest of the Whistler ski resort, at the head of Jervis Inlet). Clarke followed that with several major efforts, the most remarkable being a three-week solo ski in the virtually unexplored Klinaklini Glacier complex near Mount Silverthrone. Harkening back to the pioneer days of Coast Range ski exploration, Clarke traveled in July and endured an 11-day snowstorm.

Another fine contribution was made in 1980 when a VOC group with guidebook author John Baldwin completed a three-week "alpine" traverse of the Lillooet Icefield, which included skiing on several peaks. With better gear and the leadership of pioneers such as Baldwin and Clarke, a number of other long traverses were completed in the Coast Mountains. The frequency of ski descents also increased.

In 1985, filmmaker Peter Chrzanowski, Steve Smaridge, the late Trevor Petersen, and Beat Steiner, climbed and skied the Angel Glacier, then skied from within 100 feet of Mount Waddington's

Eric Pehota, Canadian extreme skier. *Peter Chrzanowski Collection*

Extreme skier and filmmaker Peter Chrzanowski's attempts to ski Mounts Robson and Waddington were numerous and well promoted. *Peter Chrzanowski Collection*

summit, which was capped with unskiable ice. Chrzanowski returned in 1990 with venerable Sylvain Saudan and professional extreme skier Eric Pehota. The group helicoptered to the glacier a few hundred feet below the summit "button." Pehota climbed to the summit and skied down—thus making the first descent of Waddington.

Trevor Petersen was a well known media extreme skier, and one of the Canadian Coast Mountains most prolific activists. In 1985, he joined Peter Chrzanowski, Alex Gerbowski, Steve Smaridge and Beat Steiner for several first descents on Mount Serratus in the Tantalus Range of the Coast Mountains. He did a number of first descents in the Spearhead Range of the Coast Mountains, and nailed many inspiring lines in Garibaldi Park. In 1988, he teamed up with Steve Smaridge, Eric Pehota and Peter Mattsson for firsts of several 3,000-foot couloirs on the North Face of Mount Currie, near Pemberton, British Columbia. In 1990, Petersen, along with Smaridge and Mattsson, was the first to ski the spectacular West Face of Razor-back Mountain. Petersen died in an avalanche in Europe in 1996.

One of the Coast Mountain's most impressive ski descents is the Siberian Express on Mount Atwell (a peak near Mount Garibaldi, see below). This incredible winding couloir drops 4,000-vertical feet, averages over 50°, and narrows in places to 40 feet. It's a must-do for any serious extremist. Chrzanowski, along with Peter Mattsson and Beat Steiner, authored this modern-day classic in 1991.

Presently, Coast Mountain skiers enjoy numerous classic ski descents, and traverses maintain a modicum of popularity. While recent "extreme" films have included descents on Mount Waddington and the terrain around the Whistler ski resort, skiing steep descents of specific Coast Mountain peaks has not been as popular a sport as it has elsewhere. Much of this has to do with lack of access, but the brutal climate is also a factor. Looking at the bright side, battling the weather and remoteness of this vast

wilderness should bring out the wilderness lover in all but the most jaded alpinists.

Mount Munday–Franklin Glacier

Ever since Phyl and Don Munday's first ascent of this peak in 1930, it has held a place in the heart of North American ski mountaineers. Guidebook author John Baldwin wrote that it is "without a doubt one of the most outstanding ski trips in the area."

Interestingly, Mount Munday was named *before* its first ascent. "The name *Mount Munday* had been very kindly recorded by the Geographic Board," wrote Don Munday, "rather naturally we wished to make the first ascent." The pair achieved their goal by traveling mostly on skis—in one of their legendary, continuous 24-hour pushes. With a nod to his amazing partner, Don wrote: "fortunate is he who is privileged to be abroad on such a night, the more so with a companion sensitive to the wonder of it all."

The Franklin Glacier complex. Mount Waddington is the highpoint, with Mount Munday to left and Franklin Glacier in foreground.
John Baldwin

Mount Munday is typical of the more remote peaks of the Coast Mountains. First, decide on your access style. For an extended wilderness experience you can hike in, or out, or both (see local guidebook for details). For a quick stab during a weather window, a helicopter ride to and from a glacier camp might be a more prudent choice. One such air service (see Directory) operates from Tatla Lake, a long day's drive north of Vancouver. Such commercial endeavors vary; inquire locally to find the current providers. To climb and ski Mount Munday, establish basecamp high on the Franklin Glacier. From camp, ski Corridor Glacier to the Agur-Munday Col. Continue up the moderate, south-facing glacier to the summit plateau. To reach the true summit, scramble across a notch separating it from the highest point you can reach on skis. Descend your ascent route. To optimize your chances, be prepared to wait out several days of poor weather.

Start: Scar Creek Road, or helicopter landing on glacier, elevation of Scar Creek Road 300 feet

Summit: 11,046 feet

Vertical gain: Depends on exact camp and start

Round trip distance and time: Distance dependent on access and aircraft landing, multiday

Ascent: Advanced, glacier travel

Glisse: Advanced

At the summit of Mount Munday, Mount Waddington in background. *John Baldwin*

Map: Canadian government 1:50,000 series, Mount Waddington sheet, 92N6
Guidebook: *Exploring the Coast Mountains On Skis*, John Baldwin
First ascent and ski ascent of route and peak: Don and Phyllis Munday, 1930
Weather: The Canadian Coast Mountains are one of the wettest areas on the continent. During an average January in the heart of the range, it's entirely possible to get decent weather only one out of three days. According to statistics the sunniest skiable month is May, but you can still plan on mostly stormy weather. The rain shadowed areas on the east side of the range may be drier, but committed glisse alpinists will usually find themselves aiming for the higher and wetter parts of the range, where they'll find the most majestic terrain. For weather forecasts, use local television and radio, and call the weather phone for Vancouver, listed under "weather information." Mainly, anyone traveling in these mountains should have the gear and skill to handle extended heinous weather at any time of the year. Rain is common at low elevations during every month of the year, with concurrent heavy snow at higher elevations.
Red tape: None

Mount Matier and Anniversary Glacier. *John Baldwin*

Mount Matier— Anniversary Glacier

I t can be hard to find decent weather in the Coast Mountains, and skiing more to the east side of the range can help. Mount Matier is a nicely sized glaciated peak located in the sometimes drier easterly area known as the Lillooet Range, northeast of Vancouver and the Lillooet River.

D rive to the town of Pemberton, just north of Garibaldi Provincial Park. From Pemberton, drive east on an extension of Highway 99 known as the Duffy Lake Road (all season), and park near the Cerise Creek and Cayoosh Creek confluence. Cross Cayoosh Creek, then ski into a logged area on the side of Cerise Creek. Continue several miles through timber up the east side of Cerise Creek to the toe of Anniversary Glacier. Continue 3,000 feet to the pass at the head of the Glacier, then scramble Mount Matier's short North Ridge to the summit. Descend your ascent route (the scramble section is not skiable).

Start: Duffy Lake Road, 4,100 feet
Summit: 9,100 feet
Vertical gain: 5,000 feet
Round trip distance and time: 12 miles, long day or easy overnight
Ascent: Intermediate
Glisse: Intermediate to Advanced
Map: Canadian government 1:50,000 series, Duffy Lake sheet, 92J8
Guidebook: *Exploring the Coast Mountains On Skis*, John Baldwin
First ascent of route: R. Chambers, R. Mason, C. Scott, P. Sherman, 1957
Weather: See Mount Munday above. February to March are the best months.
Red Tape: None

Mount Garibaldi—Névé Traverse

Named after an Italian patriot of the 1860s, the noble glaciated peak of Mount Garibaldi reigns over sublime Garibaldi Provincial Park, just a one-hour drive north from the city of Vancouver. Garibaldi Park was created in 1926, and has always been a popular mountain getaway for the Vancouver population. When skiing caught on in the 1940s, adventuresome Vancouver skiers began exploring the glaciers and peaks within the park. Early skiing was limited to the more accessible area around Garibaldi Lake.

In the winter of 1944, a club group made the likely first ski of Mount Garibaldi. The indomitable Mundays made lots of tracks as well. In the 1944-45 *Canadian Alpine Journal*, Don and Phyllis Munday reported a ski attempt on Mount Garibaldi with friend Phil Brock. They skied on

Phyl Munday in Garibaldi Park, circa 1945. She and husband Don did much early exploring in the Park.
Whyte Museum of the Canadian Rockies

Sphinx Glacier and climbed Panorama Ridge during the same trip. Most importantly, during this period a road was built on Paul Ridge near the small town of Squamish, thus allowing better motorized access to the highlands near Mount Garibaldi.

With easier access Vancouver skiers spent even more time on the Garibaldi glaciers. The culmination of this was the creation in the 1940s of the Garibaldi Névé Traverse, an overnight adventure that (weather permitting) can include a fine descent of Mount Garibaldi.

Mount Garibaldi: from Vancouver, drive to the town of Squamish on Highway 99, and continue 2.5 miles north to the Diamond Head turnoff. Take the turnoff, and drive the Diamond Head road 10 miles to parking. From parking, ski a snow-covered jeep trail to Red Heather Meadows, then continue on a marked trail following Paul Ridge to Diamond Head Cabin (call Park for information on cabin, see Directory). Since this is a traverse, you'll need transport from your egress point. Stash a car or arrange a pickup. From Diamond Head Cabin follow an indistinct snow-covered road to Ring Creek, then head up the east side of Ring Creek onto the actual Garibaldi Névé. Head northerly across the Garibaldi Névé, travel over the northeast ridge of The Tent, then continue north on the North Pitt Glacier. Finally, ski over a wide pass to the north of Glacier Pikes, descend to and cross to the northwest (outlet) end of Garibaldi Lake, and leave via the Black Tusk Trail.

To ski Mount Garibaldi during a traverse: After you pass by The Tent ski up Garibaldi's northeast slopes to the peak's north ridge. The ridge is a short scramble. With good conditions (stable snow and a filled in bergschrund) the adjacent Northeast Face can be skied. Maximum angle of the face is about 40 degrees. Set a high camp if skiing the peak is your goal—weather will dictate your success.

Start: Diamond Head trailhead, 3,300 feet

On the Garibaldi Névé, looking at Mount Garibaldi. *John Baldwin*

Skiing Mount Garibaldi. *Carl Skoog*

Summit: Mount Garibaldi, 8,787 feet

Vertical gain: minimum about 6,000 vertical feet

Traverse distance and time: 25 miles, multiday

Ascent: Intermediate

Glisse: Advanced (glacier travel)

Maps: Canadian government 1:50,000 series, Cheakamus River sheet, 92G14; Mamquam Mountain sheet, 92G15

Guidebook: *Exploring the Coast Mountains On Skis*, John Baldwin

First ascent of peak and route: Trorey, Dalton brothers, Pattison, King, Warren, 1907

First ski descent from near summit: Varsity Outdoor Club and Alpine Club of Canada outing, 1944

Weather: Be prepared for wet weather. The best times to ski the Traverse are the months of March and April.

Red Tape: Call Garibaldi Park (known as "Parks Branch") for information (see Directory)

Pelion Mountain–North Glacier

This rugged peak gives another taste of the exciting terrain so accessi-ble from Vancouver. It's recommended as a spring tour, and will require an overnight.

For Pelion Mountain, drive an hour north from Vancouver on Highway 99 to Squamish. Continue through Squamish. Just past the town, turn left onto the Squamish River Road. Drive the Squamish River Road to logging roads which begin at mile 20. Turn left on the Ashlu Road at mile 21 and drive 1 mile to park just past a bridge over Ashlu Creek. Hike a short bit of overgrown road to the south, then pick up a trail climbing into the hanging valley of Sigurd Creek. Skiable snow usually starts at about 2,000 feet of elevation, and subalpine terrain begins near the 3,000-foot level. Start your climb of Pelion by gaining the peak's indistinct northwest ridge at 3,400 feet in Sigurd Creek, which then fades into the North Glacier. Follow the North Glacier to the summit, with a deviation east at a notch, and a short scramble to the top. Descend your ascent route. "A nice long ski run," according to guidebook author John Baldwin.

Start: Ashlu Logging Road, 300 feet

Summit: 7,500 feet

Vertical gain: 2,200 feet

Round trip distance and time: Multiday

Ascent: Intermediate (glacier travel)

Glisse: Intermediate to Advanced

Map: Canadian government 1:50,000 series, Cheakamus River sheet, 92G14

Guidebook: *Exploring the Coast Mountains On Skis*, John Baldwin

First ascent of peak: V. Brink and B. McLellan, 1944

Weather: Best in March

Red Tape: Logging roads in this area may be closed. Call local road access numbers for information.

Pelion Mountain from the north (center of photo). *John Baldwin*

The view south from Mount Seymour, looking over Vancouver and the Strait of Georgia. *John Baldwin.*

Mount Seymour—Southwest Side

Vancouver is one of North America's finest cities. If you'd like to enjoy urban amenities, yet catch some fine backcountry ski or snowboard action, Mount Seymour is one of Vancouver's closest classics.

Drive north from the Vancouver to the Mount Seymour ski area (a small lift-served resort). Park at the ski area parking lot. Climb north up a trail paralleling the ski runs. Head past the ski area, and continue over several ridges and subpeaks to Mount Seymour. Descend your ascent route, enjoying the subsidiary bowls and peaks.

Start: Mount Seymour ski area parking, 3,300 feet

Summit: 4,758 feet

Vertical gain: 1,476 feet

Round trip distance and time: Short day

Ascent: Novice

Glisse: Intermediate to Advanced

Map: Canadian government 1:50,000 series, Coquitlam, 92G7

Guidebook: *Exploring the Coast Mountains On Skis*, John Baldwin

First ascent of peak: Gray, Chapman, Mills, Darling, Harrow, 1908

Weather: Use Vancouver radio, television, and ski reports

Red Tape: None

winter, March, ... April?

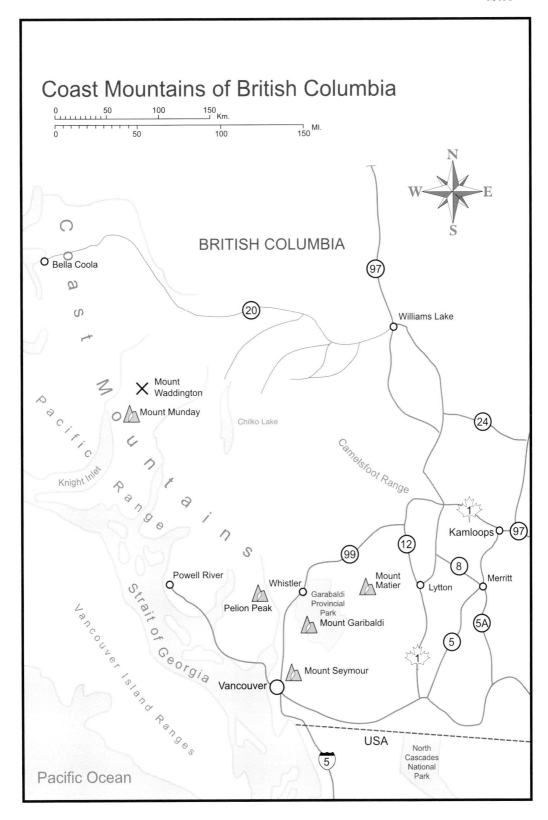

Coast Mountains of British Columbia

BRITISH COLUMBIA

Pacific Ocean

GRIZZLIES AND BIG DROPS:

ALASKA AND THE YUKON

Grizzlies and Big Drops:
Alaska and the Yukon

Alaskan mountaineers found that skis are safer for crevassed terrain. *Jonathan Waterman*

Alaska and Canada's Yukon comprise one of the world's largest wilderness areas. The region would fit the states of Texas, Colorado, and California—and still have room for the Canadian province of British Columbia. Glaciers cover about five percent of Alaska: that's 29,000 square miles of névé! Someone counted the number of Alaskan glaciers at about 100,000—a snowboard and ski paradise.

Cheechakos (Alaskan argot for outsiders) often view Alaskan mountains with a tunnel vision, believing them to be merely the higher peaks surrounding Denali, North America's highest peak at 20,320 feet. In the same manner, the Yukon mountains are often believed to be limited to Mount Logan and Mount St. Elias. Truth be told, the far northwestern region of the American continent has an astounding array of mountain ranges. Huge glaciers and lofty peaks abound—with challenges equal to those found in any other great range of the world. What's more, for glisse alpinists seeking pure fun, the lower altitude coastal peaks of the region offer lots of oxygen and reliable maritime snow.

Starting from the southern part of the region, mountains known as the Coast Ranges intrude into Alaska and the Yukon, and are often approached from the port town of Juneau. (The Coast Ranges are often confused in speech with Canada's Coast *Mountains.*) Go 200 miles northwest from Juneau and you'll probe the majestic

St. Elias Mountains. Some of the greatest mountains in the world make their home here: Mount Logan is the second highest peak in North America, and 18,008-foot Mount St. Elias hulks over the largest icefield in Alaska—1,500 square miles!

About 150 miles northwest of Mount St. Elias you enter the Chugach Mountains (a subset of the Coast Ranges). The Chugach rise as high as 13,250-foot Mount Marcus Baker, but numerous lower Chugach peaks yield some of the best glisse mountaineering in the world. Indeed, spring descents (accessed by helicopter and foot) have become a major industry in the Chugach gateway town of Valdez. The World Extreme Skiing Championships are held on peaks near the Thompson Pass Road, accessible by auto from Valdez. Nearby mountains such as Diamond Peak have achieved cult status among North American snowboarders and skiers.

In the Chugach Mountains near the city of Anchorage, the famed Alyeska Ski Resort perches on the side of towering Chugach peaks, and the closest ski mountaineering to Anchorage is on such mountains as Flattop Mountain and Ptarmigan Peak—just a short drive from downtown.

◄ Denali's 18,000-foot relief is the greatest in the world. The Wickersham Wall was first skied in 1994 by Tyson Bradley and John Montecucco. *Jonathan Waterman*

Go south from Anchorage across the sublime Turnagain Arm of Cook Inlet (where explorer Captain Cook "turned again" when land blocked his quest for the Northwest Passage), and the Kenai Peninsula holds the sprawling Kenai Mountains. Really an extension of the Chugach portion of the Coast Ranges, the Kenai are low and wet. They run about 150 miles along the southeast side of the Peninsula, with highpoints of about 4,000 feet (highest around 6,000 feet). Many of the Kenai peaks, accessible by road, airplane or train, make perfect one-day ski descents. Are these "mellow" mountains? Perhaps by Alaskan standards they are; but don't forget the Kenai's 1,700 square miles of glacier ice, and be ready for smothering coastal storms.

About 100 miles northeast from the Chugach Mountains, an inland volcanic range called the Wrangell Mountains rises to the highpoint of Mount Blackburn at 16,140 feet, and includes the skier's classic Mount Sanford. Immense glaciers of Himalayan scale stream through the Wrangells, and the range's eponymous peak is the highest erupting volcano in North America.

Return to Anchorage. About 50 miles northeast of the city, across the fertile Matanuska valley, a range known as the Talkeetna Mountains rises to its highpoint at Sovereign Mountain (8,849 feet). One of Alaska's few road-accessed alpine areas, the Talkeetnas are a small range by Alaskan standards; yet they still boast 300 square miles of glacier and a plenitude of glisse.

Finally, consider the northland's mountain crest: the Alaska Range. Ruled by 20,320-foot glacier draped Denali, the Alaska Range is a mammoth massif extending in a 400 mile arc through southern Alaska. While many of the Alaska Range's peaks are high arêtes better suited to climbers than skiers, many of the range's

glaciers make fine ski runs, and Denali has a rich heritage of skiing.

Recreational skiing came late to the great north. No doubt small amounts of pragmatic skiing were done during the turn of the century gold strikes. Thousands of would-be millionaires invaded the state at this time. Likened by John Muir to "a nest of ants stirred up by a stick," the prospectors swarmed across arctic wastes in search of Eldorado. Transportation during the gold rush was difficult. An infrastructure of trains and roads did not exist, and the vast distances made skiing or snowshoeing impractical.

The solution to Alaskan transport was dog sledding. While it's unknown if prehistoric Alaskans used dog sleds, it is certain that work dogs crossed the Bering Land Bridge with the early natives long ago.

"Mushing," as dog sledding came to be known, was quickly adopted by Alaska's early settlers. (Since then, mushing has become a northern transportation science, and has achieved status as a major international sport.) By the early 1800s, trappers were active in the Yukon and Alaskan bush, and mushing became an important part of the fur economy. When the gold strikes began, sled dogs (also known as "huskies") were in such demand that they were traded as valuable commodities. Legend holds that "no dog larger than a spaniel was safe on the streets of Seattle or San Francisco," (the port of origin for the gold rush).

Huskies were the stars of early Alaskan mountaineering. And Denali, which dominates much of interior Alaska, was often the goal. The first successful climbers on the peak, the famous "sourdoughs" of 1910, mushed 300 miles from the town of Fairbanks. They climbed the north summit while munching doughnuts, ever mindful of the bets they'd made in a Fairbanks bar. The first ascent of Denali's higher south summit was made in 1913, and dogs again

Mushing back from Denali to Wonder Lake, the key transportation for early Alaskan and Yukon mountain approaches.
Jonathan Waterman

made the trip possible by hauling the climbers and their gear to 11,000 feet on the Muldrow Glacier. In a sense, even though these early climbers didn't use skis, they brought the efficiency of glisse to the Alaskan mountains by dog sled.

In 1932 ski promoter Erling Strom and his companions (see following page) were the first to combine skis with dogsledding. In doing so they became the first to use skis on Denali, and the first to climb both summits during one trip. With that year's advent of modern mountaineering gear and aircraft, Alaska's mountains were no longer remote dreams. Instead of an expensive and time consuming sled trip, you could hop on a bush plane and be almost anywhere in the mountains in a few hours. Many later climbers stepped out of their air-taxi with a pair of skis in hand—the perfect tool for ferrying loads up long glaciers.

Modern resort skiing began in Alaska in 1959, when French benefactor Francois de Gunzberg founded the Alyeska ski resort 40 miles south of Anchorage. This major ski resort brought more skiers to Alaska, and raised the Alaskan mountaineering community's consciousness of the sport. Concurrently, the Mountain Club of Alaska (MCA) was founded by a devoted group of Anchorage locals who were as much backcountry skiers as climbers. At Alyeska and other locations, MCA skiers began to pursue backcountry skiing for its own sake, in steep terrain on serious mountains. The era of Alaskan ski mountaineering had begun.

Skiing, both at the resort and on wild snow, has remained a popular far-north pastime. Every range, from the vast Chugach, to high Alaska, to the St. Elias of the Yukon, has seen hundreds of ski descents and expeditionary ski traverses. Yet the terrain is so vast, with thousands of skiable summits, that unskied lines wait at nearly every arête, peak, and buttress.

Skiplane on the Kahiltna Glacier, Denali. Aviation has opened up Alaska and the Yukon. *Jonathan Waterman*

ALASKA RANGE

Denali—West Buttress

Denali's ski history began with the 1932 Strom expedition. Erling Strom came from Norway as a master skier, and combined his skills as an outdoorsman and skier for what has to be one of the most successful ski trips ever accomplished on the peak.

Strom was on a hunting trip in 1928 when he first viewed the "impressive giant." Locals told him that the weather on Denali was best in April, while conventional wisdom held that same month was too cold for climbing. To Strom this had the sound of skiing. Four years later, he received a message from his friend Alfred Lindley, a Minneapolis attorney who had seen the mountain and offered to organize a ski trip. With a nod from Strom, the pair recruited

The huge white bulk of Denali shouts "glisse" to all who listen. *Jonathan Waterman*

Strom, Lindley, Liek and Pearson during their successful 1932 Denali ski expedition—the first of its kind. *Whyte Museum of the Canadian Rockies*

Mount McKinley National Park Superintendent Harry Liek and a ranger named Grant Pearson.

The main reason for inviting the feds was so they'd supply the government dog teams to approach the mountain, thus eliminating a major expense. But in a telegram to Strom, Lindley pointed out a catch in the plan: the two sourdoughs were accustomed to snowshoes, and Pearson had never even been on skis. Strom's solution? Teach Pearson on the way!

At the staging area Strom and his friends were surprised to find another expedition gearing up. In an amazing coincidence, Theodore Koven and Mount Logan veteran Alan Carpé were starting their trip on the same day—to climb a mountain that had not seen a soul for 19 years.

Traveling with careful rope work, on skis, the group made short work of the heavily crevassed Muldrow Glacier. "The skis carried us across crevasses much better than snowshoes because the weight is better distributed." Strom would later write, "During an eight-hour day we could work uphill for seven hours and return to camp the last hour." How true those words ring to many thousands of subsequent Denali mountaineers.

Soon the group broached the upper Harper Glacier, and had the honor of discovering one of Denali's most famous statistics.

Nineteen years before, during his first ascent of the peak, Hudson Stuck had left a maximum/minimum thermometer on a rock at 16,000 feet. Strom's group did the unveiling: "We carefully opened the lid of the box," wrote Strom. "The thermometer was now exposed and we could see that the little float was tipped over in the bulb. It had hit bottom. The scale on the thermometer went to 95 degrees below zero, but the float had gone below that. It is fair to say the temperature had been 100 degrees below zero [Fahrenheit]."

A successful summit day followed. The group didn't ski from the top, though Strom made a few turns high on the peak "to say we'd skied above 17,000 feet." They filmed much of their trip, starting the venerable tradition of Denali climbing movies, all of which to this date contain ski segments. Sadly, the glow of success and discovery was short lived for these hard-core glisse alpinists. During their descent they skied into the midst of a tragedy.

During Strom's summit bid, Koven and Carpé had been doing cosmic ray research lower down on the glacier. Somehow, though these were experienced mountaineers, they'd developed the habit of traveling unroped. As Strom and his companions descended, they looked forward to seeing their friends. Instead they came upon an eerie sight. "As we approached their camp," Strom later wrote, "we were unhappily surprised to find snow covering their tents and obliterating all tracks around them. We hardly dared open the tents. When we did, nobody was there, but we found two empty sleeping bags and some mulligan in a pot on a stove."

A short distance below camp the group found Theodore Koven's body. "Nearby was a hole in a snow bridge," Strom explained. "On the edge of it was planted an ice ax, probably left there to mark the hole. Koven had fallen in, probably broken his skis, but been able to climb out. … Without skis to carry him over crevasses he had not dared to go far. We could see where he had walked back and forth to keep warm, but had finally succumbed at the one end of his little trail." Apparently, both men had fallen into the crevasse and died as a result. Later, Strom learned Carpé had not been using skis on the glacier, and had been walking alone and unroped. Two nearby mountains were later named after Koven and Carpé.

Skis fell out of favor for Denali mountaineering. But by the early 1970s skiing began to regain favor for the same reasons Strom had written about 30 years before. In 1972, this author joined a group of nine ski mountaineers who made the first repeat of Strom's ski trip to Denali's south summit. We used skis for all of the Muldrow and Harper glaciers, and hauled our own food and gear with no aircraft or dog teams. While the Park Service had terrified us with horror stories about Koven and Carpé, and made us carry snowshoes as a backup, we found Strom's words about the efficiency of skis to be prophetic and accurate. One by one, our snowshoes disappeared into crevasses along the way.

Starting in 1969, the number of climbers attempting Denali began a steady increase. Because of easier aircraft access most groups used a route known as the West Buttress, located on the western side of the mountain. Skis proved to be helpful on the Kahiltna, and many parties used their planks to speed the return from hauling loads up the névé.

The first complete ski descent of the peak was done in 1970 by Japanese adventurer Tsuyoshi Ueki. His feat was relatively unheralded in North America, though it received abundant play on Japanese television. Even more unknown, a partial though significant glisse descent was made in 1962 by ski instructor Hans Metz, along with his friends Willi Schmidt, Manfred Schober and Helmut Tschaffert. Schmidt and Tschaffert reached the summit on skis and skied down to 16,400 feet, where they descended steeper terrain on foot to the Kahiltna Glacier. They walked down a big chunk of the mountain, but theirs was certainly the first summit ski.

The most impressive run on Denali— perhaps the most impressive in the world— is the drop down the Wickersham Wall. One of a handful of the greatest skiable faces in the world, the Wickersham plunges 14,000 vertical feet from the mountain's north summit to the Peters Glacier. The center of the Wickersham Wall is the obvious glisse line, but it has never been descended because of avalanche danger (though it has been climbed—once). On the south side of the wall, however, a ridge line allows climbers to avoid much of the avalanche danger. The route was first climbed in 1963 by a group of Canadians that included backcountry and helicopter ski pioneer Hans Gmoser. Partly sponsored by Head skis, the expedition planned to ski at least part of the route. While fighting altitude and weather, skiing became as far down their list of priorities as the Peters Glacier was below the summit.

But the gauntlet was down; skiing the Wickersham had become the glisse prize of Denali. French extreme ski star Patrick Vallencant was the next in line. His plan, which included a kayak descent to the sea, was poorly conceived and too ambitious. After spending a fortune on a sponsored dog sled expedition to the base of the face in 1982, he looked up and said, "it is not right." Later, while scarfing burgers in Talkeetna, he told author Jon Waterman he could have climbed up and skied the West Buttress route instead; but with a French shrug of his shoulders he stated, "*Est tres facile* [too easy], *comprenez-vous*?"

Another group tried to ski the Wickersham in 1983, but the Wall awaited the next generation and a shift in thinking. Utah mountain boy Tyson Bradley and tough commercial fisherman John Montecucco had seen plenty of Alaskan mountaineering. They knew how to live on glaciers for weeks on end, and were hardy enough to make long approaches by hauling heavy cargo sleds in rough terrain. They knew how to ski, and they knew how to climb. In May of 1994, they went after the Wickersham Wall, but with a twist.

Skiers on Motorcycle Hill, West Buttress route, Denali. *Glenn Randall*

Rather than trying to climb to the north summit of Denali, then ski the whole Wickersham Wall in one continuous descent, Bradley and Montecucco applied the same rhythm used by skiers on the glaciers below. With drive and endurance worthy of the sourdoughs, they first approached up the Kahiltna Glacier then over a rough pass and down to the Peters Glacier. Taking the more conservative Canadian Route on the south shoulder of the face, they established a series of camps up the route, and skied the wall in sections as they established each camp. After skiing from the summit, they escaped the wall by heading over to easier ground, rather than descending the complete route. Arguably an odd style of "skiing" a mountain, and somewhat counterintuitive for the spectator, their method of "stage skiing" worked

and is generally acknowledged as the first ski descent of the Wickersham Wall. Wickersham one-upmanship remained alive, however, and Frenchmen Jean Urban and Nicholas Banhomme skied the Wall the next year from top to bottom. They spent one night on the route during their descent.

Denali is a glisse alpinist's mountain, and many other attempts and descents have been made over the years. In 1981, Colorado extreme skier Chris Landry retired from steep skiing after failing to ski the peak's West Rib, a route still without a complete ski descent. Every extreme skier wonders what it's like to fall down a killer slope. Landry found out. "I was bounding along, feverishly grabbing and clawing at the snow," he later told a reporter. "I eventually ground to a halt at the last possible

Riding the Orient Express, known for the number of climbers who have taken deadly falls. *Andrew McLean*

place I could have after falling some 1,000 feet. …The descent ended right there. I downclimbed the rest of the way."

One of the most beautiful glisse lines on Denali is the Messner Couloir, an incredible plunge dropping 6,000 vertical feet from the 19,600-foot plateau under the south summit. The Messner was first skied by the "father of extreme skiing," Sylvain Saudan. What could have been a glorious bit of history was tainted by Saudan's claiming to have made the first descent from the summit when he skied the couloir, when in fact he had not.

Most other high Alaska Range peaks offer little in the way of reasonable summit ski descents; but many of the glaciers and lower peaks of the range offer superb ski touring and glisse descents. The most common of such work is done on the Ruth Glacier, in a deep amphitheater behind Denali. The second highest peak in the range, Mount Foraker (17,004 feet) got its first ski descent in 1981 down the Southeast Ridge, by the French mountaineer Pierre Beghin. At the time, this was perhaps the hardest ski route yet completed in the

Alaska Range. During the same trip, Beghin's party also made the first ski descent of heavily crevassed Mount Crosson, a 12,775-foot subpeak of Foraker.

The most popular climbing route on Denali remains the West Buttress. This is also the most skied route on the peak, though most people use glisse for pragmatic reasons and don't pursue a complete descent of the route. If you do intend to snowboard or ski Denali, the West Buttress is the foundation for your best strategy, and with either minor or major variations may yield a sublime descent.

Skiing in Ruth Gorge, South Buttress of Denali in background.
Bill Stevenson

Denali: travel by train or automobile from Anchorage to the town of Talkeetna (113 miles by road), then take a ski plane to the famed landing on the southeast fork of the Kahiltna Glacier. Spend several days working your way up the Kahiltna Glacier to a huge 14,300-foot basin. Head west up the "Headwall" to the true West Buttress, and observe the Rescue Gully dropping from the head of the buttress at 17,000 feet. The Rescue Gully is the crux of doing a complete West Buttress ski descent, for it's used to bypass the unskiable portion of the buttress. Climb the regular buttress route or the Rescue Gully, continue to the summit, then ski your chosen route.

The portion of the West Buttress route above the Rescue Gully may be unskiable ice. If so, and your ski skills are up to it, consider skiing the Messner Couloir.

Start: Kahiltna Glacier, 7,200 feet

Summit: 20,320 feet

Vertical gain: 13,120 feet

Round trip distance and time: 35 miles, several weeks

Ascent: Advanced

Glisse: Advanced to Extreme, varies with conditions and exact route

Map: Boston Museum of Science, Mount McKinley

Guidebook: *High Alaska,* Jonathan Waterman

First ascent of route: Bradford Washburn, Bill Hackett, Jim Gale, Henry Buchtel, Mel Griffiths, Jerry More, Barry Bishop, 1951
First ski descent of route and peak: Tsuyoshi Ueki, 1970
Weather: The best skiing on Denali is in the spring and early summer seasons, when crevasses and icefields are still covered with snow. Be ready for arctic winter conditions and difficult snow.
Red Tape: Register with the National Park Service at least 60 days in advance, and pay a $150.00 fee

Denali from the southwest. The lower West Buttress route follows the obvious ramp-like Kahiltna Glacier. *Bradford Washburn*

TALKEETNA MOUNTAINS

Hatch Peak—
Thousand Dollar Run

Hatcher Pass broaches a fantastic alpine crest in Alaska's Talkeetna Mountains. Easily rivaling the most accessible alpine ski touring in the lower 48 states, the cirque on the east side of the pass is circled by a half dozen beautiful ski peaks, including Microdot Peak, Marmot Peak (plenty of steep couloirs), and Hatch Peak. The Thousand Dollar Run from Hatch

Peak is named for the cost of dental work incurred when a hapless skier knocked his teeth out while skiing the route. Recently, a snowcat ski operation has been using the Hatcher Pass area. With their over-snow roads and highly used slopes, the "cats" have added an element of civilization to the area. Thus far, lack of room has not been a problem; but self-powered skiers should inquire locally about both human and snow conditions at Hatcher. (It may be possible to use the snowcats for access to more remote glisse alpinism terrain, see Directory for phone number.)

On Hatch Peak, with view to Knik Arm.
Kip Melling

For Hatch Peak, fom Anchorage head north on the Glenn Highway. Go through the town of Palmer. Approximately 1.5 miles past the last stoplight in Palmer, take a left (west) on Fishhook Road, which becomes the Hatcher Pass Road. Drive 14 miles through the gorge of the Little Susitna River to the Motherlode Lodge. Here the road makes a sharp switchback and begins a 3.5 mile winding ascent to the Hatcher Pass Lodge or "A-Frame." The road is maintained year-round; however, a vehicle equipped for winter travel is advisable, i.e. studded tires, chains, four-wheel-drive. You'll find ample parking just past the A-Frame at the entrance to the Independence Mine Historical Park. To reach Hatch Peak, walk back down the main road a short distance to the Hatcher Pass Road gate, then ski up the snow-covered Hatcher Pass Road 1½ miles west to Hatcher Pass. Climb south from the pass up the east shoulder of Hatch Peak, then to the summit (4,811 feet). The road is packed by snowmobilers and well marked. For the Thousand Dollar Run, descend from the summit back down the shoulder, glisse an easterly face, then enjoy the low angled moraine paralleling the south side of Hatcher Creek, ending on the road.

Start: Hatcher Pass Lodge, 3,000 feet

Summit: 4,811 feet

Vertical gain: 1,811 feet

Round trip distance and time: 5 miles, 3 hours

Ascent: Intermediate

Glisse: Advanced (Intermediate from Hatcher Pass down Hatcher Creek)

Maps: USGS 15 minute, Anchorage D-6, D-7

Guidebook: None

Weather: The Talkeetna Mountains have a more "interior" climate than Alaska's true coastal mountains. It's generally colder than the Chugach Mountains, and a bit dryer. Interpretation of weather television will give you the best weather predictions.

Red Tape: Hatch Peak is located near the Independence Mine State Historical Park. No mountaineering registration is required.

CHUGACH MOUNTAINS

Flattop Mountain–West Side

Anchorage is Alaska's largest city. Small in terms of population, (only about 250,000 residents), the town is nonetheless influential, as almost half the population of Alaska lives there. Bordered by sea on one side and mountains on the other, the town sits like a small jewel in the hand of a giant. For starters, the municipality of Anchorage governs hundreds of square miles of raw wilderness. If that's not enough, walk north from the municipal boundary—and 700 miles of the world's finest backcountry leads you to the Arctic Ocean. Head east from Anchorage and you'll hit the western end of the Chugach Mountains, which form the east side of the "Anchorage Bowl." As the local saying goes: "Anchorage is where you get to Alaska from."

Anchorage ski mountaineers have traditionally headed for the Chugach peaks near the city. In 1944, nurse Louise Roloff was stationed at Fort Richardson Army Base north of Anchorage. She and other skiers on the base did a lot of backcountry skiing from a ski chalet that had been built a few years before near a mountain they called "Pyramid Peak." Other peaks near Anchorage were doubtless explored on skis in the early days. One such peak, Flattop Mountain, has a long and venerable ski history. Indeed, if any Alaskan peak has seen more skiing than Denali, it's probably Flattop. The Mountain Club of Alaska (MCA) was formed in the 1950s, and a group of club members did much skiing on Flattop throughout the 1960s, with an early descent by Chuck Metzer, Helga Bading, Paul Crews, and Andy Brauchli written up in a 1960 MCA newsletter. The MCA skiers were an active bunch. They ticked off descents of Carpathian Peak, did a number of trips to sublime Mount Alyeska from the Alyeska Resort ski lifts, and hit many other peaks and bowls.

The Chugach Mountains are the widest, deepest receptacle of snow in all of Alaska. *Carl Skoog*

Flattop Mountain from the southwest, Ptarmigan Ridge to right, looking up the Rabbit Creek drainage. *Louis Dawson*

Flattop Mountain: take the Seward Highway south from Anchorage. Exit on O'Malley Road. Drive O'Malley Road east for 3.5 miles, and turn right on Hillside Drive. Take Hillside Drive 1 mile, turn onto Upper Huffman Road, and drive 1.4 miles to Toilsome Hill Drive. Take a right on Toilsome Hill (4x4 with chains or studded tires required), and drive 1.9 miles to parking for Flattop Mountain at the Glen Alps Trailhead.

Start the Flattop Trail by taking the stairs at the east side of the parking lot. The summer trail traverses the north side to the summit. With snowcover, a better route might stay closer to the ridge. Take your pick of descents: several steep couloirs drop from the summit, or stick closer to your ascent route.

Start: 2,230 feet

Summit: 3,510 feet

Vertical gain: 1,280 feet

Round trip distance and time: 3 miles, 4 hours

Ascent: Intermediate

Glisse: Advanced

Map: USGS 7.5 minute, Anchorage (A-8) SE

Guidebook: None

Early ski descent of peak: Mountain Club of Alaska members, 1960

Weather: Good ski and snowboard conditions may come as early as November to the Chugach and Kenai Mountains. Midwinter glisse can be worthy as well, but daylight is scarce (about eight hours in November, December and January) and temperatures may be cold (though Alaska's coastal mountains are often surprisingly warm). The most reliable skiing is in late winter and spring: daylight is plentiful and temperatures are similar to skiing in Colorado or Wyoming. Summer glisse is available on glaciers and permanent snowfields in all of Alaska's higher mountain ranges.

Red Tape: Outside of Alaska's National Parks (where you have rescue-on-demand and subsequent bureaucracy), skiing and snowboarding Alaska's vast public lands is a exercise in freedom. Basically, you're on your own. Hire a bush plane to fly into a remote glacier. Ski from any trailhead.

KENAI MOUNTAINS

Turnagain Pass—Tincan Ridge

The Kenai Peninsula is a huge arm of mountainous land defined by Cook Inlet to the north and the Gulf of Alaska on the south. Plenty of water—plenty of snow. Even in dry years you'll find good snowboarding and skiing in the Kenai Mountains. As with most Alaskan peaks, much of the Kenai are remote and inaccessible—with two exceptions.

One easy way to reach parts of the Kenai Mountains is via Seward Highway, which was built in 1951 to connect the coastal town of Seward with Anchorage. As soon as the highway was completed over Turnagain Pass, Alaskan skiers began enjoying their nearby mountains. The tradition continues. Some of the best, most accessible glisse in the Kenai can be had on Tincan Ridge accessed from Turnagain Pass.

For Tincan Ridge, drive the Seward Highway south from Anchorage approximately 45 miles to Turnagain Pass. Park about a mile down the road south from the pass summit. The correct parking is across the creek from the base of Tincan Ridge. Identify the ridge on your topo map: it's the major feature forming the north side of the Tincan Creek drainage. The southerly side of the drainage is formed by a low ridge known as Center Ridge, which is a good tour in it's own right, and yields access to the "adult rated" glaciated peaks at the head of the drainage.

For Tincan Ridge, drop from the highway a short distance to cross Ingram Creek, then climb the series of steps forming the western end of the ridge. The first summit on the ridge is a worthy goal. You'll find skiable lines (from Advanced to Extreme) on both sides of the ridge, with the ascent route being your most conservative choice.

Start: Seward Highway near Turnagain Pass, 900 feet

Summit: 3,500 feet

Vertical gain: 2,600 feet

Round trip distance and time: 5 miles, 5 hours

Ascent: Novice

Glisse: Intermediate to Advanced, depending on exact route

Map: Trails Illustrated #760, Kenai National Wildlife Refuge

Guidebook: None

Weather: See Chugach Mountains above. Be prepared for wet weather and fast moving storms.

Red Tape: None

Above Turnagain Pass, looking west. *Louis Dawson*

On Tincan Ridge, Turnagain Pass. *Louis Dawson*

Grandview—East Side

In 1923 the Alaskan Railroad was completed from the town of Seward, on the coast of the Kenai, to Anchorage, and on to Fairbanks (Alaska's only "city" other than Anchorage). Sixty miles from Anchorage the rails punch the heart of the Kenai Mountains at Grandview. Since the early 1950s, a special "ski train" has visited the winter. Riding the ski train is a truly Alaskan social experience. Arriving in morning dark at the Anchorage station, you pile in with about 600 other adventurers. Some are planning tours near tracks at Grandview, while hard-cores will climb the glaciated peaks rising above. Still others will stay on the train, socialize, and enjoy the scenic ride. After a two-hour ride to Grandview, the train disgorges a huge crowd that quickly disperses into the wilderness like ants scouting for a sugar spill. The train leaves at 4:30 p.m.—if you're left behind there's a duffel stashed beside the tracks, containing a sleeping bag, tent, and dubious survival rations.

Such unforgiving punctuality is the stuff of legends. Rising northeast of Grandview is a huge peak known as Bruce's. During a ski train adventure a few years back, the departure whistle blew at 4:15 and someone noticed the ant-like Bruce 3,000 vertical above, atop the then unnamed peak. The news spread like an avalanche through the train. Could Bruce make it? Would he have to live on the paltry and possibly spoiled food in the survival bag? Observers crowded the observation cars. At 4:20, the rumble of the locomotive signaled imminent departure. It was then that Bruce began to ski. Plunging down the steep upper couloir he began pumping nonstop turns. Like a machine he didn't stop, he didn't fall, he didn't tire. As the astonished passengers watched, Bruce nailed his eponymous run and grabbed the handrails of his car seconds before it rolled—on time.

The ski train is about glisse, but it's also a social occasion. A polka band roams the train during the morning ride. Groups stuff themselves with breakfast goodies. Families laugh at Grandma's jokes. Young skiers and snowboarders huddle and plan their extreme adventures. The ride back is as wild as the glisse: you can "slam polka" at a dance party held in a swaying boxcar, quench your Alaskan size thirst at the essential beer bar, and buy a souvenir T-shirt—all a raucous expression of true "Alaskana."

Slam polka in a swaying boxcar, an Alaskan tradition. *Louis Dawson*

The Grandview Ski Train is organized by the Anchorage Nordic Club (see Directory) and runs twice each winter. Buy your tickets well in advance. From the train stop at Grandview, ski back north along the tracks for about ½ mile. Swing east and climb into the high basins above the valley. If you have the time and energy, several fine couloirs rise above the upper basins. Other destinations from Grandview include the Bartlett and Trail Glaciers, as well as plentiful glisse terrain on the west side of the tracks.

Start: Grandview, 1,100 feet

Summit: High bowls, 3,000 feet

Vertical gain: 2,100 feet

Round trip distance and time: 4 miles, 5 hours

Ascent: Intermediate (Advanced in high couloirs)

Glisse: Advanced to Extreme, depending on route choice

Map: Trails Illustrated #760, Kenai National Wildlife Refuge

Guidebook: None

Weather: See preceding Chugach Mountains section. Be prepared for wet weather and fast moving storms. The Kenai area may have much warmer weather than Anchorage.

Red Tape: If you're after something radical, talk with the Nordic Ski Patrol so they know what you're up to. Ski Train skiers are expected to travel in groups and be responsible.

WRANGELL MOUNTAINS

Mount Sanford—Sheep Glacier

Mount Sanford tops out at 16,206 feet in Alaska's Wrangell Mountains (see Introduction). The peak is a huge snow and ice monolith, with rotten unclimbable cliffs and heinous hanging glaciers blocking all but one route: Sheep Glacier, a skiable névé ramping a remarkable 10,000 vertical feet to the summit.

Alaska University president and mountaineer Terris Moore, along with his wife Katrina and Alaskan climber Bradford

Mount Sanford , Sheep Glacier to right. *Jonathan Waterman*

Washburn, made the first climb and ski descent of Mount Sanford in 1938. "The mountain undoubtedly remained unclimbed so long because it was considered too easy!" wrote Moore after his climb. "The discovery that you could probably drive a dog team to the summit seemed to rather cool the ardor of other prospective climbers."

But to the Moores and Washburn, all of them skiers, "the possibility of an unbroken 10,000-foot-Downhill-Ski-Ride" was irresistible. The trio drove Washburn's station wagon from Valdez to a one-house settlement known as Chistochina. There they enlisted the aid of a horsepacker, rented a dog team, and started the long slog in. No aircraft for these explorers—with the help of their dogs (for which they had to break trail in deep snow) they spent almost two weeks getting into climbing position at the base of the glacier. Moore described the alluring peak:

July 18 saw the last of the loads up at our third glacier camp, at about 10,000 feet. ...From this camp we made a short reconnaissance on skis. ...A clear route now lay open straight toward the summit, across an immense snow plateau which sloped very gradually up to the final cone.

Harsh weather drove Washburn and Moore down from their first summit attempt. Hunkered in the 10,000-foot camp, they inventoried their supplies and realized they had plenty of human food, but were running out of dog grub. Their wrangler had shot a bear during the approach, and the meat provided dog food until a huskie named Wooly got loose and inhaled a whole ursine haunch while everyone was asleep.

The group had planned to dogsled some instruments to the summit, but left the dogs at camp with Katrina Moore and dashed for the top at 1:30 p.m—reaching the summit at 9 p.m. "A temperature of –2° and

Brad Washburn (left) and Terris Moore on Mount Sanford summit during the first ascent and ski descent in 1938. *Bradford Washburn*

On the Sheep Glacier at 15,200 feet, Mount Sanford. Mount Drum in background. *Glenn Randall*

a stiff little breeze encouraged us to leave promptly," wrote Moore, "and we turned our skis away from the summit.… The return run of over 6,000 feet downhill through perfect powder snow to camp has become one of the unforgettable memories of the trip."

Moore and Washburn's descent may well have been one of the finest back-country ski runs ever made. It's not often you can combine the thrill of a premier ascent, the satisfaction of a first descent, perfect snow, relatively safe terrain, and the grand beauty of wild Alaska!

Since Moore and Washburn, the reputation of Sanford as a classic ski descent has spread throughout the world. It's often attempted, and you have a reasonable chance of success if you block out a few weeks of time, and possess the gear and downhill technique necessary for difficult snow. Apparently, the perfect powder encountered by Moore and Washburn is the exception rather than the rule. But then, on a mountain such as this—to an alpinist poised for the descent of a lifetime—there may be no such thing as "difficult" snow.

Sanford: travel Highway 1 from Anchorage to Gulkana, then fly via bush plane from Gulkana to the Windy Ridge airstrip. Contact Wrangell–St. Elias National Park for information about air travel, registration, and other details. Ask the Park Service about using the small cabin at the airstrip. From Windy Ridge walk nine miles across tundra and moraine to the Sheep Glacier. Follow the glacier to the summit, with camps arranged according to weather, ability, and acclimation. Descend your ascent route, and watch out for grizzly bears on the tundra.

Start: Windy Ridge airstrip, 3,500 feet

Summit: 16,237 feet

Vertical gain: 12,737 feet (10,000 skiable)

Round trip distance and time: 40 miles (depending on how far and which direction the grizzlies chase you), 2 to 3 weeks

Ascent: Intermediate (glacier skills required)

Glisse: Advanced

Maps: USGS 1:63,000, Gulkana A1 and B1

Guidebook: None

First ascent and descent of peak and route: Terris Moore and Bradford Washburn, 1938

Weather: The Wrangell Mountains are renowned for wind, and can be somewhat drier than the the Alaska Ranger. Plan for arctic weather on top.

Red Tape: Registration with Wrangell-St. Elias National Park is not mandatory, but a very good idea (see Directory)

ST. ELIAS MOUNTAINS

Mount Logan—King Trench

A monolith of almost inconceivable size, Mount Logan squats inside the Yukon like the hunched shoulder of Atlas. The Yukon is a vast (186,000 square mile) area of sub-arctic wilderness in northwestern Canada. (The Yukon has a population of only 28,000, with the extreme northern areas virtually uninhabited.) Logan's summit plateau is 10 miles across. The south and north walls tower 14,000 feet above vast glacier basins. Indeed, this is a mountain which holds its own against any geography in the world. Logan may only be the second highest mountain in North America, but it's by far the largest. It is also a fine ski or snowboard run.

The first ascent of Logan didn't involve skis, but it's a story we should not ignore. In 1924, Captain A.H. MacCarthy and a companion found a way to the lower slopes of the mountain—no mean feat in itself. In 1925, MacCarthy returned and began an epic that has never been equaled in the annals of mountaineering.

First, MacCarthy and a sourdough named Andy Taylor mushed through the wilds to the base of the peak—in winter—for 70 days. The pair established a chain of camps and caches for the climbing attempt. The final push began that spring, when MacCarthy and seven other climbers first horsepacked and walked 100 miles, then backpacked and climbed another 80 miles to the summit plateau, where they struggled six miles to the summit.

MacCarthy's retreat was as epic as his climb. Lost high on the mountain in a storm, the summit party survived only when luck let them stumble across their camp. With food running out, they crossed back over the deadly summit plateau in the middle of a raging arctic storm, and survived an open

Prodigious Mount Logan and the King Trench. Glisse takes some of the pain out of this epic slog. *Bradford Washburn*

bivouac. After all this, when most modern Yukon alpinists would break open their beer stash and cheer to the buzz of an airplane, they reversed the 100-mile approach, building a raft from scratch and floating out the final miles down the Chitina River.

With MacCarthy in mind, it's hard to treat the first ski descent of Mount Logan with much solemnity. Indeed, when Arno Dennig, Gerwalt Pichler, Bruno Kraker, Hans Schell, Karl Hub, Hugo Dietrich and Sepp Weber made the probable first ski of the complete mountain (including the high-est summit) in 1971, Weber wrote "It is suspected this has been done before, but no information is available."

Skis and Logan mix well. The 9,000 vertical feet from aircraft landing to the summit plateau can be a fine run, and is so easy most of it has been glissaded on a trash bag. Skis make crossing the summit plateau more efficient, and make for safer travel on the crevassed glaciers. Most of all, trying to ski or snowboard all of Mount Logan transforms a glacier slog into an elegant endeavor.

For Mount Logan, drive the Alaska Highway to Kluane Lake in the Yukon. Land a ski plane at about 9,000 feet on the Quintino Sella Glacier. Trudge the glacier up the King Trench for 5,000 vertical feet and nine miles to King Col. Continue to Prospector Pass (18,400 feet). The crux of the route occurs here, when you *drop* 1,000 feet onto the infamous summit plateau, thus losing an easy retreat. Cross the plateau and climb to the true summit. Most skiers forego launching from the exact summit; it's steep, often icy, and at high altitude. The classic start for a continuous glisse descent is Prospector Pass, but most groups get their best skiing while relaying loads from camp to camp—even if they never make the summit.

Start: Aircraft landing on Quintino Sella Glacier, 8,500 feet

Summit: 19,534 feet

Vertical gain: 11,000 feet

Round trip distance and time: 40 miles, 4 weeks

Ascent: Intermediate

Glisse: Advanced

Map: USGS Mount St. Elias, 1:250,000 scale; Mt. Logan, Arctic Institute of NA, Calgary, 1993

Guidebook: None

First ascent of route: Albert MacCarthy and 8 others, 1925

First ski descent peak and route: Gerwalt Pichler, Bruno Kraker, Hanns Schell, Karl Hub, Hugo Dietrich, Sepp Weber, 1970

Weather: Ask the authorities at Kluane National Park about what radio weather report is best received on the mountain, and carry an appropriate receiver. This is no place to predict weather by licking your thumb and holding it in the air. The best time for a ski climb is in May and June.

Red Tape: Mandatory registraton with Kluane National Park in Canada (see Directory)

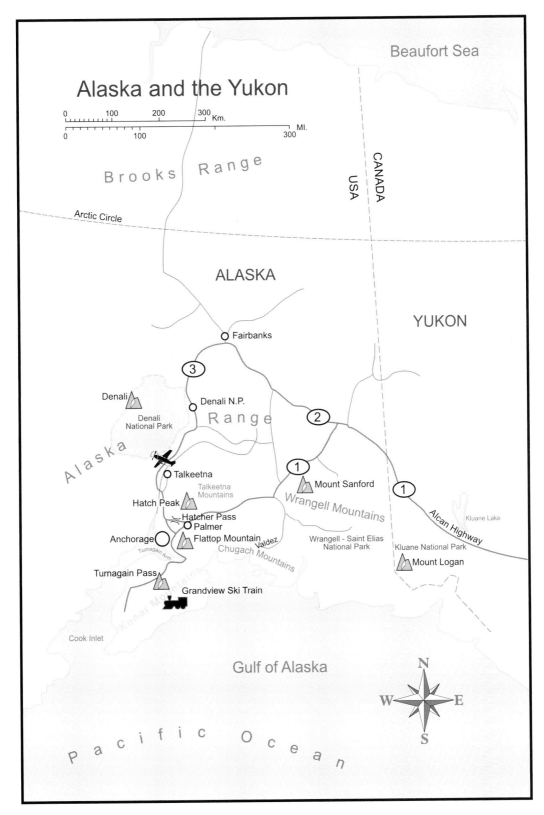

Alaska and the Yukon

Beaufort Sea

Brooks Range

Arctic Circle

ALASKA

YUKON

CANADA

USA

Fairbanks

③

Denali

Denali N.P.

Denali National Park

Range

②

Talkeetna

Talkeetna Mountains

Hatch Peak

①

Mount Sanford

Wrangell Mountains

①

Alcan Highway

Kluane Lake

Hatcher Pass

Palmer

Anchorage

Flattop Mountain

Valdez

Chugach Mountains

Wrangell - Saint Elias National Park

Kluane National Park

Turnagain Arm

Turnagain Pass

Grandview Ski Train

Kenai Mountains

Mount Logan

Cook Inlet

Gulf of Alaska

N
W   E
S

Pacific Ocean

Alaska

INFINITE GLISSE:

CANADIAN
ROCKY MOUNTAINS

Infinite Glisse:
Canadian Rocky Mountains

When Leif Ericsson sailed uncharted waters west in the year 1,000, he carried skis on his Viking ship. It's likely he used those planks in Greenland, his last stop before a gale blew him to a chance landfall in "wineland, where grapes and wild wheat grow"—later known as Canada.

Having the most robust and inspiring ski mountaineering heritage in North America is a claim easily made by the people of the Canadian Rockies. While distractions such as resort development, trail cutting, access ethics and gear plagued skiers in the United States, Canadian glisse mountaineers have simply gone out and nailed the best terrain on the continent. They've descended glaciated peaks since the late 1920s, and pioneered huge alpine ski traverses for more than half a century. Even the country's resort industry shows the region's pioneering dominance: the first North American rope tow was built in Canada in 1932, and North America's first full-time alpine mountaineering guides began service in Canada in 1899. In all, this is a country of big mountains that have inspired its citizens to alpine excellence.

The Canadian Rockies cover an area almost as large as the European Alps, and are part of the greater Rocky Mountain Range, which runs 3,000 miles from Mexico to Alaska.

Development of recreational skiing in Canada somewhat paralleled that of the United States. In the mid 1800s, skiers from Scandinavian countries no doubt brought their skills to various Canadian mountains. By 1895 Canada's first ski race was held. In 1911, well known pioneer climber Conrad Kain started a ski club in Banff, a Rocky Mountain gateway town. But skiing as a mountaineering endeavor was slow to be accepted. When famed pioneer mountaineer and Alpine Club of Canada officer Alexander "A.A." McCoubrey tried to take a group of skiers into the Rockies that same year, the idea was met with "jeers." But the "success of the experiment," he later wrote, "resulted in another trip three years later to the Selkirks. … But the way of the pioneer, like that of the transgressor, is a thorny one."

Luckily for modern day skiers and snowboarders, the enjoyment of glisse was adequate compensation for the pioneers. With people like Kain and McCoubrey involved, Canadian skiers soon took up ski alpinism at a more advanced level than anywhere else on the continent.

In 1885, the Canadian transcontinental railroad was completed over Rogers Pass in the heart of the Rockies at Glacier National Park. Rail travel to the mountains was popular, and the Canadian Pacific Railroad soon built the famed Glacier House Lodge near the summit of the pass, with an inspiring view of the Great Glacier spilling from the vast Illecillewaet Icefield. In 1899, the railroad imported a crew of Swiss guides to work out of Glacier House, thus creating a direct connection to European alpine culture. At the time, Europe was the fountainhead of mountaineering and skiing.

◀ The indomitable A. A. McCoubrey, pioneer of Canadian skiing. "The way of the pioneer," he wrote, "is a thorny one." *Whyte Museum of the Canadian Rockies.*

The first Swiss guides came to Canada in 1899, and brought European alpine culture to North America.
Whyte Museum of the Canadian Rockies

Aileen Harmon skiing near Mount Assiniboine, 1934.
Whyte Museum of the Canadian Rockies

The guides' continental influence, combined with the remote and glaciated Canadian Rocky Mountains, resulted in state-of-the-art alpinism. Mountain pioneer A.O. Wheeler wrote of these guides:

> They take the veriest embryos on any and every climb; they haul them up cliffs, lower them down precipices, place their hands and feet where they should go, soothe their ruffled feelings, carry their paraphernalia and cheerfully assume the responsibilities of life and death; then, just before reaching the summit, they stand to one side, take off their hats and say, "After you sir."

High-level skiing in the Canadian Rockies was inaugurated in 1928 by Erling Strom, when he and the Marquis d'Albizi led a ski group to huge Mount Assiniboine. Strom was a tireless promoter of all things skiing; he would lead Denali's first ski expedition several years later (see Alaska chapter). In the 1920s Strom also operated a popular ski lodge on Lake Magog under Mount Assiniboine. Strom entertained his guests with "tests," such as skiing around the lake as quickly as possible, working the sides of a gully like a modern day halfpipe, and schussing from the base of Mount Assiniboine to the lake (a feat only com-

pleted once, according to one reporter). By 1930 backcountry skiing had truly caught on in the Canadian Rockies. That year five men skied 200 miles from Jasper to Lake Louise: an amazing accomplishment for the day, and one that still inspires.

The Alpine Club of Canada (ACC) greatly influenced Canadian ski mountaineering. Soon after the club was founded in 1906, ski articles began to appear in the club's publication, *The Canadian Alpine Journal*. In 1931, a special "Ski Section" was added to the *Journal*. That year's reports included a race for roped skiers, and the important first ski descents of Snow Dome and remote Mount Resplendent.

The ACC has operated North America's largest alpine hut system for almost a century. In the 1930 *Canadian Alpine Journal*, visionary A.A. McCoubrey wrote "a factor of the utmost importance in the development of alpine skiing in our mountains is the necessity for numerous, well placed cabins." The first hut managed by the ACC was the Hermit, built in 1904 by Swiss guides in Glacier National Park. By 1986, the club would be operating more than 18 huts in the Rockies and more in other Canadian mountain ranges. They even manage a hut in the United States. The huts range in design from austere glacier shelters to luxurious hostels, and are extremely popular. Because of the northland's serious alpine weather, such a string of shelters has been essential for development of ski mountaineering in the Canadian Rockies.

Some of the Rocky's highest and most desirable ski terrain lies in the cordillera of stupendous peaks sprawling 150 miles between the towns of Jasper and Banff. In the early days, a primitive pack trail was the only route through this rough wilderness. In 1940, an amazing alpine road opened through the mountains and connected both towns. Now known as the Banff/Jasper Highway, or Icefields Parkway, the route started as a primitive dirt track. Winding just feet from the toe of colossal glaciers, and bringing skiers to perfect trailheads for hundreds of routes, this is a road to the promised land. In 1961 the parkway was paved and is now an all-season road. Indeed, considering the parkway and another similar road that was completed over Rogers Pass in 1962, it's safe to say Canada has the best automobile mountaineering access in North America.

Canada's age of modern glisse alpinism began with the alpine highways and continued with a flock of new huts. Among others, the Great Cairn Hut was built in 1963 near Mount Sir Sandford, the Bow Hut and Balfour huts on the popular Wapta icefields were completed several years after, and the Fairy Meadow Hut was built next to Granite Glacier and the popular tour to Friendship Col.

In 1958, inspired by the ski trudgers of the past generation, New England ski instructor and guide Bill Briggs (see Teton chapter) ushered in a new era of Canadian high traverses and ski descents. In years past, Briggs had made several mountaineering trips to the Bugaboo Mountains, a subrange of the Canadian Rockies near Rogers

Pass. He loved the "Bugs," and in a mountain epiphany Briggs conjured an expedition to combine skiing, climbing and exploration in one grand 100-mile traverse from the Bugaboo Mountains to Glacier Station (near Rogers Pass in British Columbia).

At the time most of the area was not mapped, and only one hut provided shelter along the way. What is more, no expeditions of this sort (using skis in an aggressive style on technical glaciers and passes), had been attempted in North America. Not that ski expeditions were unheard of. Briggs knew of Fridtjof Nansen's traverse of Greenland in 1888, and of the last generation's long Canadian traverses, but his plan took the concept of a ski traverse into steeper and more technical terrain—a modern application of an old concept. As a consummate skier and mountaineer, Briggs had found what a fine tool the ski was. He wanted to share his insight with his mountaineering community. "There was something to be said," he remembers.

Briggs was operating a ski school in Woodstock, Vermont. For instructors he'd hired his climbing buddies from the Dartmouth Outing Club, including Barry Corbet, Roberts "Bob" French, and Sterling Neal. All were superb mountaineers, expert skiers, single, and ready for adventure. Briggs brought his Bugaboo ski traverse idea up with his crew. "I didn't have to do any persuading," he remembers, "these were all climbers and Exum Guides, and the idea was to go into an unexplored area—to be the first mountaineers there."

Inventor Howard Head gave the men his latest metal skis, and they drilled holes in the tips so they could tie the skis together as tent supports and make an emergency sled if necessary. The group knew weight was critical, and Briggs whittled the gear list to lank essentials, even questioning the inclusion of French's harmonica (which

Bill Briggs, Barry Corbet, Sterling Neale and Bob French (L to R) during their visionary high traverse of the Bugaboo Mountains in 1958.
Bob French

they allowed). Food was planned at an anorexic one-and-a-half pounds per day. With everything loaded, they started out with 43-pound packs—unheard of for a 10-day trip in the 1950s.

With all their skill and planning—and luck with weather—the men's visionary ski traverse went off mostly without a hitch. For 10 days they climbed and skied through some of Canada's most rugged, unexplored mountains. They descended couloirs, crossed glaciers, forded rivers, and even chased a cougar.

"We were at the head of a gentle glacier, and we spotted a cougar down on the névé," remembers Briggs with a hearty laugh. "We were in a playful mood, so we decided to give chase. We were going like mad down the glacier—the cougar would run away, look over his shoulder, then run farther. So there we are, schussing down this glacier, playing in the mountains and throwing caution to the wind. Then I look

Barry Corbet fords a river during the Bugaboo traverse of 1958.
Bob French

down and notice we're crossing a few small crevasses. Soon we skim a crevasse about a foot wide, then another that's a couple of feet. We've forgotten about the cougar. Soon we're jumping over wide crevasses and going too fast to pull around and stop. It really was something else. I remember thinking, 'are these going to get too big?' Lucky for us the angle eased off and the crevasses never got any bigger."

During the last day of the trip, Briggs made his crowning achievement as a navigator by bringing the group across the Illecillewaet Glacier in a fog, using only map and compass (this section was one of few covered by a map). His heading dropped them into a narrow couloir, where the visibility improved and they made glorious turns to within yards of the foot trail leading down to the Glacier train station. The group had accomplished the first "high ski traverse" in the Canadian Rocky Mountains, and such ski traverses would continue to gain popularity to the present.

The next year Austrian guide Hans Gmoser teamed up with five others and attempted another Canadian expedition, known as the Great Divide Traverse. The idea with this ambitious, indeed astounding, route is to stick to the high icefields and passes of the Continental Divide between the towns of Lake Louise and Jasper. It's 185 miles long, crosses nine icefields, and stays classically true to the heart of Canada's greatest skiable alpine wilderness.

Gmoser and his crew made a valiant effort, completing the southern half of the route in 25 days. Grueling trailbreaking, harsh storms, and food shortages brought them short of the complete line.

Despite the Gmoser group's failure to complete the route, they had a fine adventure. Gmoser wrote an augural article about the trip in the 1961 *Canadian Alpine Journal*, and thus ignited the imagination

The first to complete the 185 mile Great Divide Traverse: Don Gardner, Chic Scott, Charlie Locke, Neil Liske (L to R). *Chic Scott Collection*

of a whole generation of ski mountaineers. Someone had to complete the route.

A Canadian backcountry skier named Don Gardner rose to the challenge. Gardner had watched Gmoser's group start their trip, and the idea festered for seven years in the young mountaineer's brain. In 1967, Gardner teamed up with fellow university students Neil Liske, Charlie Locke and Chic Scott to try the complete route. The crew made meticulous preparations, including seven months of route study and numerous cache placements. Since the idea of these traverses is to cover distance, the men used lightweight Nordic ski gear instead of the much heavier alpine touring equipment of the day. The group achieved a great success, as Chic Scott later wrote:

> We began our journey up the Whirlpool River several miles south of Jasper. Over the next 21 days an incredible adventure unfolded as we wended our way up beautiful and almost unknown valleys, over many an unknown col revealing ever new panoramas. … The complete high level route, from Jasper to Lake Louise, is a treat I heartily recommend … it had been the finest experience of my life.

Traverses of Great Divide magnitude have never achieved great popularity. Only a

On the Great Divide Traverse, at the Alexandra Icefall. *Chic Scott Collection*

young ski mountaineer with legs of iron and a will of steel can call such a route a "treat." Such huge ski traverses simply take too much time, commitment, and physical ability. What's more, most of today's ski and snowboard mountaineers are more concerned with how much vertical they can climb up and slide down, rather than how many miles they cover. Nonetheless, long Canadian ski traverses have continued to be somewhat of a cult activity since the 1960s, and shorter traverses are regularly completed.

The whole Great Divide Traverse has only been repeated once, but sections of the route, especially that from Columbia Icefield to Kickinghorse Pass, have been done several dozen times. Other traverse routes, such as that between the Bugaboos and Rogers Pass, are run as guided trips and repeated with greater regularity. Still other routes pioneered by the likes of Scott and Gardner have achieved varied degrees of vogue.

Presently, ski and snowboard mountaineering are popular and accessible sports in the Canadian Rocky Mountains. Each season, mountaineers from over North America flock to the Rockies and enjoy glisse ranging from helicopter-accessed luxury hut vacations, to vagabond tailgate skiing and snowboarding, and yes, to lengthy ski traverses for the hardcore. And for inspiration, regular reports of harsh extreme skiing come out of the region.

One of the better known Rockies activists of the past decade has been Calgary fireman and ski racer Doug Ward. His list of firsts includes the North Face of Mount Quadra in the Valley of the Ten Peaks, the Aemmer Couloir on Mount Temple, and recently the Skyladder route on Mount Andromeda (in 1996).

Perhaps the greatest prize in Canadian extreme skiing is 12,972-foot Mount Robson, a stupendous icy fin higher than all else in the Canadian Rockies. Robson was first

skied from the summit by filmmaker and promoter Peter Chrzanowski in 1983, but to do so he had to downclimb the Kain Face, a huge plaque of snow that looks like one of the best ski runs in the world, but is usually best enjoyed as an ice climb. In 1981 Chrzanowski also made the first descent of Mount Athabasca via the North Face (with John Reed and Bart Ross), and has since scribed first turns on numerous other Canadian peaks (see Coast Mountains chapter).

For both extreme skiers and climbers, Robson's North Face is the plumb. This fluted snow and ice precipice approaches 60 degrees, rising from hanging glaciers like a colossal 3,000-vertical-foot playground slide. The face has repelled numerous ski attempts over the past decade. Doug Ward failed when guide Mike Sawyer lost a hand to a helicopter blade. Defeat also

Troy Jungen on the first descent of Mount Robson's North Face—a "last great problem" of North American glisse alpinism.
DBH Productions

stalked the dream team of film star Scot Schmidt, filmmaker Eric Perlman, producer-cum-skier Peter Chrzanowski, and the late Trevor Peterson. Chrzanowski became obsessed with skiing the face, but all five of his attempts ended in angst.

The crux of the descent is that the face is rarely in condition for skiing—it's usually a shining shield of sinister ice. Just climbing the route is considered a fine accomplishment. The key for a successful glisse of the face is having the patience to wait for the right conditions—to go at a moment's notice.

Young "ski bohemians" Troy Jungen and Ptor Spricenieks played the waiting game in 1995 by living near the peak and staying poised for a quick start. A seemingly endless series of storms blasted the peak that year, and by fall the face boasted an unusual coating of snow that Jungen and Spricenieks deemed skiable.

On such terrific snow the climb was trivial and the pair reached the summit ridge in four hours (from high camp), but turned around before summiting so they could catch the face in prime condition. Then their testicular shrivel began. Without ropes, they skied a terrifying 60-degree pitch, then enjoyed the relaxed 50-degree skiing below, with a final drop off a 15-foot bergschrund. Done: one of the most relentlessly steep, ropeless ski descents yet accomplished in North America.

Where does Jungen and Spricenieks' descent fit into modern ski alpinism? Most certainly, the pair proved that patience, the time honored skill of the alpinist, is how standards are pushed and life preserved. Moreover, the North Face of Robson, at an average angle of 57 degrees for almost 3,000 vertical feet, is one of the steepest faces of its length yet skied in North America. Is this the extreme descent of the decade? Perhaps so for North America. Nonetheless, descents of equal angle and

vertical have been done elsewhere. Still, Robson's North Face was one of the North America's last great unskied lines, and Jungen and Spricenieks deserve respect and praise for their inspiring accomplishment. What's more, the two alpinists emphasize the personal and spiritual gains they gain from facing such challenges— a refreshingly soft voice in the present din of commercial alpinism.

JASPER AREA

Mount Resplendent— Northwest Slopes

Located at the north end of the famed Icefields Parkway, the small mountain town of Jasper is the gateway for the grand mountains of Mount Robson Provincial Park and Jasper National Park. Jasper's ski history began in the 1930s, when tough mountaineers such as Ron Burstrom, Rex Gibson and Joe Weiss spent their spare time establishing trails, building huts, and trying to rope their friends into the sport they held so dear.

Mount Resplendent is a classic ski peak located near Mount Robson, about 100 miles west of Jasper. Northern Rockies ski mountaineering began on Resplendent in the 1930s.

In 1932, Rex Gibson teamed up with Jasper skier Joe Weiss to make what they thought would be the first winter ascent of Resplendent. Naturally, skis would be their tool of choice. In February, the pair made the long approach to bivouac in a small cabin at Berg Lake, below Mount Robson. Winding through crevasses and making a final push on crampons, the pair arrived at the summit in mid afternoon. "Then came the great moment of the day," Gibson wrote. "Off came our crampons and on went our skis for the glorious thrill

of the descent of nearly 5,000 feet of glacier under perfect snow conditions."

Gibson and Weiss skied from the summit, and thus made the first ski descent of Resplendent, but they had a surprise when they arrived back at the cabin. They'd missed the first winter ascent by two years. Written on a wall they found an inscription by Pete Parsons they had not noticed earlier, detailing a winter ascent of the peak: "Beautiful, February day, with some skiing … sure had some sport."

Rex Gibson, circa 1930. He did a huge amount of early Canadian ski mountaineering. *Whyte Museum of the Canadian Rockies*

For Mount Resplendent, drive from Jasper 55 miles west on Highway 16 to the obvious turn for the Mount Robson trailhead. Drive the short secondary road to parking. Make the long backpack approach 11 miles to Berg lake and the Berg Lake Shelter on the north shore of the lake. (Enjoy outstanding views of Mount Robson's famed North Face.) To avoid the long approach to Berg Lake, it's possible to hire a helicopter for a drop-off (see Directory).

From the Berg Lake Shelter (5,375 feet) ski across the north end of the lake, then to the toe of the Robson Glacier. Ski up the Robson Glacier 5 miles to the col between Robson's Southeast Ridge and Mount Resplendent. Continue east then southeast to the summit of Mount Resplendent. Conditions vary, and crampons rather than skis may be appropriate for the upper sections. The last bit to the exact summit is almost always done on foot while roped.

Start: Berg Lake Shelter, 5,375 feet

Summit: 11,240 feet

Vertical gain: 5,865 feet

Round trip distance and time: Multiday

Ascent: Advanced (glacier travel and possible ice)

Glisse: Advanced (roped)

Map: Canadian Topographical Series, 83 E/3 Mount Robson

Guidebook: *Summits & Icefields,* Chic Scott

First ascent of route: C. Kain and B. Harmon, 1911

First ski descent of peak and route: Rex Gibson and Joe Weiss, 1932

Weather: Use Jasper radio and television for weather, and call the Mount Robson Provincial Park for latest weather phone numbers and reports they may have. The best seasons for skiing on Resplendent are late winter and early spring. Remember: once the Canadian days lengthen in June, snow can melt fast and not solidify at night.

Red Tape: Little or no red tape. For information call Mount Robson Provincial Park (see Directory).

COLUMBIA ICEFIELD

Snow Dome—Athabasca Glacier

"The Columbia Icefield is one of the premier ski mountaineering locations in Canada," wrote Chic Scott in *Summits & Icefields*. Scott was modest. If you like solitude and rustic style, the Columbia Icefield is one of the premier places on the *planet* for glisse alpinism.

An immense cap of glacier, the Columbia Icefield lies like a titanic starfish on a high plateau in Jasper National Park. Eleven of Canada's 22 highest peaks surround the field: hulking giants such as ice-shrouded Mount Columbia, the lurking pyramid of Andromeda; the enigmatic Snow Dome and Mount Kitchener. The eminently skiable southern reaches of these peaks contrast their north cirque pits, which host the greatest ice climbs in North America. At 90 square miles, the Columbia is the largest icefield in the Canadian Rockies. It feeds six main outlet glaciers. The Icefield is the hydrographic apex of North America, meaning water melting from the Columbia Icefield glaciers flows to the three great northern oceans—the Arctic, Atlantic, and Pacific.

Mount Resplendent from Lynx Mountain. *Whyte Museum of the Canadian Rockies*

The first European mountaineer near the Columbia Icefield was probably Scottish botanist David Douglas. In 1827 he trekked through Athabasca Pass, then bragged about the 17,000-foot mountains he'd discovered there. With dreams of such high peaks, mountaineer Arthur Coleman followed 65 years later. Upon reaching the area, Coleman immediately knew he'd been "humbugged" by Douglas's chest beating. Later, in 1896, mountaineer Walter Wilcox came close to the Columbia when he climbed over Wilcox Pass. Soon, other mountaineers began visiting the region, no doubt still inspired by Douglas.

Then in 1898 Norman Collie and Hermann Wolley summited Mount Athabasca. They made an astounding discovery: "We were looking on a country probably never before seen by human eye. A vast snow-

Chic Scott, guidebook author and traverse pioneer, circa 1967. *Chic Scott Collection*

Camp on the Columbia Icefield, circa 1935. *American Alpine Club Collection*

field, feeding many glaciers, lay at our feet, rock-peaks and snow-covered mountains were ranged around it, whilst, far away to the westward we could just see through the haze of the valley of the Columbia River. This great snowfield, from which the Saskatchewan Glacier takes its rise, also supplied the ice for another glacier at the headwaters of the Athabasca; whilst to the west we saw the level snows bending over to flow down more than one channel, feeding, when melted, the rivers that empty themselves into the Pacific Ocean."

Collie and Wolley were also the first to see Mount Columbia, the Canadian Rockies' second highest, "on the opposite side of the snow-field. ... Chisel-shaped at the head, covered with glaciers and ice, it also stood alone, and I at once recognized the great peak I was in search of."

The pair continued their quest and summited Snow Dome several days later: the easiest peak on the Icefield, but a worthy goal even by today's standards, considering the harsh environment and glacier travel. The men wanted Mount Columbia as well, but were thwarted by the deceptive distances across the Icefield. The majestic Columbia would finally yield to James Outram and guide Christian Kaufmann four years later.

The first ski descent of Snow Dome was a momentous event in North American glisse alpinism. In 1925, Russell H. Bennett, a devoted ski alpinist, studied new maps of the Rockies with a "professional eye" and noticed the "eminent, if not spectacular suitability of portions of the Columbia Icefield as skiing ground."

Bennett tried to ski on the Icefield in 1930, but was skunked by poor planning and bad weather. In March of 1931, he teamed up with Clifford White and Jasper ski fanatic Joe Weiss. The trio spent 11 days traveling more than 200 miles "by devious route" to camp near the Saskatchewan Glacier toe, south of the Athabasca Glacier. At camp they could cover their eyes, point in any direction, and come up with a potential first winter ascent. But as Bennett explained in the 1931 *Canadian Alpine Journal*, skiing was their true goal:

> There is really in the mere attainment of distance very little reason for a winter venture into the mountains. ... There is but little more reason in the attainment of altitude. The vital element, the animating force, of the sport of down-hill running, and the energies of the ski-explorer in the Rockies should be devoted to finding the runs of greatest magnitude, judged by the high standards of the Swiss and Austrian schools.

The Saskatchewan Glacier looked like a poor ski run to the pioneers, so they scouted the Athabasca Glacier and were struck by its glisse promise. Starting at 7:30 A.M., the trio of hardmen humped huge packs to the base of the Athabasca Glacier, thinking they'd need to camp there. But after arriving at their "advanced camp," they decided to push on, continuing up the Athabasca Glacier and climbing Snow Dome. After reaching the summit late in the afternoon, Bennett would later write they "proceeded to enjoy the reward of a climb," and "got into the skier's ideal, light powder snow." They soon reached the Athabasca Glacier, where they paused for a "bite and nip," before continuing on back to their camp. Arriving at 11:00 P.M., they then set about enjoying a hearty campfire meal.

Their repast was well deserved: the men had completed their round trip in an astonishing push of 30 miles and 5,000 vertical feet in 15½ hours! How did these men get so fit? "The two-hundred-odd miles we had covered by devious route since leaving Jasper 11 days before had put us in good condition," Bennet explained, in classic understatement.

Bennett considered the Snow Dome descent to be "without a doubt the highlight of our trip. … The run is of greater magnitude than any that we, in a combined experience covering over five thousand miles on ski in the Canadian Rockies, have encountered. In fact I believe it can be classed among the few great ski runs of the world. … It is one, we believe, all ski enthusiasts will want to include in their experience."

Snow Dome is still a prize; indeed, it is one of the most eloquent and classic ski descents in Canada. Success requires every mountaineering skill, from snow camping to glacier travel—not to mention solid ski or snowboard technique. Failure is common: alpinists are often humbled by weather, difficult snow, or deceptive distances. It should be noted, however, that extended northern daylight makes long pushes possible for mountaineers with the requisite endurance. In other words, go to the Icefield when you're fit, make a high camp on the névé, and you may catch Snow Dome in a quick push during a short spell of good weather.

The breathtaking North Face of Mount Bryce greets you topping out above the Athabasca Glacier onto the flats of the Columbia Icefield. *Louis Dawson*

Snow Dome viewed from the east, with the Athabasca Glacier below. The route ascends the obvious ramp at the head of the glacier, then swings around up the low-angled slopes. *Clive Cordery*

Most people approach Snow Dome via the Athabasca Glacier, which flows 3,000 vertical feet and four miles down from the Icefield. Start the trip by driving the Icefields Parkway (Highway 93) to the Icefield Center. Speak with a park warden to get the latest information on trailhead parking, snow conditions and weather. (The Icefield Center is closed in winter and early spring, in which case speak with wardens in Lake Louise or at the Poboktan Creek Warden Station about 15 miles north of the Columbia Icefield.) The best route onto the Athabasca Glacier is to walk the road used by the snow coaches, buses with giant tires which take tourists out on the névé. It's also possible to climb from the toe of the glacier. Rope up for the glacier, and know your crevasse rescue tricks.

Swing right to pass the first steps in the glacier, then take an obvious ramp just to right of center on the upper headwall. Much of the route is threatened by the Snow Dome icefall, so keep moving. Once you top out on the vast Icefield, begin wanding your route as you travel to a camp within striking distance of Snow Dome, usually below the mountain's broad southern slopes. From camp, climb the broad slopes to Snow Dome's rounded summit. Wand your route, and return via your ascent route.

Start: Athabasca Glacier parking lot, 6,400 feet

Summit: 11,322 feet

Vertical gain: 4,922 feet

Round trip distance and time: Multiday

Ascent: Intermediate (roped glacier travel)

Glisse: Advanced (roped glacier travel)

Map: Canadian government topo, 83 C/3

Guidebook: *Summits & Icefields* by Chic Scott
First ascent of route: J.N. Collie, H. Woolley, Bill Peyto, Hugh Stutfield, 1898
First ski descent of route and peak: Russell Bennett, Joe Weiss, Clifford White, 1931
Weather: For enjoyable skiing, good snowcover on the névé is essential. Late winter or early spring are good bets. By June, the long northern days may have turned much of the Athabasca Glacier into an ice walk.
Red Tape: Register with wardens at an open Warden Station, and listen to their advice. This is adult alpinism.

WAPTA ICEFIELDS

Mount Gordon and Bow Hut

The Bow Hut on the Wapta Icefield. *Charlotte Fox*

With five cozy huts to choose from, and easier approaches than the Columbia Icefield, the Wapta Icefield is the tame alternative. It includes two icefields: the Waputik and Wapta. Located about 75 miles southeast of the Columbia Icefield, the Wapta covers about 230-square miles. Numerous climbable and skiable peaks pop their heads out of the névé, and the huts can be linked with several fine ski traverses.

In May of 1932, ACC skiers A.A. McCoubrey, brothers Ferris and Roger Neave, and Campell Secord spent a week skiing the peaks of the Wapta. On May 9th they skied up the Yoho Glacier and summited Mount Gordon via the peak's moderate north slope. "A gentle glide, followed by a steeper dive over a well filled bergschrund, took us down to a point just below Vulture col," Ferris Neave wrote of their ski climb and descent.

The Wapta also lends itself to ski traverses. Ferris and Roger Neave traversed Yoho Peak (a smaller subsidiary mountain) during their 1932 trip. In 1936 a party made a blitz traverse that started at Bow Lake and included a ski ascent of Mount Balfour, the Wapta's highest peak (and still termed "real prize" by guidebook writer Chic Scott). Hans Gmoser's 1960 ski traverse also drew attention to ski possibilities on the Wapta.

Presently, the Wapta Icefield is one of Canada's most popular areas for alpine ski mountaineering. Alpinists connect the huts with four exquisite traverse routes, while base skiing and climbing from any of the five huts is also a popular activity. Any of the huts and nearby peaks are classic; a good sample is Mount Gordon from the Bow Hut.

Drive the Icefields Parkway (Highway 93) to the turnoff for Num-Ti-Jah Lodge, and park in the public parking area. The route to the Bow Hut takes the drainage feeding Bow Lake, and follows a circuitous route. Ski across the frozen lake, then take a trail up a subsidiary drainage to avoid the first canyon of the main drain. Stay on this trail as it leads you back into the main drainage. Climb the second canyon by following the creek. After ½ mile, head left out of the drainage and climb though light timber to the cirque below Mount Saint Nicholas. Take a southerly route across the cirque and climb

Skiing the slopes of Mount St. Nicholas near the Bow Hut. *Jonathan Waterman*

a steep hill to the hut. The hut approach is 5 miles and 1,280 vertical feet.

To climb Mount Gordon, head northwest from the hut and cruise west beside Mount Saint Nicholas. Swing toward Mount Gordon and take the peak's right shoulder to the summit ridge. Follow the ridge to the summit, and descend your ascent route.

Start: Bow Hut, 7,644 feet

Summit: 10,508 feet

Vertical gain: 2,864 feet

Round trip distance and time: 15 miles, 10 hours

Ascent: Intermediate (glacier travel)

Glisse: Advanced (glacier travel)

Map: Touring the Wapta Icefields, Murray Toft

Guidebook: *Summits & Icefields*, Chic Scott

First ski descent of route and peak: A.A. McCoubrey, Ferris and Roger Neave, Campell Secord, 1932

Weather: Late winter to early spring. Use local television and radio for weather, call the Banff weather phone.

Red Tape: Register with the Lake Louise wardens, and make your hut reservations with the Alpine Club of Canada (see Directory)

Mount Gordon may be nondescript from this side, but offers fine skiing. *Clive Cordery*

LAKE LOUISE AREA

Mount Field—East Flanks

If a glacier tour sounds too complicated, this glacier free classic in Yoho National Park is a good bet. It's got good access, plentiful terrain, and is easily done in one day. The first to use skis for a Mount Field climb and partial descent were Norman Brewster and the indomitable A. A. McCoubrey, in 1937. "A month of foul weather in the Yoho district ... had put two of us at least in a desperate mood," wrote Brewster, "McCoubrey and myself felt that we simply must climb something, no matter what." After reaching Mount Field's summit, a "splendid open run," and a "veritable downhill race" back to town, gave the pair came to reflect that "although a mountain may be practically in your back yard it may still provide good fun."

A wild skier of the early years rides his stick.
John Moynier Collection

McCoubrey and Brewster took a fairly direct line from the town of Field to Mount Field's summit. Theirs is not as good a ski route as a more roundabout course on the east side of the mountain. For the easterly ski route, drive the Trans-Canada Highway (Highway 1) to the Yoho Valley turnoff 2.5 miles east of Field. Park a short distance up the turnoff. From parking, ski up the Yoho Valley Road 2½ mile to a set of switchbacks. Climb the switchbacks, then turn southwest and climb the left edge of an avalanche path to timberline. Work northwest into a large basin, then swing left (south) toward the summit. Traverse below a cliffy area just below the top, climb to the summit ridge, and continue to the apex. Descend your ascent route.

Start: Yoho Valley parking, 4,380 feet

Summit: 8,645 feet

Vertical gain: 4,265 feet

Round trip distance and time: 10 miles, 11 hours

Ascent: Intermediate

Glisse: Advanced

Map: Canadian government topo, 82 N/8 Lake Louise

Guidebook: *Summits & Icefields*, Chic Scott

Early ascent and ski descent of route: Pierre Lemire, late 1970s

First ski descent of peak (partial): Norman Brewster and A. A. McCoubrey, 1937

Weather: Late winter to early spring. Use local television and radio for weather, call the Banff weather phone, and speak with park wardens when you register.

Red Tape: Register with Yoho National Park (see Directory)

ROGERS PASS

Youngs Peak—
Seven Steps of Paradise

Rogers Pass broaches the apex of the Selkirk Mountains (a subrange of the Columbia Mountains). This area catches Pacific storms before the main Canadian Cordillera, and wrings moisture out of the clouds like a giant twisting a sopping dishrag. Epic snow is the rule—it's a backcountry powder hound's heaven.

The Rogers Pass area is one of Canada's several major hut mountaineering centers. One of the area's oldest alpine huts, the famed Glacier Circle Cabin, was built in the 1920s when Fred Pepper mushed a dog team over the Illecillewaet Glacier to the hut site—accompanied by his wife and infant daughter. Rogers Pass is also known for its snowslides. One of North

Digging out the train tracks at Rogers Pass, circa 1938. The area is known for deep powder—and deep avalanches.
American Alpine Club Collection

America's most deadly avalanche accidents occurred in 1910 when a slide snuffed 62 men clearing snow off the railroad tracks near the pass.

Modern history of Rogers Pass (see Introduction) begins in 1962 with the completion of the Trans-Canada Highway through the pass. Since then, glisse alpinists have touched virtually every peak, drainage, slope and icefield available from the pavement. One such slope will lead you to Paradise in just seven steps.

For Youngs Peak, drive the Trans-Canada Highway (Highway 1) to Glacier National Park and Rogers Pass. Drive to the Glacier Park Lodge (at the pass summit), the best starting point for finding trailheads. From Glacier Park Lodge, take the highway west 2.2 miles and park at the Hotel Gun Site parking area, on the south side of the highway.

From parking area, ski southeast a short distance up the Illecillewaet drainage, then swing right and head 3 miles up the Asulkan drainage to an area known as the "practice slopes." Continue on a more or less direct route south then southeast to a final steep section below the summit of Youngs Peak. With stable avalanche conditions continue to the summit, or forego the summit if you deem the steep section too hazardous.

Descend your ascent route, which is the sublime Seven Steps.

Start: Hotel Gun Site parking, 4,085 feet

Summit: 9,252 feet

Vertical gain: 5,167 feet

Round trip distance and time: 19 miles, 14 hours

Skier looking at Youngs Peak and the Seven Steps of Paradise. *Brian Litz*

Ascent: Advanced

Glisse: Advanced

Map: Touring at Rogers Pass, Murray Toft

Guidebook: *Summits & Icefields*, Chic Scott

Weather: Check television and radio weather, and discuss conditions with a park warden at the warden office. Mid winter through spring offers the best skiing.

Red Tape: Register your trip at the warden office at the summit of Rogers Pass across from Glacier Park Lodge (see Directory).

SOUTHERN COLUMBIA MOUNTAINS

Mount Brennan—Lyle Creek

*C*olumbia Mountains is an inclusive term embracing the major subranges to the west of the main Canadian Rockies, and isolated by several major drains. The area around the town of Nelson, located in the Columbia Mountains just 75 miles north of the U.S. border, gets immense snowfalls. It is a powder pilgrim's mecca. Because of the thick snowpack, early spring skiing and snowboarding in this area are also sure bets. What's more, most of the routes in the Nelson area do not involve glacier travel. It's hard to play a favorite when so many classics stud such a small area. For a sample, guidebook writer Chic Scott suggests Mount Brennan, "a terrific ski descent … with a tremendous amount of relief."

Descending Mount Brennan, Mount Lyle in background. *Paul Heikkila*

For Mount Brennan, use either Canadian Highway 6 or 31, drive Highway 31-A to Retallack. Park in a turnout on the south side of the highway a short distance east of Retallack. From Retallack, ski a series of confusing logging roads east to Lyle Creek, and continue up Lyle Creek. Use your map and road signs to find your way. The roads end at a steep pitch in the Lyle Creek drainage. Climb the steep section to a good campsite. From camp, climb north then northwest over moderate ground to the Mount Brennan summit. Descend your ascent route.

Start: Retallack, 1,312 feet

Summit: 7,480 feet

Vertical gain: 6,168 feet

Round trip distance and time: 10 miles, overnight

Ascent: Advanced

Glisse: Advanced

Map: Canadian government topo, Roseberry 82 K/3

Guidebook: *Summits & Icefields*, Chic Scott

Weather: Do this tour during early spring, and time your ascent to avoid afternoon thaws on avalanche slopes. Use local television and radio for weather reports.

Red Tape: None

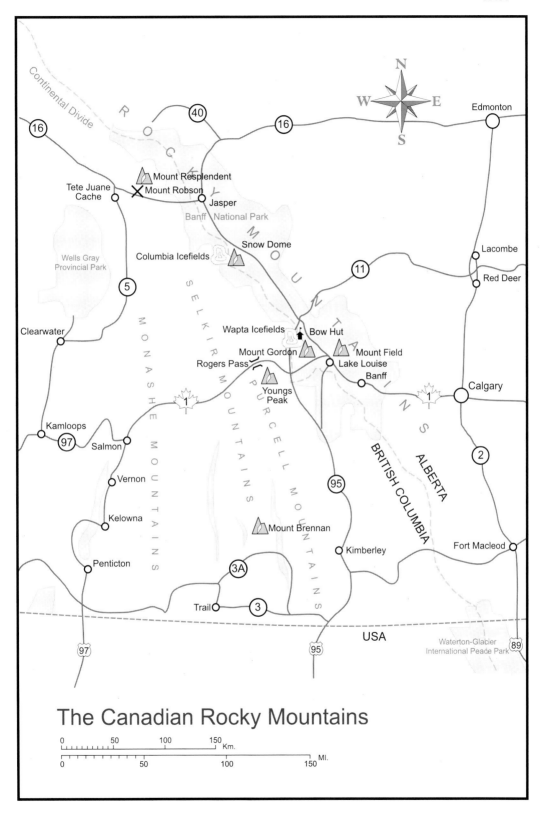

The Canadian Rocky Mountains

STEEP, ROCKY AND WILD:

TETONS OF WYOMING

Steep, rocky and wild:
Tetons of Wyoming

You always remember your first view of Wyoming's Teton mountains. Foothills don't hide them. You enter the valley known since pioneer days as Jackson Hole, and astounding peaks such as the Grand Teton and Mount Moran hit your face like a splash of cold glacial melt-water. Without question, you know these alps define North American mountaineering.

The first non-native to see the Tetons was most likely fur trapper John Colter, almost 200 years ago. Mountain men such as Colter did most of the early exploring in the Jackson area. They trapped beaver to support the booming hat industry back in civilization, and blended their Anglo technology with the ways of the Indians. The roughneck trappers were recruited by explorers of the day such as Captain Louis Bonneville, a French-born U.S. Army officer who, in Washington Irving's words, "became so excited by the tales of wild scenes and adventures … that an expedition to the Rocky Mountains became the ardent desire of his heart." The mountain men who signed on were, according to one reporter, "a piebald mixture, half civilized and half savage. … As they passed the straggling hamlets and cabins that fringe the frontier, they would startle their inmates by Indian yells and war-whoops."

Like the trappers of old, mountaineers of the twentieth century find the Tetons irresistible. The first ascent of the Grand Teton, the area's highest and most stunning peak, is shrouded by controversy. In 1872

Nathaniel Langford and James Stevenson made a high reach—Langford claimed they stood on top. By 1898, Franklin Spalding and Billy Owen had made a documented climb, and the Tetons became a mountaineering center. Since 1931, one of the two oldest and most respected technical guide services in North America, Exum Guides, has operated in the Tetons. Another unique Teton amenity, the American Alpine Club Grand Teton Climbers Ranch, has long provided affordable lodging for alpinists (see Directory).

Skiing in the Tetons began more than a century ago when trappers used hand-carved planks to cross the winter's snow. By 1872 mailmen were slogging over Teton Pass and making their winter deliveries on skis. In the 1930s government water surveyors worked on skis while measuring snowpack depths—some logging 600 miles in one winter.

Recreational skiing no doubt paralleled the workaday variety, and by the 1920s locals were schussing hills near the town of Jackson. Soon after, pioneer mountaineer and skier Fred Brown was promoting the region as a ski destination and taking his friends to the classic backcountry runs on Teton Pass. In 1938, Brown, Allyn Hanks, and Park Naturalist Howard Stagner made the earliest recorded high tour in the Tetons, when they skied 45 miles from Beaver Creek to Granite Canyon and back, eating pre-cached food and using ropes to safeguard steeper slopes.

Mechanized skiing came to the Tetons in 1939 with a rope tow on Snow King (a small and amazingly steep ski area near the town of Jackson). Such simple beginnings

◀ The Grand Teton with Bill Briggs's first tracks, 1971.
Bill Briggs Collection

evolved to the present day plethora of steel girding the area's three ski resorts.

Early backcountry skiers gravitated to the land near the ski lifts. As a result, Teton exploratory skiing was relatively dormant in the decades from the late 1930s to the 1960s. Even so, a group of locals kept the faith. Tenth Mountain Division veteran Grant Hagen explored Cascade Canyon with Fred Brown, and in 1953 a group built a classic ski hut in the Sheep Creek drainage east of the town of Jackson. Another local, Olympic veteran Betty Woolsey, backcountry skied Teton Pass for three decades and guided many people to find the joy of hiking for perfect powder and corn snow.

Modern glisse alpinism came late to the Tetons. The birth year of the sport was probably 1961, when Eliot Goss and Ann

Gannett Peak, Wyoming's highest, is a remote but worthwhile glisse destination in the Wind River mountains. Dolores LaChapelle views the peak during a 1948 ski expedition.
Ed LaChapelle

LaFarge skied precipitous Buck Mountain with Exum Guide Barry Corbet. The Cascades' Mount Rainier had felt the steel edge a few years before, Canada had hosted several high ski traverses, and Otto Schniebs had long since marked Castle Peak in Colorado.

By 1966, Teton ski mountaineering had caught up with the rest of the continent, and mountaineers from every corner of North America were flocking to the "American Alps." Many would pioneer rock and ice climbing routes at world-class standards. A no less committed but smaller group would pioneer steep skiing. Bill Briggs was one such pilgrim.

William Morse Briggs was born December 21, 1931, in Augusta Maine. Briggs entered the world without a hip joint—at two years old surgeons chiseled out a socket in his pelvic bone. Despite his hip the boy was a natural athlete, and taught himself to ski at an early age. After a boyhood of outdoor living and winters of skiing on local New England hills, Briggs entered Philips Exeter Academy. There, Briggs met English teacher Bob Bates, the man who became his most influential mentor. Bates was a devoted mountaineer—an active member of the American Alpine Club and a K2 survivor. Moreover, Bates was an inspiring leader with a resoundingly positive attitude. Briggs decided that if alpinism had something to do with the character of Bob Bates then he'd take up the life himself.

Briggs went on to Dartmouth College, where he immediately joined the famed Dartmouth Outing Club. During his first winter at Dartmouth in 1951, he and several Outing Club members traveled west on a ski trip. "At Sun Valley we paid for a lesson with Stein Erikson," Briggs laughs, "Basically you just followed him down the mountain—if you could keep up."

Bill Briggs competed with Bob Dylan for audience during the 1960s in New York City, then jammed with the man later in Jackson Hole. *Bill Briggs Collection*

During winters at Dartmouth Briggs made many trips to Tuckerman Ravine on Mount Washington, and skied progressively steeper terrain. "It scared the pants off me," he says, "so I developed a slow speed turn with an uphill-stem and a jump off both tails to quickly get into a turn." Briggs discovered that the same attitudes behind successful mountaineering also applied to steep glisse: risk assessment, careful planning, training, conservative yet athletic technique. "It all came about because of a mountaineering attitude," he states. Practice paid off. Roberts French, Briggs's later companion during the famed Bugaboos ski traverse (see Canadian Rocky Mountains chapter), says "Brigger was the most controlled, precise skier I've ever seen."

At Dartmouth the young Briggs realized he didn't fit in when, in a philosophy class, the professor asked all of the students who believed in free will to raise their hands. "I raised my hand immediately," says Briggs, "and no one else did!" He and Dartmouth soon parted ways. The parting was not easy and Briggs fell into suicidal depression. "I found I couldn't kill myself —I didn't have the courage," he explains. "Since I had to live, I decided to make the

most of life, to simply go with what I found most pleasurable: climbing, skiing, and music." Briggs received his ski instructor certification in 1955, and immediately went to work teaching in New England and for a period in Aspen.

But the mountain's call was Briggs's siren song; he did several trips to the Canadian Rockies and found "the best way to get around was on skis." During a visit to Aspen in 1956 he skied the classic high tour between Aspen and Crested Butte (first skied during the mining days of the late 1800s). Briggs was also spending a lot of time climbing, and in 1958 was hired by Exum Guides.

Briggs did his well known Bugaboo Mountains traverse in 1959, but his hip had become a painful disability. In 1961 he decided to have the joint fused. The medicos said at best he'd need to change to a sedentary life—at worst he'd be in a wheelchair. In what can only be called hubris, before the operation Briggs built a cardboard splint which locked his hip. Then he went skiing. Much to his delight and amazement he could make turns with the immobilized joint! Even so, he knew he probably couldn't lead the outdoor life he had in the past, and after the operation he sank into depression. The owner of Exum Guides assumed he would be unable to do physical work, so Briggs lost his job as a guide. His fiancée had left him and married another, and a girlfriend he proposed to also left. Briggs tried to change careers while convalescing in Greenwich Village, and played guitar in the Folk City Coffee House. "The problem with that," laughs Bill, "was just down the street a guy named Bob Dylan was packing them in; the coffee shop where I played was deserted."

"Things were grim," continues Briggs, "I went up to Hunter Mountain and tried to ski, but I sprained my knee getting off the chairlift. I could barely walk. Then a friend of a friend, Heidi Lockwood, came to my place and did a 'Touch Assist,' which is a part of Scientology which relieves physical trauma by using touch and visualization. The treatment completely eliminated the pain and reduced the swelling. From my point of view this was a miracle—I wanted to know more about where this came from."

After this experience Briggs involved himself in Scientology, and subsequently found that many fears he'd had, such as speaking in front of groups, could be eliminated. He also experienced a marked improvement in physical ability. "I thought, there's hope!" Briggs remembers. Soon he grabbed a pair of wire cutters and hacked off his cast, resumed teaching skiing, and got married.

With his new-found athletic prowess Briggs knew he could continue mountaineering and skiing, so he moved back to Jackson Hole, began guiding again, and in 1966 became director of the ski school at Snow King Mountain. Once back in Jackson, he pursued the outer limits of ski mountaineering, especially skiing the

steeps. "I was trying out my new abilities, testing, seeing what I could do, surprising myself," remembers Briggs, "I'd been scared on Mount Washington's Tuckerman; I was now skiing things just as steep, such as Buck Mountain, and it was not that scary anymore. My focus was incredible."

During those formative years Briggs skied numerous peaks in the Tetons. In the spring of 1968, along with several other mountaineers, he made the first ski descent the Teton's most striking classic: Mount Moran via the Skillet Glacier (covered as a featured classic). Rising 6,500 vertical feet from the glistening waters of Jackson Lake, the Skillet begs to be skied, and is counted as one of the five most classic ski descents in the Tetons. But that was only a warm-up for the Grand Teton.

Briggs first tried to solo his climb and descent of the Grand, but weather and snow conditions turned him back. He then enlisted the help of John Bolton, Jorge Colón and Robbie Garrett, and on June 15, 1971, Briggs clipped his ski bindings at the top and started down the 1,000-vertical-foot snowfield on the upper East Face of the peak. "I'd planned

The stunning Teton Range viewed from the east, Grand Teton with banner cloud, Middle Teton and South Teton to left. *Louis Dawson*

very carefully," he remembers, "but you can't predict everything. I didn't know just how steep the skiing would be—it was really steep—and I didn't know how much the snow was going to slough off when I traversed across." Later Briggs wrote, "gusts of wind made balance uncertain, so I used great caution to get off the summit block. The snow above Ford Couloir was good for a few turns. Then I broke through and the skis sank about a foot into the snow unexpectedly and caused my first fall. I fell downhill, quickly rolled over, and stood up on the skis again. From there on the snow was deep corn but quite skiable."

A man ahead of his time, Briggs cut turns above fall-you-die cliffs, gingerly funneled into the narrows of the Stettner Couloir, rappelled the big chockstone and icefall to another skiable section, then finished on the bonus bowls of the Tepee Glacier.

The "Grand" was an impressive ski descent; but the Jackson locals were nonchalant, if not skeptical, about Briggs's feat. "I said, 'I skied the Grand yesterday,'" he remembers, "and people said 'uh huh.'" Briggs needed proof, so he drove to the airport for a good view of the upper snow face. To his delight he could see his tracks with binoculars, so he called a photographer at the Jackson Hole News. The resulting photograph, clearly showing his tracks, is still a best-selling poster.

After his Grand Teton descent, Briggs continued guiding and climbing, but took a break from hard-core ski mountaineering. "It was hard to top the Grand," he says. Then in 1974 the steep skiing bug bit him again, and he and Boomer McClure (who later died while trying to ski the Matterhorn) climbed Mount Owen with a ski descent in mind. "I didn't do as good a job as I'd done on the other peaks—I took a fall skiing for the camera," remembers Briggs. "Luckily I

arrested before I got in too much trouble. That shook me up, and this was before the hard part which was a super-steep traverse going to the right; the wrong side with my fused hip. I had no choice but to do it strictly on my uphill ski, so I took a belay. But even with the rope, if I'd fallen on that side I wouldn't have been able to get back up! I was past my prime." The pioneer knew it was his time to retire from radical glisse, and he did so with grace. Briggs didn't retire from skiing, however, and continues to teach the sport and develop a method of instruction held in high esteem by some of Jackson Hole's best guides and ski instructors.

After Briggs skied the Grand Teton, backcountry skiing grew at a healthy rate throughout the Jackson area. The Tetons' almost dream-like isolation and focused mountaineering atmosphere attracted scores of excellent ski mountaineers, and the rowdy locals ticked most of the area's skiable summits. Ironically, many Teton backcountry skiers of the 1970s were attracted back to the ski areas by the promise of easy vertical—but with a twist. By intention or default, they'd dress as skiing hippies, act like mountain men of John Colter's era, and drive the ski resort owners to distraction with their dirtbag lifestyle and belligerent telemarking. One crew even lived at the base of Grand Targhee ski resort in straw-lined snowcaves. In 1977, Targhee banned the skiing hippies, whom they called "snow maggots," from their slopes—ostensibly because free-heel skiing was somehow unsuitable for resort skiing, but most likely because of the skier's looks and behavior. The wormy skiers forced the ski area to allow free-heelers when they produced a video showing there was no difference between free-heel and fixed-heel skiing—a prescient event considering today's blending of the two techniques.

In 1978, filmmaker Bob Carmichael was "turned on" by Bill Briggs to the possibilities of extreme skiing in the Tetons. Carmichael, then of Boulder, Colorado, envisioned an art film called *Fall Line* that was something of a day in the life of a winter alpinist. Carmichael cast his net for a film subject, and caught an Aspen ski-shop mechanic and mountaineer named Steve Shea. A man somewhat ahead of his time in the American alpinism scene, Shea was traveling to France each year, where he wowed the Chamonix locals with his vertical ice climbing technique. The French in turn wowed Shea with their extreme skiing. "I got to be good friends with Jean-Marc Boivin," says Shea. "The stuff he was skiing even back then was unbelievable." Shea practiced the European ski techniques. When Carmichael offered to pay Shea for his skiing and climbing, the vagabond alpinist put off his next trip to Chamonix, and began performing in America's Alps—the Tetons.

The final film, which still exists on the shelves of ski bistros around the world, is a 12-minute montage of Teton ski descents, with most shots made in the environs of the Middle Teton Glacier. While filming, Shea made first ski descents of Middle Teton's Pinnochio Couloir and classic Glacier Route, and Kochs Couloir. Since Shea was being paid, this was the first professional extreme skiing done in North America—the precursor to today's lucrative "extreme" film industry. With judicious editing Carmichael used his disparate footage to illustrate a ski descent of the Grand Teton, which Shea did for the cameras, making the second descent in the process. What's more, he skied the Grand for the cameras once again he next spring, thus making the third ski descent! Shea says he was "scared shitless above the Stettner Couloir," and belayed some of the skiing even though he preferred skiing "pure." At the time, he didn't know Bill Briggs had used ropes for parts of his first

descent, "I just figured Briggs had gonads of steel," Shea recalls.

Fall Line won an Academy Award Nomination for Carmichael, and was profitable for the distributor. In an ironic way, it became one of the most watched ski films ever made—at least a few seconds of it. A short sequence in the film depicts Shea taking a certain-death fall down Kochs Couloir on the Middle Teton. For several years, a cut of the fall was repeatedly shown on ABC television as a lead-in for a popular show called *American Sportsman*.

After Briggs and Shea, Teton ski mountaineering went through a somewhat stagnant decade. A small number of skiers focused on backcountry accessed via the ski area tramway, while others were sidetracked by the one-upmanship of using free-heel equipment to repeat ski descents previously done on fixed-heel gear. This resulted in some athletic feats, but the

Bob Carmichael's *Fall Line* was one of the first movies to feature extreme skiing. *Bob Carmichael Collection*

Steve Shea (inspired by the European extremists) during filming for *Fall Line. Denali Productions*

greatest effect of such gear obsession was to distract skiers from exploring new lines. Several skiers, however, were not so distracted. One such pioneer was a young mountain guide named Jeff Rhoads. In 1978, Rhoads skied the Grand Teton at only 21 years old, then climbed the peak again the next day and made the first descent of the difficult Ford Couloir with Brad Peck. Another important glisse event occurred two years later, when Jorge Colón, Mark Wolling, and Dean Moore skied one of the most obvious lines in the Tetons: Mount Moran's southwest couloir.

The modern spirit arrived in the Tetons in the 1990s, in the form of three young men: Stephen Koch, Mark Newcomb and Thomas Turiano. Koch, a former California surfer, made his tool the snowboard. With the climbing skills and fitness of a Euro super-alpinist, he "surfed" first descents on technical, cliff-banded routes. One such line, the Bubble Fun Couloir, involves making turns down a 50-degree slope to the top of a deadly cliff, where you shuck your glisse tools and make several rappels to exit. Another modern desperate, the Apocalypse Couloir on Prospectors Mountain, was done in 1994 by Koch, along with Mark Newcomb, a lifelong Jackson resident and another "new-age" glisse alpinist. Before their descent, Newcomb had seen an unusual view of Prospectors, and locked his eyes on an unknown couloir dropping from one of the peak's ridges. The pair dodged an ice avalanche, raced warming snow to the summit, and launched off the top. Then, as guidebook author Thomas Turiano wrote in classic understatement, "they continued through the 10-foot-wide, icy, 50-degree crux." The Apocalypse is one of the longest, most continuous extreme descents in the Tetons, and unlike other modern descents does not require rope work to link discontinuous snow.

A recent first descent of the Hossack-MacGowen route on the Grand Teton, skied by Mark Newcomb and Hans Johnstone in 1996, may be the most impressive line yet done in the Tetons. The route starts at the summit and has less rappel distance (only four short ones) than any route yet skied on the Grand. "The … couloir plummets over 3,000 feet from the commonly skied upper East Face to the Teton Glacier in sheer hanging snowfields and 65-degree, single-ski-width snow hoses," wrote Thomas Turiano in *Couloir* magazine. "It was Newcomb's vision to try the route during winter when the snowpack is deep and consolidated. … Not only was it the first ski descent of the Grand in winter, but the pair were the first to ski the mountain in one day!"

Thomas Turiano himself is one of the Teton's most prolific modern activists. Born in 1966 and raised in New York State, Turiano moved from Colorado to Jackson Hole in 1985 to "get more into mountaineering." Turiano worked as a ski instructor at Snow King, and under the tutelage of Bill Briggs and widely traveled mountaineer Tom Bennett he became a superbly fit alpinist and consummate skier. In 1986 Turiano made his first ski descents on classics such as Buck Mountain and Mount Moran. "On those peaks, I discovered something I was good at—I could do it with total comfort," he recalls. At the time, Turiano also began doing long tours through the Tetons in a high and light style. Eventually, he was spending up to 80 days a year on such trips, and marked his routes on a map now covered with a spider web of ink.

In 1990 Turiano made his first premier descent down remote Mount Wister, just north of Buck Mountain. His route was a steep exposed face with no obvious line. Turiano has made many other first descents of Teton summits and routes, including Spalding Peak in 1993, the intricate South

Guidebook author Tom Turiano launching off Thor Peak, Tetons. *Tom Turiano Collection*

Face of Mount St. John, and Racing the Sun Couloir on Raynolds West, a 45-degree gully Turiano calls "one of the most striking mountain features north of Mount Moran." Turiano has found guidebook writing a logical extension of his mountaineering career, and now that his *Teton Skiing* is published, he's working on books for other areas in Wyoming.

Located in the northwest corner of Wyoming, one of America's least populated states, the Tetons are a small range. A liberal definition would put the length at about 50 miles, with a width of only half that. Moreover, within this small area, the high peaks of jagged rock do not offer the almost infinite count of ski descents you find in the Sierra Nevada or Colorado Rockies. Indeed, because of the Teton's limited terrain, the art of finding discontinuous ski lines, sometimes connected with rope-work and down climbing, has become more highly devel-

oped in the Tetons than any other North American mountain range. Nonetheless, the Tetons offer a number of classic descents with no rappels, long vertical, and deep history. A few of the best are detailed below.

Mount Moran—Skillet Glacier

Mount Moran isn't the highest peak in the Tetons, but it's by far the most spectacular. On the east side of Moran, dropping 6,500 vertical feet to the riffles of Jackson Lake, the Skillet Glacier offers the most classic descent in the Tetons—perhaps the most classic in the conterminous United States. The Skillet has everything. A challenging summit couloir keeps you honest. The huge bonus bowl below makes you whoop with joy when the snow is good—or drip tears when you face 4,000 vertical feet of guano. Views of silky lakes and gnarled precipices astound you.

Mount Moran and Skillet Glacier from the east. *Louis Dawson.*

Bill Briggs, Peter Koedt, Dick Person and Fletcher Manly made the visionary first descent of the Skillet in 1968, and since then more than 300 people have skied it. Don't let the numbers fool you; the Skillet is always hot, and you might get fried. The summit couloir is extreme, and the whole run can be an avalanche trap—or be covered with trap-crust. Early-season skiers get the classic vertical, but pay the price of crossing the lake without using a boat: a snowmobile ride, perhaps a long slog, at worst a dangerous epic.

Early morning climb of the Skillet Glacier, Mount Moran. Jackson Lake below. *Andrew McLean*

In early season, drive through Grand Teton National Park to Colter Bay on Jackson Lake, and endure the long slog across the lake ice to camp at the base of the Skillet near Bearpaw Bay. If the lake is well frozen, it's possible to cross via snowmobile. After the lake opens, a boat ride is your best bet (see Directory). Negotiate the lower reaches of the route by following lateral moraines to the glacier. Punch the long climb up the "handle," then trend left and exit the upper handle at a small notch at the top. Continue a short distance south from the notch to the summit.

With good snowcover, it's possible to start your ski descent at the summit. Yet, as Thomas Turiano wrote "the essence of the descent is the first turn off the notch!" This may require a cornice drop or at least a few turns down a steep headwall. Use a rope if need be. After the steep upper section the angle eases, but the early eastern sun may trigger avalanches, so keep moving.

Start: Jackson Lake, 6,772 feet

Summit: 12,605 feet

Vertical gain: 5,833 feet

Round trip distance and time: 4 miles, long day from basecamp

Ascent: Advanced

Glisse: Extreme (Advanced without exact summit start)

Maps: USGS 7.5 minute, Mount Moran; Grand Teton National Park visitor map

Guidebook: *Teton Skiing*, Thomas Turiano

First ascent: L.H. Hardy, Ben Rich, Bennet McNulty, 1922

First descent of peak and route: Bill Briggs, Peter Koedt, Dick Person, Fletcher Manly, 1968

Weather: The Tetons are a high-altitude range, at a northerly latitude and tucked away from ocean warmth. Winter lasts more than half the year. Snow is deep, and prevailing winds from the southwest blast the upper reaches. Storms are often severe and dangerous, but are periodic and interspersed with regular stretches of good weather. Nightly temperatures often fall below –25° F in midwinter, but the dry air eases the cold's bite. Interestingly, though the Tetons have an inland climate, they have less of a problem with dangerous sugar snow then other interior ranges, such as those of Colorado. The reasons for this vary, but the result is that steeper ski descents can be made in late winter as well as spring. Nonetheless, the best time for skiing the Teton classics is the spring snow season, which in the Tetons runs roughly from May through June. Weather reports for the Tetons are available by phone (see Directory), television and commercial radio. Such reports offer general guidelines, but do not detail conditions on the high peaks.

Red Tape: Mountaineering registration is required. Do so in Grand Teton National Park at the Moose Visitor Center or Jenny Lake Ranger Station.

Middle Teton—Southwest Couloir

Jutting just south of the Grand Teton, Middle Teton (12,804 feet) is perhaps the most skiable of the Teton high peaks, with routes of various difficulties on all sides. The first glisse descent of the peak was made in 1967 down the Southwest Couloir, by the indomitable Bill Briggs. In the late 1980s, a troop of Boy Scouts survived a trash-bag glissade of the couloir. Don't let down your guard—the Southwest Couloir includes a 45-degree narrows.

In Grand Teton National Park, drive the Teton Park Road to the well-signed Lupine Meadows Trailhead. Endure a long slog up Garnet Canyon to Garnet Canyon Meadows, then continue west toward the base of Middle Teton. Just before the base (9,600 feet) climb a short, wide, and steep gully into the South Fork of Garnet Canyon. Take the South Fork around Middle Teton, then climb several headwalls to the saddle at the head of South Fork (11,300 feet). From the saddle, take a narrow ridge north to a bench below the Southwest Couloir, then climb the Couloir. Glisse your ascent route.

Start: Lupine Meadow Trailhead, 6,732 feet

Summit: 12,804 feet

Vertical gain: 6,072 feet

Round trip distance and time: 18 miles, full day or overnight

Ascent: Intermediate

Glisse: Advanced

Maps and guidebooks: See Mount Moran, preceding

First ascent of route: H. O. Christensen, M. Christensen, Irven Christensen, 1927

First ski descent of route and peak: Bill Briggs, 1967

Weather: See Mount Moran, above, for a description of Teton weather. The best skiing on Middle Teton is during the spring season.

Red Tape: See Mount Moran, above

Buck Mountain—East Face

The Buck Mountain massif is a snowy arête forming the southern end of the Teton high peaks. The classic East Face route was first skied in 1961 by guide Barry Corbet and two clients. Corbet's descent didn't turn any heads at the time, but it was one of the earliest ski descents in the United States to tackle steep alpine terrain. The upper part of the route is just under 45 degrees, and a huge cliff yawns below, waiting to punish those who botch.

Barry Corbet and Ann LaFarge below Buck Mountain after their first descent in 1961. *Tom Turiano Collection*

Drive the Moose/Wilson Road northeast from Teton Village or southwest from Moose. Turn north on the well-signed Death Canyon Road, and drive 1½ miles to parking at the Death Canyon Trailhead. Hike the trail west to the third footbridge, then leave the main trail and head north to Stewart Draw. Climb Stewart Draw to Buck Mountain's East Face. A gully on the right side of the face yields a route next to the infamous cliffs. Descend your ascent route.

Start: Death Canyon Trailhead, 6,780 feet
Summit: 11,938 feet
Vertical gain: 5,158 feet
Round trip distance and time: 6 miles, long day

Static Peak (just to left) and Buck Mountain (highpoint) from the east. *Louis Dawson*

Ascent: Advanced
Glisse: Advanced/Extreme (exposed skiing)
Map: USGS 7.5 minute, Grand Teton
Guidebook: *Teton Skiing*, Thomas Turiano
First descent of peak and route: Barry Corbet, Elliot Goss, Ann LaFarge, 1961
Weather: See Mount Moran, above, for weather description. Beware the sun baking this eastern aspect.
Red Tape: See Mount Moran, above

Static Peak—Southeast Face

S tatic Peak is the southern bump of the Buck Mountain massif. It's easier than Buck, and the standard introduction for skiing on the high Teton peaks. The earliest recorded descent of Static was made in the 1970s via the peak's East Face, by Jorge Colón and Tom Raymer. The first ski of the Southeast Face route may be lost in history; early descents were made by a number of Jackson Hole skiers in the late 1970s. In 1983, several skiers were exploring and noticed two bighorn sheep disappearing over the north side of the peak (a herd lives in the vicinity of the mountain).

Following the sheep, they discovered a good extreme route down the North Face—the first recorded sheep-guided descent.

Static Peak from the east. *Tom Turiano Collection*

T o climb and glisse the classic Southeast Face, take the same approach from Death Canyon Trailhead as described above for Buck Mountain. Instead of traversing to Stewart Draw, climb the Static Peak draw. Continue northwest and climb the obvious Southeast Face of Static Peak. Descend your ascent route.

Start: Death Canyon trailhead, 6,780 feet
Summit: 11,303 feet
Vertical gain: 4,523 feet
Round trip distance and time: 5 miles, medium day
Ascent: Novice
Glisse: Intermediate
Map: USGS 7.5 minute, Grand Teton
Guidebook: *Teton Skiing*, Thomas Turiano
First descent of peak: Jorge Colón and Tom Raymer via East Face
Weather: Late winter and spring are the best seasons for this route. See routes above for other weather information.
Red Tape: See other routes above. May be closed to protect bighorn sheep.

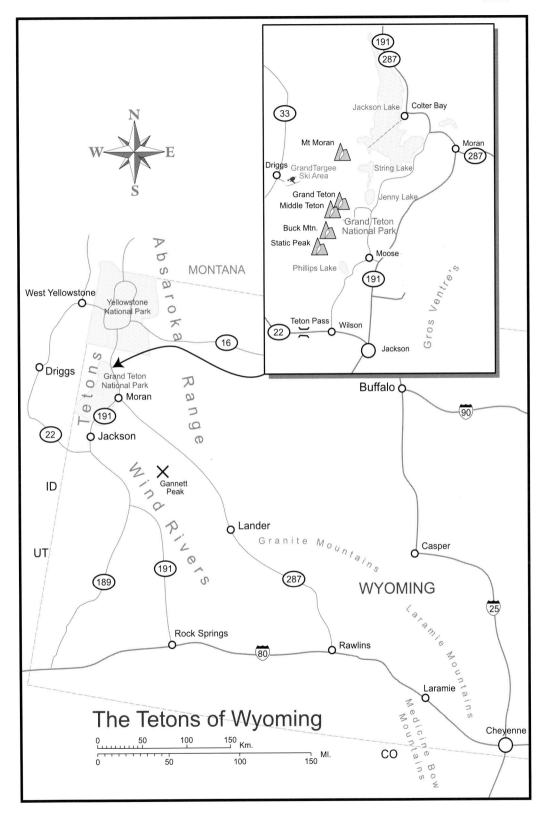

The Tetons of Wyoming

POWDER PERFECT:

UTAH'S WASATCH MOUNTAINS

Powder Perfect:
Utah's Wasatch Mountains

With a lurch of your legs, push with your poles and launch. At your first turn the fluff washes your knees, then your waist disappears. You cut your first curves harsh and almost fall. Three turns later you click back. As fluff boils around you like a cascading mountain river, your skis seem to turn your feet. Soon you're an observer in a trance. Your skis take on a life of their own, and you move beyond thought as the mountain skis you. You've become a powder skier.

Powder was not always such sought-after glisse. In the early days of skiing, telemarkers and arlbergers alike preferred wide open slopes of hardened wind pack or corn. They'd deal with powder slopes by making long swooping turns that didn't work for narrow chutes and couloirs—turns only the best skiers could pull off with consistency. Indeed, the European motherland of alpine skiing is not known for powder, and early texts of skiing mention little if any ecstasy associated with fluff. The powder skiers of Utah's Wasatch Mountains would change that.

A small interior range, the Wasatch Mountains run 250 miles south from the Bear River in Idaho, extend past Salt Lake City, and end at the San Pitch River. The range's highest peak is 11,877-foot Mount Nebo. As the first major inland barrier to moist Pacific storms, the Wasatch gets huge amounts of snow every winter. In 1965, a seven-day "loading event" spewed nine feet of snow on the high Wasatch. Storms with equally intense snowfall, but of shorter duration, are common. Unlike North America's coastal mountains, however, the snow comes down drier on the inland Wasatch. Moreover, winter storms, while energetic, usually last just a few days and are separated by good weather.

As with many other areas in the continental United States, skiing came to the Wasatch during the mining days of the late 1800s. In 1893, a Mormon named Florence Merriam wrote of her visit to the Alta mining camps, and recorded the words of a miner who "astonished us by saying he had ridden it [a steep nearby mountain] on his skees [sic]. It was dangerous but exciting work, he said. … He had been up and down most of the mountains around Alta." Sporadic skiing continued into the early 1900s, with Scandinavian miners usually gripping the poles. Soon the northern Europeans were organizing jumping contests and ranging far and wide on their "Norwegian Snowshoes."

After the late 1800s silver crash, most of Utah's mining died a quick death. But the state's urban areas were gaining population, and outdoor recreation became a desirable commodity for the urbanites. Skiing fit the bill. Various groups and clubs were organized to teach the sport, provide transportation, and whip up enthusiasm. No ski lifts were available until the Alta ski resort's first in 1938, so most of the skiing until then was backcountry style.

The Wasatch Mountain Club (WMC) is the best known and most influential of the Utah's early ski-oriented outdoor groups. The club began in 1912, when Brigham Young University coach Charles Stoney

◀ Dick Durrance at Alta in 1940, where modern powder skiing was invented. *Margaret Durrance*

started a loosely organized outdoor recreation group. By 1917 his club was officially organized and scheduled ski trips in the foothills near Salt Lake City. It's amusing to note that a group of high school students known as the Rough Neck Ski Club—presaging North America's extreme skiers—made Utah newspapers two years prior to Charles Stoney's group. Headlines not unlike today's coverage of extreme skiing described the Rough Neck's death-defying antics.

The Wasatch Mountain Club folks knew abundant snow was available for the taking above the Wasatch foothills. Access was the key, so they organized North America's first "ski train" when they chartered a locomotive to haul them up into Parley's Canyon for a day of snow frolic in 1924.

In 1935, the WMC members proved themselves as the most visionary of Utah's ski pioneers when they built a comfortable lodge at the high Wasatch mine and lumber town of Brighton. Brighton's history included some of the earliest skiing in Utah, and the lodge continued a venerable tradition. In the late 1930s the federal government became involved when the Works Progress Administration improved the Brighton access road and started a "winter sports improvement program" that would refine ski amenities all over the Wasatch.

By 1938 skiing was entrenched as Utah's most popular winter outdoor recreation. Mechanization followed, with the area's first ski lift hauling skiers at Alta that year. Nearby, Brighton became one of Utah's most popular ski locations, and has developed into a modern-day mechanized skiing complex.

Alta began in 1871 as a mining area. The town boomed to a population of 3,000, then went through several busts, culminating in 1892 with the demonitization of silver. During the Great Depression the town's population dropped to almost

nothing. Then skiing began to gain popularity across North America. Around 1936, with Sun Valley as inspiration, a group of Salt Lake City outdoors people and entrepreneurs decided to create a ski resort at Alta. Problem was, they needed to buy most of the private land in the area, and money was short.

A man named George Watson bought much of the Alta land in the 1920s. Ten years later, with mining never making the comeback he had envisioned, Watson was deep in hock. He sold his mining rights to his creditors, but for the sum of "One Dollar" sold surface rights for his considerable holdings to the U.S. Government. With public land now available, the consortium from Salt Lake City was able to build lifts and create what became the chief among North America's publicly operated ski areas. Without a strong profit motive, ticket prices stayed low. Perfect powder snow falls on Alta like manna, and the congregation of modern powder skiers comes every winter to partake.

Backcountry skiing remained somewhat popular in Utah for a few years after 1938, then stagnated until the 1960s as it did in most of North America. A victim of this transition was what could have been one of North America's finest ski hut systems. In 1941, Alta ski resort founder James Laughlin proposed an amazing chain of 14 ski huts in the Wasatch. "Until we have them," he wrote, "American skiers will never know what it means to tour and, as anyone knows, ... touring is the real cream of skiing." Wasatch Mountain Club president William Kamp was also of this opinion, noting that "huts so located in a string ... would do more to stimulate ski touring than anything else." Only three of the proposed huts were ever built, and one still exists today. But as it turned out, with the present teeming network of roads and ski lifts providing one-day access to most of the Wasatch, such ski huts have been unnecessary for the appreciation of the "real cream of skiing" in these mountains.

Also in 1941, Utah's first ski tourer avalanche occurred in a steep gulch at Alta ski resort known as the Snakepit. The victim tried to race the white death, and failed. Indeed, because of great snow accumulations and lack of subsequent consolidation, deadly avalanches occur with alarming frequency in the Wasatch Mountains. In recent years, Utah has been third behind Colorado and Alaska in the number of annual avalanche deaths.

With a few ski lifts and the "best snow on earth," the stage was set in Utah for the invention of modern powder skiing—and the subsequent resurrection of Wasatch backcountry skiing.

When Alta's first lift cranked up in 1938, only a minority of superb skiers knew how to handle steep powder. For most, skiing at the ski area meant repeating runs down a narrow strip of packed snow. A movie was made at the time, *Marjorie of the Wasatch.* "The film will break your heart," wrote pioneer powder skier Dolores LaChapelle in her book *Deep Powder Snow*, "in scene after scene … one sees wide open slopes without a single track in every direction— forever. And it's all perfect Alta powder."

But skiers soon partook of the cornucopia. One of the first was a mechanical engineer named Fred Speyer, who came from Europe to Alta in 1939 to debug the ski lift (its old mining hardware was fraught with problems). Speyer also was active with the Wasatch Mountain Club, and showed the locals a powerful arlberg ski technique that worked better in the powder.

Another early enthusiast was famed racer Dick Durrance, took over management of the Alta ski school. Though known as one of the era's most powerful skiers,

Durrance soon found his technique was not ideal for Alta's steep powder, especially in the narrow chutes where wide shoulder-driven turns were impossible. Being a mountaineer as well as a skier, Durrance was familiar with the technique of "heeling" down steep scree-filled couloirs. Ever the innovator, Durrance molded his scree technique into a quick heel-thrust turn on skis, which by some accounts also included a step similar to today's peddle turn. He called it the "single dipsy" after a rhythmic song of the era. Durrance's technique was remarkably effective and quickly caught on.

During World War II some of the best and most influential skiers in North America came to Alta to help Durrance teach skiing to 150 Army paratroopers. At heart, this was an experiment to determine if it would be easier to "make skiers out of soldiers" rather than "soldiers out of skiers." When only a few of Durrance's troops learned to ski effectively, the War Department decided to work with the National Ski Patrol to recruit skiers for the future 10th Mountain Division (see Colorado chapter). But, despite the failure of the project, the media loved the idea of these "Wild Men From Heaven" who carried "enough dynamite to blow the top off Pikes Peak."

The real success story of Alta's war years was that dozens of fine skiers learned Dick Durrance's single dipsy. They then shared the turn with their friends—and applied it to some of the most consistent and abundant natural snow in North America.

Around 1945, Norwegian champion ski jumpers and racers Alf and Sverre Engen began working with the Alta ski school. The Engens refined the single dipsy by using both skis as a solid platform for each turn (termed the "double" dipsy). "It looked like a very light floating, almost in the fall line, with the two skis moving absolutely as one," remembers Jay Laughlin. "To see one of

Dick Durrance teaching the soldiers at Alta, circa 1940. *Margaret Durrance*

these lads come down High Rustler or the Chutes of Baldy in new snow was something you would never forget." Modern powder skiing was born.

By 1952 other skiers at Alta, such as instructor Junior Bounous, had established the double dipsy as today's modern parallel powder turn. Refined techniques followed, such as using minimal upper body movement, and starting a run by jamming ski tails in the snow, facing downhill, and pushing off with your ski poles (now known as the "Alta Start").

The new powder skiing methods developed at Alta spread around the world like pollen in strong wind. "I'm told that when they [the Engens] first turned up in Europe," says Jay Laughlin, "the European

Steep skiing started in places like Alta's Baldy Chutes, and evolved to steep drops such as this: Otis on Thunder Ridge. *Andrew McLean*

professionals were amazed. They had never seen anything like it." In the early 1950s Dolores LaChapelle, who lived and learned in Aspen and Alta during these pioneer days, took the new turn with her to Davos, Switzerland, where the entire ski school learned to mimic her technique.

Through her years with Alta's legendary snow LaChapelle literally became one with the earth by letting "snow and gravity together" turn her skis. She was one of the West's most prolific and best known early powder skiers, and developed a radical personal philosophy that meshed tightly with the branch of environmentalism known as "deep ecology." LaChapelle explains by using a powder skiing metaphor: "There is no longer an I and snow and mountain, but a continuous flowing interaction … that's deep ecology!"

The cultish tradition and technique of deep powder skiing are Utah's lasting legacy to backcountry glisse. Complete social groups are built around the sport. Skiers and snowboarders seek out deep snow as the religious seek the Word; and the source of the powder gospel is the Utah backcountry. LaChapelle wrote:

> Powder snow skiing is not fun. It's life, fully lived, life lived in a blaze of reality. What we experience in powder is the original human self, which lies deeply inside each of us, still undamaged in spite of what our present culture tries to do to us. Once experienced, this kind of living is recognized as the only way to live–fully aware of the earth and the sky and the gods and you, the mortal, playing among them.

Dolores LaChapelle and other Alta denizens—such as her husband Ed, George

Dolores LaChapelle at Alta. *Ed LaChapelle*

Sormer, Peter Lev, Ted Wilson, and Rick Reese—did a lot of Utah ski touring in the 1950s and 1960s. Much of this was on terrain initially accessed by ski lifts, but almost every skiable summit in the Wasatch also felt the touch of glisse. Indeed, the area received national recognition in a 1956 *Summit Magazine* article entitled "Alta—the Hub of Deep Powder Touring." Nonetheless, backcountry skiing in Utah remained a cult activity until the outdoor recreation boom of the mid 1960s, when interest in ski touring increased all over North America. By 1965, ski tourers were exploring most of the Wasatch backcountry. That same year, North America's first modern backcountry ski guide service was operated as part of the Alf Engen Ski School at Alta. The school brochure listed various ski tours, including the "Alta-Brighton-Alta" trip.

Most of the ski tourers of the 1960s and 1970s were more concerned with covering distance rather than doing ski descents. A small cadre of mountaineers, however, soon focused on making backcountry turns and skiing from peaks. One of the era's most prolific was a young Alta ski racer, Rick Wyatt.

Later to become an avalanche safety consultant and mountain guide, Wyatt grew up as a Utah skier. In 1973, at 17 years old, he got his first taste of a classic descent when he skied Mount Superior, the majestic peak rising to the north of the Alta ski area (see following routes). After a series of knee injuries he quit skiing, then met George Sormer, a 10th Mountain Division veteran who'd been an avid Utah backcountry skier for several years. With Sormer as his mentor, Wyatt started exploring the Wasatch as a ski tourer. In doing so he became part of the backcountry ski renaissance sprouting all over North America. Like many other backcountry skiers of the time, Wyatt started touring more as an adjunct to wilderness travel, rather than with specific intent to climb and make turns.

"I was getting into the mountains and climbing more," remembers Wyatt, "so this was another part of mountaineering … more to get in the mountains … to go for a walk. And then slowly, after three years I was starting to ski down hills again; but that wasn't really the goal, it was just part of cruising around the mountains." Nordic skis were the obvious choice for such "overland" use, since the alpine gear and ski mountaineering gear of the day was unwieldy, if not entirely dysfunctional.

But the Wasatch mountains are not flat, and Wyatt soon became a glisse alpinist. By 1975 he was able to ski down just about anything he wanted on super-lightweight gear: low-top leather boots and Nordic-width skis that were virtually flatland planks being forced into turns. With the technique to enjoy turns on such weightless equipment, Wyatt again discovered the joy of ski descents. He signed hundreds of Wasatch summits with his tracks, and for a period made his reputation by skiing extreme routes such as Wyoming's Grand Teton on his flimsy gear. "I was interested in skiing from summits, but I didn't think much about whether something had already been skied—that was irrelevant," says Wyatt, "The goal was … to climb big peaks. The most efficient way down was to ski, so that's what we did." Wyatt and his friends skied Superior often, descended Twin Peaks from almost every direction, and eventually skied virtually every major summit in the Wasatch—a number as firsts. Some of the routes were steep, perhaps extreme, but many were simply glorious descents any advanced skier could enjoy, such as Lone Peak's south slopes and the high peaks of Mount Nebo and Mount Timpanogos.

Unlike the Northwest, Sierra, or Colorado, where difficult snow is often the rule in mid winter, perfect winter powder is the Wasatch norm. It's snow so good that, with a modicum of practice, anyone can enjoy it with almost any gear—including the free-heel bindings that frustrate all but the best skiers in Colorado trap-crust or Sierra cement. What's more, much of the Wasatch vertical is a direct climb up and ski down from your car, without the endless flat slogs that discourage glisse alpinists in other ranges. Thus, as Wyatt and his peers re-discovered the convenient Wasatch trove, Wasatch touring rapidly gained popularity.

As a marker of Utah's leadership in ski touring, in 1976 Alexis Kelner and David Hanscom published the area's first backcountry ski guide. Replete with excel-lent photos and hundreds of modern-style ski tours, *Wasatch Tours* was the first ski mountaineering guidebook in North Amer-ica to include complete graphic illustration with more than a small selection of ski

Thunder Ridge, where the Wasatch extremists play. Otis to right, Dover in center. *Andrew McLean*

Andrew McLean. His "chute skiing" hobby started with a Department of Transportation guide to the avalanche chutes of Utah. *Mark Holbrook*

descents (several other guides had been published, but they were limited in scope).

With mass quantities of terrific snow and the terrain to support it, present glisse alpinism in Utah is a broad mix of touring, short climbs and descents, and summit drops. On the fringe, a cadre of alpinists are pushing the limits of glisse on the steeper terrain of the Wasatch. One such activist is Andrew McLean.

When McLean started looking for his type of ski descent he found the standard guidebook lacked the information he needed. To his delight, he discovered that none other than well-known mountaineer and avalanche consultant Peter Lev had written the Depart-ment of Transportation (DOT) guides to the avalanche paths of Little Cottonwood Canyon and Big Cottonwood Canyon. "When I first saw the DOT guides," says McLean, "I thought WOW, this is it! It has all the vertical, distance, angle, aspect—everything you need. The Little Cottonwood DOT book mentions 36 slide paths that threaten the road, … which of course means 36 ski runs." McLean is working on his own guidebook to what he calls "chute skiing," and gets a chuckle out of the fact that he can trace the roots of his sport back to the Utah Department of Transportation.

McLean and other extremists such as alpine climbing specialist Alex Lowe ("the father of Wasatch rap' skiing"), Mark Holbrook, Loren Glick and John Whedon are hitting improbable descents such as the Northwest Col of the Pfeiefferhorn, the vertical shaft of Otis (named after an elevator company), steep lines in the cirques of Mount Wolverine near Brighton ski area, and Argenta; "the biggest baddest chute in Big Cottonwood Canyon." For the super-extremist, McLean authored a line on Cardiac Ridge called Lightning Bolt, which involves survival skiing on 64-degree snow above cliffs. "It's really good," he says with a demonic laugh.

Politics have also become an important part of Utah backcountry glisse. The Wasatch is a small mountain range, and winter sports such as backcountry skiing, helicopter skiing, snowmobiling and lift skiing must rub knees in limited terrain. While the Utah Wilderness Act of 1984 reserves dozens of pocket wilderness areas throughout Utah, much of this land is only suitable for advanced glisse alpinism. Thus, people enjoying moderate ski and snowboard touring sometimes crowd with snowmobiles and helicopters. Currently, backcountry skiers and snowboarders have rallied around the slogan "heli-free Wasatch," and are attempting to restrict helicopters from many non-wilderness areas. Interestingly, in their co-written guidebooks, authors Alexis Kelner and David Hanscom include a strong dose of invective against all forms of development; but they insightfully realize that some mechanized use, when oriented toward the backcountry, may have its place. For example, about snowmobiles they write:

"Because they enjoy the same public lands for their recreations, snowmobile operators and ski tourers have a common interest in protecting those lands from excessive commercial exploitation. … Stopping to socialize with snowmobile operators provides opportunities for exchange of vital information. … It also builds good will and trust, which should result in a more pleasant experience for all."

History and politics aside, and whatever your choice of gear, technique or terrain, the truth of Utah glisse remains: "One can never be bored by powder skiing because it is a special gift …" wrote Dolores LaChapelle, "… it only comes in sufficient amounts in particular places …" One such place is the Utah backcountry. Go.

Mount Olympus— Mount Olympus Couloir

Mount Olympus is Salt Lake City's signature mountain, rising from the municipal outskirts like its namesake, the lofty home of the Greek gods, rose in the imagination of the ancients. You don't have to be Zeus to ski Salt Lake City's Mount Olympus, but you do need a modicum of fitness, and the patience to wait for good snow conditions on this low-elevation mountain. While many ski routes grace Olympus, the most visible line is a slanting couloir dropping to the west from a saddle between the peak's twin summits. This is known as the Tolcat Couloir, and with good snow conditions it is probably the simplest way to get an aesthetic couloir descent from near the summit of Mount Olympus. When asked how best to ski Olympus, the locals will often recommend a clone of the Tolcat Couloir, starting at the same saddle, but dropping to the north. This is known as the Mount Olympus Couloir.

While the Mount Olympus Couloir drops into Norths Fork and then Neffs Canyon, the lower reaches of Neffs Canyon are too brush-choked to make a good ascent route. Thus, it's better to use the Mount Olympus Trail up Tolcat Canyon, and climb the Tolcat Couloir to the saddle at the head of both couloirs. From there, descend the aesthetic part of the Olympus Couloir, climb back up, then head down the Tolcat Couloir. Drive to the Mount Olympus Trailhead on Wasatch Boulevard in Salt Lake City. Hike the Mount Olympus Trail as it takes a climbing traverse into Tolcat Canyon and leads to the base of the Tolcat Couloir. Climb the couloir. At the summit saddle, decide on your descent options according to snow conditions and your fatigue from the long climb.

Start: Mount Olympus Trailhead, 5,400 feet

Summit: 9,026 feet

Vertical gain: About 5,000 feet (includes climbing back up Olympus Couloir)

Round trip distance and time: 7 miles, 12 hours

Ascent: Advanced

Glisse: Advanced/Extreme

Map: Wasatch Touring Map # 1, published by Alpentech

Guidebook: *Wasatch Tours, Volume 2*, Hanscom and Kelner

Weather: Ski the steeper lines in this area from late winter through early spring. Due to its low elevation, Mount Olympus may offer safer skiing when avalanche hazard is high at upper elevations. For weather information, use local television, radio, ski reports, and avalanche forecasts (see Directory).

Red Tape: None

The Wasatch slot couloirs are found between vertical rock ribs such as this. *Bill Stevenson*

Glade skiing is popular among Utah backcountry skiers and riders; find a good patch of fluff, then do laps. *Bill Stevenson*

Peak 10,420

When steep alpine peaks such as Superior and Timpanogos (see the following routes) are deemed too avalanche prone to enjoy, the Wasatch offers many summits and ridges with fine powder skiing, where lower angles and timbered slopes yield minimal avalanche danger. Peak 10,420 is one such destination. Located on the divide separating the resort town of Park City from Big Cottonwood Canyon, the mountain offers beautiful powder glades for a day of glisse around its summit, or you can do an "interconnect" tour to the town of Park City.

Drive from Salt Lake City up Big Cottonwood Canyon. Past Solitude Ski Area, turn left on Guardsmans Pass Road. Drive to parking at the snowplow turn. Ski the road to Guardsmans Pass, then follow a ridge south to the summit of Peak 10,420. Ski runs seen on the way up. An alternative route takes the peak's northwest ridge.

Start: Guardsmans Pass Road, 8,900 feet

Summit: 10,420 feet

Vertical gain: 1,520 feet

Round trip distance and time: 5 miles, average day

Ascent: Novice skiing

Glisse: Intermediate

Map: Wasatch Touring Map #1, published by Alpentech

Guidebook: *Wasatch Tours, Volume 2*, Hanscom and Kelner

Weather: Use local television, radio, ski reports, and avalanche forecasts (see Directory). On average, mid winter to early spring are the best times to ski this route.

Red Tape: None

Mount Superior—South Face

The stunning peak of Mount Superior, located in full view of the Alta ski area, is one of Utah's most attractive steep-ski descents. While the harsh slopes of Superior's South Face were seldom, if ever, skied in the early days, Superior's stupendous south side graced countless early photographs of the Alta region. The mountain became somewhat of an icon—or at least a "wannabe." In an amusing incident of the 1970s, Utah travel promoters produced an illustrated matchbook to show off the state's mountains. Superior was the obvious candidate for stardom. But much to the delight of Utah's competitors, what ended up on the matchbook was none other than Colorado's famed Maroon Bells. Such a faux pas aside, Mount Superior is the "superior" ski moun-

Mount Superior looms above Alta ski area, 1964. Original rope tow and lodge are shown. *Peter Lev*

tain, and if not the king of North America's classic steep descents, it's certainly a member of the high court.

Naturally, as soon as ski equipment and technique were up to the task, the looming face of Mount Superior was cut with tracks. While no record exists of who first skied the face, early descents were made by Alta skiers such as Elizabeth Woolsey, George Haldemeir and Darwon Stoneman. Peter Lev, who worked as an Alta ski patrolman in the late 1960s and early 1970s, described Stoneman's ski of the face as a "real descent ... with balls ... other people sort of minced around on Superior, Darwon skied it."

Getting psyched to drop down off the summit of Mount Superior, with Alta below. *Andrew McLean*

For Mount Superior, drive up Little Cottonwood Canyon to the vicinity of Alta Ski Resort. Glisse alpinists use several routes to reach Superior's summit for descents of the South Face. A reasonable route starts at the Forest Service garage on the Little Cottonwood Canyon Road, near Alta Lodge. Take a snow-covered road up to a power line, follow the power line to Cardiff Pass on Superior's East Ridge, then take the ridge to the summit. With compacted spring snow and low avalanche danger you can climb a route known as the East Shoulder, which ascends directly from Little Cottonwood Canyon up a shoulder to climber's right of the South Face, gaining the East Ridge at Black Knob. This climb can involve a section of hand-and-foot climbing on rotten rock. To avoid that possibility, wait until spring and climb directly up the South Face ski route on early morning compacted and frozen snow. Before and during your climb, pick a route that avoids cliff bands and other difficult terrain features. Bring crampons and ice ax for the direct route, and a lightweight rope for the ridge route.

Start: Little Cottonwood Canyon Road, 8,000 feet

Summit: 11,132 feet
Vertical gain: 3,132 feet
Round trip distance and time: Several miles (varies with exact route), average day
Ascent: Intermediate on ridge, Advanced on face
Glisse: Advanced/Extreme
Map: Map: USGS 7.5 minute, Dromedary Peak, Brighton
Guidebook: *Wasatch Tours, Volume 2*, Hanscom and Kelner
Weather: See other routes above
Red Tape: While no steep face should be skied or snowboarded with unstable snow, doing so on Superior could get you shot at. Artillery is used to blast avalanches from the face. Glisse during periods when the snowpack is widely acknowledged to be stable.

Little Cottonwood Canyon— Y Couloir

The Y Couloir out of Little Cottonwood Canyon gives a taste of a classic Wasatch style: with deep snow and stable avalanche conditions, you simply pick a likely looking gulch or couloir above the narrow defile of Little Cottonwood Canyon, climb it to a highpoint on a ridge, then descend. Not a summit ski descent, but then, with 3,000 vertical feet of fine Wasatch snow to play in, why quibble?

Upper section of the Y Couloir viewed from across Little Cottonwood Canyon. *Tyson Bradley*

Drive from Salt Lake City up the Little Cottonwood Canyon Road. About 2.6 miles from the mouth of the canyon, the Y Couloir rises south from the road up the face of Thunder Ridge, a short distance to climber's right of Hogum Fork Canyon. It's easily identified as the most classic line in this area. Park to the side of the road as close as you can get to the Y Couloir. You'll usually find a plowed pull-out on the south side of the road. Climb and descend the couloir, maximum angle is just over 40 degrees. Farther downvalley from the Y Couloir, the forbidding brush-choked defile of Coalpit Gulch climbs the mountainside. Coalpit has become somewhat of a testpiece for hardcore Wasatch skiers. Above the bushwhacking it provides a ski descent with lots of vertical, but it's not as direct and accessible as the Y Couloir. Amusingly, in the *Wasatch Tours* guidebook Coalpit is covered as a non-route that "neither author … has ever toured (or descended) … for good reasons!" With a description like that, what extremist could resist? Yes, Coalpit gets its share of glisse, but take your familiarization tour on the Y.
Start: Little Cottonwood Canyon Road, 6,500 feet
Summit: 9,800 feet

Vertical gain: 3,300 feet
Round trip distance and time: 2 miles, 5 hours
Ascent: Advanced
Glisse: Advanced/Extreme
Map: Wasatch Touring Map #2, published by Alpentech
Guidebook: *Wasatch Tours, Volume 2*, Hanscom and Kelner
Weather: Ski the Y Couloir with a stable late winter or early spring snowpack. For weather information, use local television, radio, ski reports, and avalanche forecasts.
Red Tape: None

Climbing the Y Couloir. *Andrew McLean*

Lone Peak is located in Utah's first legal wilderness.
Bill Stevenson

Lone Peak—South Summit and South Side

Termed the "gemstone of Utah's first wilderness" by the *Wasatch Tours* guidebook, Lone Peak is a truly alpine mountain with numerous snow climbs and glisse descents. While shorter routes to Lone Peak from Little Cottonwood Canyon exist, this route leads to a vast array of southerly slopes that produce good corn snow early in the spring, and are less extreme than the peak's north reaches.

For Lone Peak, drive south from Salt Lake to Alpine, then northeast several miles to the Hamongog Trailhead. The latter part of this drive can be confusing, use your map and inquire locally. From parking, take the Hamongog Trail north to the high southern flanks of Lone Peak. Descend terrain you scouted during the climb.

Start: 6,900 feet

Summit: 11,253 feet

Vertical gain: 4,353 feet

Round trip distance and time: 6 miles, 8 hours

Ascent: Intermediate

Glisse: Intermediate

Maps: USGS 7.5 minute, Lone Peak; Trails Illustrated, Wasatch Front, #709

Guidebook: *Wasatch Tours, Volume 2*, Hanscom and Kelner

Weather: Late winter and spring are the best seasons for skiing Lone Peak. For weather information, use local television, radio, ski reports, and avalanche forecasts.

Red Tape: None

Mount Timpanogos from the southwest. The classic route takes the other side, but is very similar. *Tyson Bradley*

Mount Timpanogos—North Peak

One of the highest and most alpine of the Wasatch peaks, Mount Timpanogos yields fine descents for alpinists willing to work. As a bonus, while most of the Wasatch has a rather short season of spring skiing, you can find good ski and snowboard snow on "Timp" Glacier well into summer.

Mount Timpanogos was named in 1776 by a Spanish expedition, the odd moniker being an adaptation of the name of the Timpanogotzis Indians. The mountain was probably first climbed by Indians or early settlers. An organized annual climb known as the "Timp Hike" started in 1912, when 19 mountaineers reached the trailhead by via horse transport and hiked to the summit. Twenty years later, 1,460 people summited during the 1932 Timp Hike! For skiers, the big event was the 1941 hike, when the Timpanogos Summer Ski Classic race was held on the Timpanogos Glacier. Ski races on the glacier were held for several years after that, and contributed to the popularity of summer skiing on the Timp Glacier, which continues to the present. In 1970 Timpanogos was loved to death when 3,500 people made the summit during the Timp Hike, heavily damaging the trails in the process. After that, the event was discontinued.

For Mount Timpanogos, drive south of Salt Lake on Highway 189 up Provo Canyon to the town of Wildwood. Turn northwest on the Alpine Scenic Loop Road to Sundance Ski Resort. Drive 5 miles to the Aspen Grove Trailhead, indicated by obvious signs. The trail starts as pavement, then becomes a beaten path to the toe of the Timp Glacier (about 10,400 feet, mostly a permanent snowfield but may have deep bergschrunds). At the base of the glacier you'll find a famous old structure known as the Timp Shelter. It's decrepit and missing the front door, but makes a good bivouac. Climb the glacier to a saddle, then take the ridge northwest to the north summit if you want to claim a true climb of "Timp." You'll find the most reliable skiing by starting at the saddle and heading down the glacier, with variations viewed during your climb. With good snowcover, skiing directly down the drainage below the glacier can yield a huge and exciting ski descent that's been compared to a "halfpipe." Be aware that late-season snow in the canyon gets hollow over several waterfalls. A number of hikers have died after falling through these hazards.

Start: 8,040 feet

Summit: 11,750 feet

Vertical gain: 3,710 feet

Round trip distance and time: 10 hours

Ascent: Intermediate

Glisse: Advanced

Maps: USGS 7.5 minute, Timpanogos Cave and Aspen Grove (for greatest detail); Trails Illustrated, Wasatch Front, #709

Guidebook: *Mount Timpanogos*, Michael R. Kelsey

Weather: Ski Timpanogos in the spring and early summer. For weather information, use local television, radio, ski reports, and avalanche forecasts.

Red Tape: Beware of early spring and winter road closures

Climbing the northeast side of Mount Timpanogos.
Andrew McLean

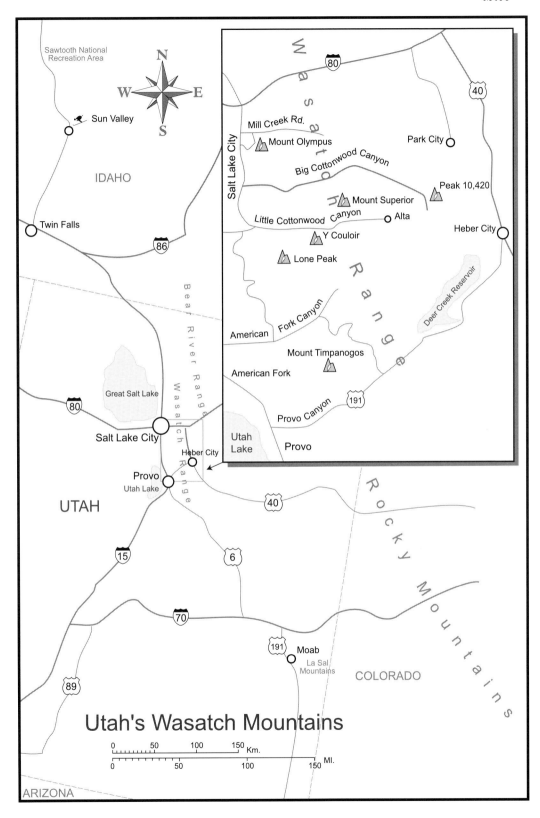

Utah's Wasatch Mountains

FOURTEENERS AND SNOWSLIDES:

COLORADO ROCKIES

Fourteeners and snowslides:
Colorado Rockies

A winter satellite view of western Colorado shows a wide snowy stripe extending from the state's southern to northern borders. As if in a glisse alpinist's dream, a thousand major skiable peaks stud this expanse of the Colorado Rockies.

Until the 1800s, the high peaks of the Colorado Rockies—including the 54 famed 14,000-foot peaks known as the "fourteeners"—were regarded more as landmarks and obstacles than recreational destinations. Even so, most of the accessible summits were first climbed by Indians, mountain men, or prospectors. In the mid 1800s the Colorado mining boom brought thousands of people to the state. True mountaineering during this period was uncommon, but miners prospected high on the peaks and opened many access routes that exist to the present. The men of the famous Hayden and Wheeler federal surveys (from 1873 to 1876) also did a number of first ascents when they scrambled to many of the easier summits.

The first documented use of skis in Colorado was during the Marcy military expedition of 1857, when guide Jim Baker carved a pair of planks with his sheath knife, then tried to lead his lost and starving charges to safety. This was not a particularly auspicious beginning for the sport, however, for the expedition was ultimately saved when guide Miguel Aloña took over and led the group on foot over Cochetopa Pass to safety.

After the mining boom population growth of the late 1800s, skis were common

in mining camps such as Crested Butte, Breckenridge, Ouray, and Aspen. In 1886, Colorado's first ski races were held on the hill behind Crested Butte. In 1919, miners at the Eureka mine near Telluride rode the ore cars to a highpoint, then skied down a high backcountry valley. (Several decades earlier, California ore car riders became the first "lift" skiers in North America.)

The powder was good and the sky often blue, but Colorado's winter snowpack was, as it is to this day, arguably the most avalanche-prone on the continent. Huge slides plagued Colorado's high mining camps. When a legendary blizzard hit central Colorado in 1899, snowslide-marooned muckers on Independence Pass put out a sign reading: "Wanted—1000 pair of Norwegian snowshoes." (Skis were known by this moniker at the time.) But avalanches rarely provided such occasions for humor. The first U.S. skier to die in a snowslide, in 1863, was mail carrier John Armstrong, on Mosquito Pass near Leadville. (Armstrong's successor, Methodist minister Father Dyer, went on to become Colorado's version of California's famed postman-cum-skier Snowshoe Thompson.) The first documented fatality in North America caused by a skier-triggered avalanche also occurred in Colorado, when, in 1905, two playful miners were caught in a slide near the town of Silverton.

From about 1900 to 1910, famed naturalist and mountaineer Enos Mills skied the backcountry around Longs Peak in northern Colorado, and wrote of his adventures in a series of essays (often compared with those of John Muir). Mills had his own ski encounters with avalanches, including

◀ Skiing Richmond Ridge, Hayden Peak in background.
Michael Kennedy

one "magnificent monster ... comet-tailed with snow-dust" that gave him a race for his life. Many glisse fanatics have fantasized such a situation, although few caught in such a race manage to survive. Mills was one of the fortunate few, leaping a "forty-odd-foot" wide gorge to safety.

Enos Mills went on to become an inspiration for the next generation of Colorado ski mountaineers. Many of these mountaineers were also involved with the Colorado Mountain Club (CMC), formed in 1912. By 1916 the CMC had established a

A happy Colorado Mountain Club skier at Berthoud Pass in 1933; still a popular destination for backcountry glisse. *Colorado Mountain Club Collection*

tradition of backcountry ski outings, including the use of huts, that continues to this day. The club's journal, *Trail and Timberline*, soon became *the* venue for reporting first ascents, major explorations, and backcountry ski trips, and thus drove the complete exploration of the Colorado alps.

The Colorado mountaineers of the twentieth century also found a unique appeal in bagging the summits of the state's numerous 14,000-foot peaks, and the "fourteeners" would become the focus for many of the early explorations reported in *Trail and Timberline*. In the golden years of fourteener climbing, from about 1907 to 1910, Percy Hagerman and Harold Clark climbed all the fourteeners in the challenging Elk Mountains between the towns of Crested Butte and Aspen. In the same period, William Cooper and John Hubbard were making many demanding scrambles in the San Juan Mountains to the south. The fourteeners would also become tantalizing objectives for ski alpinists; in 1921, 17-year-old Graeme McGowan and two teenaged friends made the first ski descent from the summit of Pikes Peak, a fourteener with a long history of attracting interest.

The ever popular pastime of climbing all the fourteeners as a goal in itself began with pioneer Colorado mountaineers Carl Blaurock and William Ervin, who in 1923 became the first to do it (though the count was 49 at the time). As the years went by, climbing all the 54 fourteeners became an appealing goal for the state's mountaineers—and for some an obsession. To date more than 700 climbers have officially recorded their bagging of the 54. Doubtless many others have completed their hunt yet not recorded their bag . Other climbers go for repeats and see how many "times around" they can make in a lifetime. The current record stands at more than 10 circuits. Still other fanatics see how fast they can climb all 54 in one push, with the current record at under 15 days.

Fourteener pioneer Carl Blaurock was a skier as well, and in 1934 he made ski descents of fourteeners Mount Bierstadt and Mount Evans. Since then, the fourteeners have played an essential role in Colorado glisse alpinism.

An important part of Colorado backcountry ski history was a series of visits to the Elk Mountains by ski promoter, coach, author and instructor Otto Eugene Schniebs. A disciple of ski maestro Hannes Schneider, Schniebs had come to the United States from Germany in 1928, with an eye on opportunities in ski instruction and coaching. A tireless promoter, Schniebs founded his own system of ski instruction, and also promoted what he thought were the best places to ski in the country. One such place was the area between the towns of Crested Butte and Aspen, where he and his companions did a huge amount of forward-thinking ski alpinism (see Castle Peak route description that follows). Schniebs wrote extensively of his Colorado sojourns in his classic book, *American Skiing*.

By Schniebs's day, better gear and technique had made skiing easier for the masses, and recreational skiing had become popular in the northeastern United States. The eastern skiers wanted terrain more closely matched to that of Europe; but without the 10-day sail. So to Colorado they came, and "snow mining" (as wags called the ski industry), replaced much of the shrinking mineral industry. Several years before the U.S. entered World War II, the state's first mechanized ski areas were established at places such as Cement Creek outside of Crested Butte (where Colorado's first chair lift was built), Berthoud Pass, Loveland Pass, and Winter Park. Others were in the planning stages. Then, the Japanese attacked Pearl Harbor.

Early in World War II, officials in the U.S. War Department realized mountain warfare was a blank in the U.S. Army's repertoire. A unique recruiting effort ensued, including the requirement of reference letters, and by 1943 more than 10,000 would-be mountain troops were living at a huge training facility called Camp Hale, located in a high valley north of Leadville. During their two winters at Hale, the soldiers of the 10th Mountain Division skied mountains such as Homestake Peak on the Continental Divide. At least one group (including pioneer climber Paul Petzoldt), did a 50 mile ski traverse over the mountains to Aspen, and a couple of die-hards skied to 14,005-foot Mount of the Holy Cross and did the first winter ascent.

After heroic combat in Italy, many veterans of the 10th returned to settle in Colorado. Aside from their amazing involvement in the ski resort industry (see Introduction) scores of 10th veterans figured in the development of Colorado's mountaineering tradition, both with skiing and climbing. Fritz Benedict, for example, was the principal founder of the 10th Mountain Division Hut System. Extreme skiing pioneer and Aspen newspaperman Bil Dunaway was another 10th veteran.

With plentiful ski resorts and an enthusiastic ski public as customers, Colorado glisse alpinism hibernated during the late 1950s and most of the 1960s. A few long yet low-altitude ski traverses were made, but the high peaks saw little action.

Athletes in Crested Butte revived the telemark turn in the late 1960s, but doing so distracted many of these skiers from mountaineering. In an ironic twist, most days would find the "tele revivalists" riding ski lifts while dressed in their backcountry outfits, endlessly refining the sexy but difficult telemark. To their credit, a core group of the Crested Butte Nordic downhillers, including

A 10th Mountain Division patrol on Homestake Peak. Many came back after the war and pioneered the state's ski industry.
Louis Dawson Collection

ski patrolman Rick Borkovec and his friends Doug Buzzell, Koli Kazarinoff and Greg Dalby, made early descents of local peaks. The group's first winter and spring of high activity was 1972, when they nailed a long list of local classics including Red Lady Mountain, Gothic Peak, Whetstone Mountain and Teocali Mountain.

The Alfred Braun Hut system between Aspen and Crested Butte saw a fair amount of use at this time, and skiers repeatedly traversed the high-lines between the two towns. These are serious alpine routes that involve much high-altitude weather, difficult snow, steep terrain—and enough flat ground to make the hybrid Nordic-downhill gear of the day the appropriate choice.

In 1965, Colorado's first lengthy high-altitude ski traverse was made by Chamonix guide and pioneer skier Jacques Sineau and

19-year-old Colorado mountaineer Paul Sibley. The pair started in northern Colorado then headed south for 140 miles through the Gore Range and Sawatch mountains to Aspen (with several food resupplies). At one point a huge storm plunged the two into a whiteout for five days. After wandering in circles and running low on food, they finally found a snowbound ranch house with nobody home. "The heat was on, the freezer was full of pies and turkeys, and the phone worked!" Sibley recalls. "So I called the operator and said, 'I'm kinda lost, can you tell me where I am?' I wasn't surprised when she said, 'are you the skiers everybody is looking for?'" The lost skiers had become a media event, and when they later came out of the mountains for a resupply they were greeted by a bunch of reporters—and the sheriff.

Colorado glisse alpinism came out of hibernation in the early 1970s with the contributions of Fritz Stammberger. In 1970, I was with a group winter camping on Hayden Peak. We had pitched a tent in view of a steep (45 degree), avalanche-prone headwall. We had never considered skiing this face, it was just a place where we watched avalanches. Suddenly someone voiced a startled cry and pointed to the wall. It wasn't a slide this time, but a skier coming down! He'd make a powerful traverse, knock off a good-sized avalanche, then turn around and make a few turns where the slide had scoured. Then he'd do it again. We watched in amazement, the way Native Americans must have watched the arrival of Columbus. It was skiing completely out of our experience—transcending reality. That encounter stands as my enlightenment as a ski mountaineer—that day I became as much a glisse alpinist as a climber. The skier we watched, of course, was Fritz Stammberger.

Stammberger was an imposing man with a weight-lifter's physique, thick German accent, and the poise of a rugged individualist. He'd immigrated to the U.S. from Germany in the early 1960s, and settled in Aspen as a printer and ski instructor. Fritz was a true alpinist and a bold skier. In 1964 he became the man with the highest ski descent to that date when he skied from 24,000 feet on Cho Oyu in Tibet (after making the first ascent of that 8,000-meter peak, the seventh highest mountain in the world). Unfortunately his accomplishment was marred by controversy: he skied down Cho Oyu to get help for two companions who died on the mountain, and pundits later claimed the deaths were caused by Stammberger's neglect. History seems to exonerate Stammberger, but his mountaineering career was dogged by that initial debacle.

During his years in Aspen, Stammberger spent countless days skiing mountains such as Hayden Peak and Grizzly Peak

Fritz Stammberger cut a wide trail in the 1960s and 1970s.
Chris Cassatt

(a 13,988 peak with a beautiful couloir dropping from the summit). His training was legendary. On all but the coldest days he would ski without gloves, and he'd walk around town with dripping snowballs clenched in his hands. Almost any winter morning, you could see Stammberger's tall figure striding impossibly fast *up* the ski area on his alpine touring skis—his favorite training. Like a Nietzschean Übermensch, he'd wait until winter, then make first winter ascents of mountain walls as visionary and difficult as any climbs of similar size done elsewhere in the world. In 1969 he made the first winter climb of dagger-like Pyramid Peak, one of Colorado's last fourteeners without a winter ascent. In late winter of 1972, he skied with Gordon Whitmer to the north wall of 14,130 foot Capitol Peak, where the pair made a bold directissima.

While Stammberger's creativity was fabulous, mixed with his aesthetic and playful spirit was no small amount of self promotion and one-upmanship. In Aspen politics he soon established himself as a radical, chaining himself to a tree to prevent a building from going up, and marching in a parade with a sign reading "Public Castration for all Bycicle Thiefs [sic]."

He was obsessed with trekking and climbing in the Himalayas, and the only way to raise money for such trips was to make a name for himself. He'd heard of the European extreme skiers who were creating their own legends. Moreover, he was good friends with Aspen newspaperman Bil Dunaway, who'd done pioneer extreme skiing in Europe, and who had a good sense of mountaineering politics. No doubt, Stammberger's association with Dunaway inspired what followed. Fritz could ski and climb as good as anyone, so he did.

Outside of Aspen is a double-topped fourteener called the Maroon Bells. Known

Fritz Stammberger made his pioneer 1971 descent down the center of the right hand face of North Maroon Peak (to the right), traversing over the lower cliffs. *Louis Dawson*

as the "Deadly Bells" to local mountain rescue teams, the mountain has claimed scores of lives, and makes casual climbers quake with fear. It's steep, striated with relentless cliff bands, and built with rock so loose the climbing is often like scrambling up a gravel pile. With the tight snowpack of spring, however, the Bells mutate. They're safer and easier to climb for those knowing snowcraft, and they become skiable.

In 1971 few people knew the secret of Maroon Bells snow, but Stammberger did. On June 24 he cramponed up the North Face of North Maroon Peak (the north Bell), donned his planks, and skied back down. Even by today's standards the descent wasn't easy: Stammberger fell over a 15-foot cliff, and skied a narrow section exceeding 50 degrees. Moreover, he used no ropes and had no support team. Stammberger's feat amazed the locals and was trumpeted in the Aspen newspaper. Yet as with the coverage of Bill Briggs's Grand Teton ski that same spring, the Maroon Bells ski descent was too far from North American ski reality to receive much press.

After his Maroon Bells descent Stammberger endured a frustrating series of failures in the Himalayas, eventually meeting his end while solo climbing in 1975 on Tirich Mir in Pakistan. A year before he disappeared, Fritz married Janice Pennington, a former Playmate and television starlet. Pennington became obsessed with finding Fritz. Convinced by visions and psychics that he was still alive, she enlisted the help of everyone from private investigators to Elvis Presley. Despite the best efforts of his friends and family, Fritz was never found. Bil Dunaway is convinced he died on Tirich Mir. Pennington went on to write a book about her search for Fritz, concluding that he'd been recruited by the CIA, then died in Afghanistan during the jihad fighting of the early eighties. Whatever the

case, Stammberger's spirit lives on among North American glisse alpinists.

After Stammberger's Maroon Bells descent, interest in Colorado ski descents picked up. Two parties repeated North Maroon the year after Stammberger's feat, and skiers started to tackle moderate fourteeners such as Redcloud Peak in the San Juan Mountains and the easily-skied humps of the Sawatch Range. In 1977, Colorado Springs guide Brian Becker made an early descent of the Railroad Couloir on the North Face of Pikes Peak. The same year, Vail residents Tom and Jim Carr made the first ski descent of the famed Cross Couloir on Mount of the Holy Cross, another lofty fourteener. In the San Juans, the circuitous Snake Couloir on 14,150-foot Mount Sneffels was skied. Then, a year later, Chris Landry made the descent of the decade with his amazing run down the East Face of Pyramid Peak.

Chris Landry grew up in Aspen. The lean athlete started climbing in the Elk Mountains at an early age, and ski raced extensively during high school. Aspen's climate of European alpinism in the 1970s nurtured Landry's mountaineering skills. A bent towards ski alpinism was the inevitable result. After practicing in the Elks, skiing ever steeper lines, Landry set his sights on Pyramid Peak, a steep 14,018-foot arête resembling the blade-hand of a karate fighter. The sides of the peak are riven with countless couloirs and blocked by cliff bands. People who fall down the peak are picked up in pieces.

The line Landry chose on Pyramid's East Face was easily a generation beyond the descents of Bill Briggs and Fritz Stammberger. Indeed, it was equivalent to the radical descents being done in Europe at the time. Super steep, with a number of 60-degree sections, the face is long and discontinuous. Just getting up the thing is a hairy technical crampon ascent, and seldom done. Moreover, Colorado's east-facing pitches are notorious for poor snow conditions—a face such as Pyramid East may only come into good skiing condition several days a year.

After climbing the route with photographer Michael Kennedy in the wee hours of May 15, 1978, Landry started down at 8:30 in the morning. "I didn't decide [to ski] until I got to the top," Landry recalls, "I knew all along what I wanted to do, but it wasn't until that moment I knew I would." On the 60-degree, 15-foot-wide patch of thawing crud near the summit, Landry sometimes had to stop and back up in order to gain enough room to make his next turn. Several

In 1978, Chris Landry skied 60-degree slopes above certain-death cliffs when he made the first descent of Pyramid Peak's East Face.
Peter Kelley

times slabs big enough to knock him down would break loose, resulting in at least one close call. Much of Landry's skiing on Pyramid was performed within several feet of 300-foot cliffs. The crux of the route was stopping above a near-vertical ice face, changing mode to crampons, downclimbing a short distance, then changing to skis again. Kennedy, who was climbing down the route while Landry skied, remembers he was "too gripped to watch Chris go off the summit." Seven hours after they started the pair arrived back at their camp at the base of the face. "I'm still shocked by it," Landry stated a few months after making the descent, "It was the first time I'd ever skied something where, if I fell, I died. I wonder sometimes—like anyone—exactly what I was doing there." Landry went on to make notable descents in California and Washing-

Chris Landry at the summit of Pyramid Peak before his descent.
Michael Kennedy

ton, then retired from extreme skiing after a near-death fall (see Alaska chapter).

Aside from his legacy of 1970s limit pushing, Landry has been attributed with the oft repeated phrase "if you fall you die" as a definition of extreme skiing. It's a catchy axiom, but a misquote. According to Landry, writing in *Couloir Magazine* in 1993, the snip appeared after he was interviewed by writer Oscar Johnson for an article in *Sports Illustrated*. Johnson asked how Landry would define extreme skiing, and Landry explained that "In Europe, the French would probably say something like, 'It's when if you fall, you …'" Landry explains he'd also told Johnson "that's about the worst possible definition. … It's not about killing yourself. … I think of it in more personal terms, as a kind of personal evolution, combining two of my favorite disciplines into a new one I feel is natural to pursue." In Landry's estimation, "it was expedient, not to mention spectacular, to lead the story with that short, simple and near-bizarre phrase. … I was disappointed."

The 1980s in Colorado were a somewhat dormant time for ski alpinism. In 1983 writer John Harlin made the first ski descent of Longs Peak, a craggy fourteener in Rocky Mountain National Park. Early in the decade, a group of Aspen and Crested Butte skiers made several aggressive mid-winter traverses of the Elk Mountains. Using several caches, these trips attempted to follow the spine of the range, climbing 14,000 foot peaks and skiing deadly avalanche slopes in the process. Years later, one of those skiers would share that "we were really a bunch of fools. … I'm amazed we didn't get killed in a slide." Also in the 1980s, a more sane group of skiers completed a traverse they dubbed the "Colorado Grand Tour" which connected a string of ski resorts by traveling the backcountry between. The concept was good, but with ski area boundaries to cross

John Harlin on the first ski descent of 14,255 foot Longs Peak in 1983, during a time of relative dormancy in steep ski mountaineering.
John Harlin Collection

and expensive lodging to buy, the Grand Tour never became popular.

Rather than using Colorado alpine ski resorts as a base, the future of general back-country skiing in the state was the wilderness ski shelters that came to be simply known as "huts." While such cabins had existed since the middle 1930s near Berthoud Pass, and the Alfred Braun huts mentioned previously were mostly built in the 1960s, the shining light of the 1980s was an amazing boom in hut building. The 10th Mountain Hut Association built its first two huts in 1982, and completed 10 huts within the decade. In 1984, one of Colorado's finest ski cabins, The Friends Hut, was built in a rugged alpine area between Crested Butte and Aspen. Numerous shelters such as temporary yurts and teepees were erected in other parts of Colorado during the decade. For the most part, the Colorado huts are easy to reach and are located in gentle terrain compared to Canadian and European

huts. Thus, while committed ski alpinists are often surprised at the lack of terrain they can access from a hut such as the McNamara near Aspen, locating shelter in such mellow terrain has resulted in unprecedented popularity. The 10th Mountain Hut Association boasts more than 20,000 user nights each season. In Colorado, the words "hut trip" have entered the vernacular of everyone from Aspen socialites to Denver carpenters.

Back to ski descents: Landry's Pyramid ski stands without a repeat, though this author and Jeff Mauss used the upper part of his route in 1989 for a second ski descent of the peak. By then I'd been skiing four-teeners since 1978, when I'd enjoyed an eye-opening run from the summit of Castle Peak near Aspen. Before then, alpinism had been an important part of my life; but I'd never known the freedom of hanging ski tips off a summit, then cutting loose to fly, rather than plod down. Castle hooked me, and by the early 1980s I was climbing, then skiing, every peak I could. In 1987, I realized that several of the fourteeners had never had ski descents, and no one had ever skied them all. My goal was set.

My effort to ski all the fourteeners was a solitary endeavor, done alone or with whatever partner I could roust. While enjoying each descent was important, "skiing them all" was like a larger mountain rising above the foothills. Moreover, looming on that horizon were summits unskied by anyone, such as Capitol Peak. I was eager to meet those impossibles. If they were unskiable, then the whole project was moot. "Brutal" was what one cohort called my style. Because weather was hard to predict I preferred doing the peaks as marathons with no overnight camps. Catching good weather was usually the result, but more than one route tired me to the point of falling to my knees in tears.

Finding the fourteeners in skiable condition is usually the crux of a descent.

I knew of others who'd taken more than a half-dozen tries for certain 'teeners, and given up after being chased by avalanches and access nightmares. At first, my unbounded optimism counted such problems as trivial. Not so. Snow coverage on the peaks varies with Colorado's fickle winters and shifty storm tracks. Moreover, the state's avalanche-prone winter snowpack dictates that survivable extreme skiing must be done in spring or during rare midwinter periods of stability. The resulting combination, limited season and unreliable snow, makes skiing all the fourteeners a problem in logistics as much as an athletic challenge.

As a result, my fourteener ski quest was an ironic combination of elated moments and expensive time-consuming failures. But then, are those not the ingredients of any worthwhile mountaineering project? Mount Elbert, Colorado's highest, yielded a wondrous 3,000-vertical-foot corn snow feast I'll dream about for the rest of

The author collapsed in exhaustion during an 18-hour solo push, skiing a southern fourteener. *Louis Dawson*

my life. Winter ascents of a half dozen peaks had their sublime moments, such as watching the moon set through the branches of bristlecone pines, and enjoying that special solitude only the icy season can deliver. A few first descents of routes and peaks came my way. Little Bear Peak, which I skied in 1991, was the last unskied four-teener and thus a milestone. Crestone Peak was another unskied summit, as was Capitol Peak in the Elk Mountains. Climbers laughed at my plans to ski Capitol, but I'd been there in the winter and seen how the famous two-inch wide Knife Ridge was buried by a skiable cornice.

Optimism, religion, and a solid marriage kept me going, but most of the peaks were harder than I'd planned. The worst were the Sangre de Cristo mountains. El Diente Peak required six attempts and the seven other fourteeners in the "Sangres" took at least two tries each. Avalanche danger turned me away three times. Several other times the peaks were bone-dry and unskiable.

On May 9, 1991, I stood atop Kit Carson Mountain—the last of 54 ski descents. Photographer Glenn Randall and I had left the town of Westcliffe eight hours before, blitzed our way over a high divide into Spanish Creek, then climbed Cole's Couloir to the summit. As I stood on that apex, it felt as if all the fourteener ski pioneers joined me to gaze over the sea of jutting peaks I call home. Then, with a backdrop of that deepest azure which only 14,000 feet can bring, I dropped through the deep slot of Cole's Couloir to the base of the face. A long hot slog back to the car brought me to my senses, but as far as I get from that day, both in distance and time, the call of those 54 ski descents, capped by Kit Carson Mountain, orders my life.

Glisse alpinism in Colorado has an exciting future. Ski resorts have begun opening their boundaries to skiers and snowboarders. What's more, a number of ski areas have vast amounts of "extreme" terrain within their permit areas, and they've realized opening such terrain is another way to sell tickets. Huts are still being built at a steady pace, and it's easier to find consistently plowed roads to important trailheads. Ski lifts and roads aside, the future of Colorado glisse alpinism lies in its huge number of skiable summits. While it's undeniable that Colorado glisse alpinists have been biased toward descents on the fourteeners, the state also has 636 major peaks above 13,000 feet, most of which have several top-to-bottom glisse lines. If you use up those you can move to the several hundred peaks above 12,000 feet, which again offer incredible skiing or snowboarding. Indeed, with such options, most committed Colorado skiers must hope for reincarnation—it's impossible to do even a fraction of the best runs in one lifetime.

Colorado's high-altitude snow remains deep, unconsolidated and dangerous well into late winter. As a result, until the state's snow compacts in spring, descents are hard to bag with reasonable safety. Thus, while certain times during every Colorado winter allow steep skiing with minimal avalanche danger, most of the state's best descents are made during the spring snow season, usually from April through June, and some years into July. Colorado mountaineers have learned to live with their snowpack—the alternative is to die in it. Rather than force the issue when the mid-winter snow is bad, there is hut skiing at lower-angled terrain, or traveling to other, safer mountain ranges. As the snow of Utah melts and snowline in the Northwest rises high above the parking lots, we return to Colorado and enjoy high altitude spring and summer corn snow descents on the state's glorious peaks.

Buffalo Mountain—Silver Couloir

Interstate 70 splits Colorado like the belt on a sumo wrestler's stomach. Climbing over bulging mountains, dipping through river chasms, sneaking through a tunnel now and then, I-70 yields access to the heart of the Rockies. In central Colorado near the Continental Divide, the highway's route has served as a transportation corridor for all recorded history, and heavy prehistoric use by the Ute Indians is shown by artifacts that turn up during construction projects. In recent history, the most astounding transmogrification on Interstate 70 was the creation of the Vail ski resort. In the early 1960s a two-lane road would take you slowly past peaceful meadows, small gas stations, grazing deer, and potholes. A uranium prospector named Earl Eaton thought the area would make a good ski resort, and a furious development project ensued with 10th Mountain Division veteran Pete Seibert at the helm, and 10th vet Fritz Benedict doing design work. In just a few years, where cows had quietly chewed their cud, a complete city stood below a cleared and developed ski mountain.

Vail only civilized one mountain in the area. As saving grace, dozens of other nearby peaks still provide wild snow with skiing as good or better than Vail. Of course, you get the pleasure of earning your turns on those—as most glisse mountaineers

Buffalo Mountain from the northeast. The Silver Couloir drops from the summit down the center of the face. *Louis Dawson*

prefer. One such destination is Buffalo Mountain, a humped peak rising north from I-70 and west from the town of Silverthorne.

The north side of Buffalo Mountain is split by a long 3,000-vertical-foot couloir which necks down to 50-feet wide at one point. This run, known to some as the "Silver Couloir," is one of the best ski descents in Colorado, and should be on every expert skier or rider's list.

Drive Interstate 70 west from Denver or east from Vail, and take the Silverthorne exit. Drive Highway 9 north, and take a left at the first intersection. Drive the Wildernest Road up through houses and condominiums to parking at the start of the Willow Creek Trail (at the highest level the road will take you). The trail starts on the northeast side of a major curve in the road. Trailhead signs exist, but may be covered by snow. (Traveling in the conifer forest here may be confusing—pay attention to map and compass.) Take the trail a short distance to the Buffalo Cabin Trail, climb ½ mile to Buffalo Cabin, then climb west up open avalanche slopes 2,000 vertical feet to the summit. Head a few hundred feet northwest from the summit, then drop northeast into the couloir. The crux of the descent is a steep narrows near the bottom. After the couloir

Skiing the Silver Couloir, Buffalo Mountain. *Louis Dawson*

widens at the base, take the right (east) edge of the avalanche run-out, and intersect an aqueduct at 9,700 feet near the bottom of the avalanche path. With snowcover, the aqueduct looks like a small shelf leading through the timber. Don't miss the aqueduct: it defines a trail you must follow 1½ miles back to parking. About ½ mile along the aqueduct, climb southeast a few hundred vertical feet back to the trail you started on, then descend to parking.

Start: 9,760 feet

Summit: 12,777 feet

Vertical gain: 3,017 feet

Round trip distance and time: 4 miles, 7 hours

Ascent: Intermediate

Glisse: Advanced

Maps: USGS 7.5 minute, Dillon, Willow Lakes, Vail Pass

Guidebook: *Skiing Colorado's Backcountry*, Brian Litz

Weather: Ski and climb this route on compacted spring snow (see route descriptions that follow). Be at the top of the peak by sunrise, as the northeast aspects in the couloir get sun immediately. The best weather reports are those on NOAA weather radio.

Red Tape: Be aware of private property near the trailheads and approaches

Quandary Peak—East Ridge

Quandary Peak is perhaps the easiest of the Colorado fourteeners to climb and ski with significant vertical. The route is a classic line up and down the mellow ramp of a long sinuous ridge.

But don't let Quandary's eastern pitch fool you. The West Ridge of the peak is a tricky scramble, and the South Face is a challenging extreme ski. Incidentally, because of the peak's easy access and popularity, at least three *wannabe* extreme skiers have fallen down the South Face. All were badly beaten, with pulverized shoulders, snapped legs and bruised brains—their sur-

Quandary Peak, the East Ridge heads to the right, South Face to left. This is one of Colorado's best "entry level" fourteener descents. *Louis Dawson*

vival was a miracle. Stick with the East Ridge unless you're a qualified extremist, and climb the route you plan on descending.

Enraptured after a fine section of descent on Quandary Peak's east ridge. *Glenn Randall*

For Quandary Peak, drive north on Highway 9 from Fairplay, or south from Breckenridge to the Monte Cristo Creek switchback on the north side of Hoosier Pass. This switchback is 2.2 miles from Hoosier Pass and 8.2 miles from Breckenridge. At the lower (northern) portion of the switchback, turn west onto the Monte Cristo Road. Drive .5 mile and park where another road turns to the right, or at snow closure.

Climb ½ mile north to the broad ridgecrest. Avoid posted land. The best route up the ridge follows the left side of the peak's broad eastern flank. Descend your ascent route. Skiers in the learning stages should leave their planks at the step beneath the upper face of the summit.

Start: 10,900 feet

Summit: 14,265 feet

Vertical gain: 3,365 feet

Round trip distance and time: 6 miles, 7 hours

Ascent: Novice

Glisse: Intermediate (Advanced from exact summit)

Map: USGS 7.5 minute, Breckenridge

Guidebook: *Dawson's Guide to Colorado's Fourteeners, Volume 1,* Louis Dawson

Weather: This route can be climbed and skied with stable winter snow, but spring is a better season for skiing on Quandary. See chapter introduction and other Colorado route descriptions for more weather information.

Red Tape: Park with care for private property

Castle Peak—Montezuma Glacier

When most people envision Colorado's Rockies, they see the Elk Mountains. Other ranges in the state have peaks as steep, other ranges have more square miles, but no other range matches the Elks' bulk of raw rocky topography. The Elks were one of the last areas of Colorado to be explored. William Brewer got close enough to "that terra incognito" in 1869 to see some of their "nameless, untrodden and unknown peaks" spiking through the distant haze. Dr. Ferdinand Hayden, while mapping the Elks during his famous 1873 survey, observed that "the great variety of colors of the rocks, the remarkable and unique forms of the peaks, and the extreme raggedness, all conspire to impress the beholder with wonder." Like gigantic backbones, the scraggy ridges of the Elk Mountains reach to airy 14,000-foot

Castle Peak from the east, with a fine extreme route down the center curving couloir. Montezuma Basin is in the valley hidden by the right hand ridge. *Louis Dawson*

alps. Glacial valleys filled with lush stands of aspen and spruce are home to some of North America's most prolific elk herds, giving the range its name.

Three of this chapter's featured classics are located in the Elk Mountains, and with good reason. For resort skiers and

The original Tagert Hut at the base of Montezuma Basin, circa 1948. *Dick Durrance*

snowboarders, the Elk Mountain resorts offer some of the state's most challenging terrain on Mount Crested Butte, Aspen Mountain, and Aspen Highlands. In the backcountry, much of North America's ski mountaineering history was written on such Elk peaks as the Maroon Bells, Pyramid Peak, and Castle Peak.

Castle Peak is located on the high divide between the towns of Crested Butte and Aspen. It was one of only two four-teeners climbed by the Hayden Survey, when Henry Gannet and his cohorts made an amazingly hard scramble route on the peak's south side. Colorado has no true glaciers, but a handful of large permanent snowfields provide glacier-like skiing last-ing well into the summer. One such snow-patch exists on Castle Peak, in the huge amphitheater known as Montezuma Basin.

The first skiing done in Montezuma Basin was probably in 1937, when Andre Roch reported he "climbed alone to the summit of Castle Peak … the descent was a series of basins and steps, one more rewarding than the next." Starting in this same period, ski pioneer Otto Schniebs began making ski mountaineering trips to Montezuma Basin and environs. In the spring of 1938 Schniebs organized a crew of three, who staged a virtual military expe-dition to the Castle Peak area of the Elks. First, the locals assisted by dynamiting avalanche debris off the approach road so the skiers could drive to snow closure. Then the expedition spent 13 days moving 1,600 pounds of supplies (including fresh eggs and movie cameras) 12 miles to an old cabin at timberline below Castle Peak, where Schniebs set up his base of opera-tions. (This cabin would later burn, to be replaced by the Tagert Hut, a popular mod-ern destination for ski mountaineers.)

Schniebs and his friends hammered the Elks for a month. They skied from high

on Castle Peak several times, then enjoyed climbs and descents on dozens of orbit peaks. Heading east, they made an early ascent of 13,521-foot Star Peak via a tech-nical snow route. The crew cut turns on every skiable slope they could reach, and enjoyed the classic high traverse over Pearl Pass toward Crested Butte.

Castle Peak reigned over a dormant land for the next several decades. World War II passed by, then the skiing at nearby Aspen was developed. In the early 1960s, an Aspen lodge owner named Rick Richards bought land in Montezuma Basin and installed a small ski tow for a summer ski training camp. Richards would plow the Montezuma jeep trail every June, then ski with his groups on into summer. Legend holds that the first summit descent of Castle was done by a young racer attending one of the ski camps, via the upper East Ridge and a couloir on the North Face, the classic route described below.

To the west of Castle Peak, a wilderness hot spring soothes weary skiers, Michael Kennedy and Graeme Means. *Louis Dawson*

For Castle Peak, start from the town of Aspen on Highway 82. A short distance out of Aspen turn off to Castle Creek and Maroon Creek roads. Take an immediate left onto the Castle Creek Road, and drive 12 miles to its end. Park at the start of the Pearl Pass Jeep Trail, indicated on the right (west) side of the road by a sign board and four-wheel-drive sign. With a high clearance vehicle you can continue .7 miles to parking below a rough hill that's obvious four-wheel-drive terrain. With a 4x4 vehicle, you can continue up the Jeep Trail to snow closure, parking at almost 13,000 feet near Montezuma Glacier. Assuming you park at the beginning of the Pearl Pass Jeep Trail, travel on foot up the Jeep Trail 3¼ miles to another fork, where the Montezuma Road continues into Montezuma Basin. Climb the basin to 12,800 feet, then head up snow slopes of the Montezuma Glacier to Castle Peak's North Face. Climb the obvious couloir up the left (east) side of the face. From the top of the couloir, follow the ridge to the summit. Descend your ascent route. With good snow cover, it's possible to glisse from the exact summit, down the summit ridge to the notch at the head of the couloir, then down the couloir.

Start: Two-wheel-drive parking, 9,800 feet

Summit: 14,265 feet

Vertical gain: 4,465 feet

Round trip distance and time: 11 hours, 10 miles

Ascent: Advanced

Glisse: Advanced on glacier, Extreme from summit

Map: USGS 7.5 minute, Hayden Peak, Pearl Pass

Guidebook: *Dawson's Guide to Colorado's Fourteeners, Volume 1,* Louis Dawson

Weather: Ski Montezuma Glacier during the spring and summer snow season, from early May through July. See other routes in this chapter for weather information.

Red Tape: None

Skiing early summer corn snow in Montezuma Basin. *Louis Dawson*

Hayden Peak—Sawyer Creek

Most skiers have heard of Aspen. Now an elite playground for the wealthy, the area's ski mountains have humble beginnings: rich history with an underpinning of ski mountaineering in Aspen's local alps. One such mountain is Ski Hayden Peak, located in the Elk Mountains.

It's amazing how close Ski Hayden came to being Aspen's developed ski mountain. In the late 1930s, just before World War II, a group of private investors (Tom Flynn, Billy Fisk, Ted Ryan, and others) formed the Highland Bavarian Corporation to build a ski area near Aspen. Ryan had met Fisk at a bobsled race, and gained a great respect for Fisk's aplomb and athletic ability. The two had commiserated over having to "spend ten days in a boat to go downhill skiing," and then had determined to search the U.S. for the best spot to build a European-style ski area. During his subsequent travels, Fisk met a man trying to sell silver mine shares in Aspen, traveled to the town, and got his first look at the Elk Mountains. He returned to Ryan with photos of "country above the timber, like Davos, Switzerland." Fisk and Ryan moved to Aspen and built Highland Bavarian Lodge on nearby Castle Creek, at the base of a massif known as Mount Hayden.

The investors hired famed French mountaineer and ski area engineer Andre Roch as a consultant. Roch and his assistant Gunther Lange surveyed the area, and they named Ski Hayden Peak (one of three Hayden summits) as the best ski mountain in the area. The men knew Averell Harriman was spending a million dollars building his hotel at Sun Valley, and Fisk envisioned one-upping Harriman by spending "a million dollars on the tramway alone." Interestingly, the group had also worked out gov-

Hayden Peak highest in center, Hayden Peak's North Summit to right. The route takes the obvious face. *Michael Kennedy*

ernment financing. But World War II intervened. Fisk died in the war and the efforts of the corporation fizzled, to be replaced later by another group who developed the brush-covered ridge behind Aspen, now known as Aspen Mountain—a far cry from the ski mountain the Hayden Massif was then, and continues to be, for those who earn their turns the hard way.

Andre Roch's companions from the Los Alamos Ranch School, on the first ski descent of Hayden Peak, 1937.
Aspen Historical Society

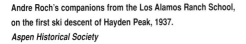

Drive Highway 82 west out of Aspen for Hayden Peak. A short distance out of town you will see the well-signed turnoff to Castle Creek and Maroon Creek roads. Take a hard left onto the Castle Creek Road. Drive 8 miles to a slightly widened shoulder on the road. The correct trailhead is not obvious, but may be identified by a good view of Hayden's North Summit.

The ascent route generally follows the Sawyer Creek drainage. At the parking area you'll be about ⅛ mile downvalley from the Sawyer Creek-Castle Creek confluence. Ski a short distance down and cross Castle Creek. You may find a log crossing or snowbridge. Once on the west side of Castle Creek, follow a marked trail southwest on an easement across private property, then intersect an obvious roadcut. Follow the old road as it leads up the Sawyer Creek drainage, crosses the creek at 9,480 feet, then ends at a flat area (9,600 feet). Bear left and find a more obscure trail leading to the base of a narrow gulch. Stay out of the gulch by crossing to the right, then continue climbing with the gulch on your left. Continue up the drainage to an area where the timber thins just below timberline—the Lunch Spot (11,300 feet). The steep Stammberger Face is above to the south. Swing west, climb the rib between the Twin Gullies, and continue up the huge bowl and face to the North Summit. Descend your ascent route.

Start: Castle Creek Road, 9,000 feet
Summit: 13,316 feet
Vertical gain: 4,300 feet
Round trip distance and time: 10 miles, 9 hours
Ascent: Intermediate
Glisse: Advanced
Map: USGS 7.5 minute, Hayden Peak
Guidebook: *Colorado High Routes*, Louis Dawson

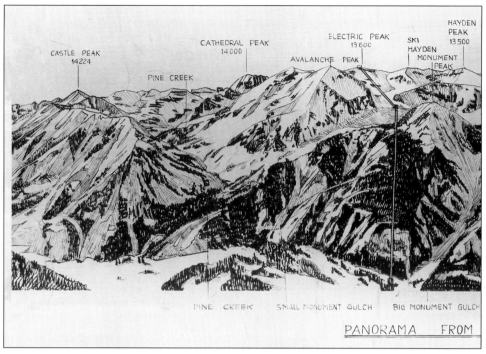

Andre Roch's design for the most far-sighted ski area in North America. Fortunately for glisse alpinists, it was never built.

First ski descent: Andre Roch and Los Alamos Ranch School students, 1937
Weather: The best forecast for the Aspen area is NOAA weather radio broadcast from the city of Grand Junction. Traditionally, Ski Hayden is skied in winter. Such adventures require astute avalanche hazard evaluation. Skiing on the peak is safer in spring.
Red Tape: The easement across private land was created specifically for skiers. While skiing the easement (first ¼ mile of the route), stay on the trail and move quickly and quietly.

Mount Sopris— Thomas Lakes Bowl

Drive Interstate 70 to the town of Glenwood Springs, then head up the Roaring Fork Valley toward the town of Carbondale. If you're in a car full of glisse alpinists be prepared to pull over. Rising before you will be colossal Mount Sopris, western bastion of the Elk Mountains (see preceding Castle Peak description), and one of Colorado's most tempting ski descents. Sopris is not a fourteener. It's not even a thirteener. Nonetheless, in a vertical thrust seldom seen in western Colorado, Sopris

rises 6,000 vertical feet from the Crystal River Valley in just three miles. Five glorious cirques radiate from its double topped-crown: two summits 1½ miles apart and both 12,953 feet high.

While the names of many Colorado summits have boring or mundane histories, Sopris is an exception. The peak is named after Richard Sopris (1813-1893), one of Colorado's early explorers. Sopris was born in Pennsylvania and migrated west in 1858 with the gold boomers. In spring of 1860 Sopris organized a group of 15 gold prospectors to explore west of the "Snowy

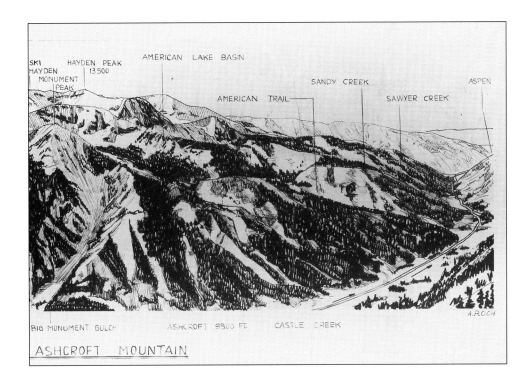

SKI HAYDEN PEAK
HAYDEN 13500
MONUMENT
PEAK

AMERICAN LAKE BASIN

SANDY CREEK

AMERICAN TRAIL

SAWYER CREEK

ASPEN

A. ROCH

BIG MONUMENT GULCH

ASHCROFT 9500 FT.

CASTLE CREEK

ASHCROFT MOUNTAIN

Mount Sopris from the Crystal River Valley. Thomas Lakes Bowl is buried in ridges to far left. *Louis Dawson*

Range," the huge barrier of the Continental Divide west of Denver. The crew took a roundabout route, eventually traveling over the hills south from the Vail area to the Roaring Fork Valley, then to the base of the stunning mountain they named Sopris Peak. The journey wasn't over. They headed downvalley and discovered the famed Glenwood Hot Springs, then spent several months swinging through southern Colorado. While the Sopris expedition didn't find gold, they helped make the first functional map of Colorado. Richard Sopris went on to a life of farming and politics in the Denver area.

Mount Sopris is easy to climb. The recorded ascent was made in 1873 by Dr. Albert Peale and other Hayden Survey workers, and it was doubtless climbed by Native Americans before then. During the Elks' mining boom of the mid 1800s, the area around Mount Sopris was the district's bread basket. During this time a network of roads developed around the north side of the peak, with one track ascending to Thomas Lakes, a pair of tarns at 10,200 feet. In the 1950s and 1960s, spring skiers such as Aspenite Bil Dunaway jeeped to Thomas Lakes and skied Mount Sopris. The Thomas Lakes Road was closed to summer vehicle traffic in the 1970s, although it's still open to snowmobiles up to the wilderness boundary at Thomas Lakes. While the road closure was a disappointment to older skiers such as Dunaway, Sopris skiing is still popular among glisse alpinists in the Roaring Fork Valley, and is approached on foot as well as snowmobile via the old road.

For Sopris, drive Highway 82 for 22 miles upvalley (southeast) from Glenwood Springs or downvalley (northwest) 18 miles from Aspen to the Emma townsite. Turn south at obvious signs indicating "Emma Road and Sopris Creek Road," then take an immediate left (east) on the Sopris Creek Road. Drive 1.1 miles to a T intersection, then turn right on the West Sopris Creek Road. Drive 5.3 miles to a parking area (winter closure) at a switchback below Prince Creek Divide. During spring snow season the road may be open another .5 mile to the Prince Creek Divide (8,110 feet). At the Prince Creek Divide, take a left (south) on the Dinkle Lake Road (Forest Service Road 6A), and follow the Dinkle Lake Road 2.1 miles to obvious parking on another divide (8,640 feet); this is the late spring and summer trailhead, Dinkle Lake Divide. Take the old Jeep trail, climbing the northern flanks of Mount Sopris 4 miles to Thomas Lakes. From the west side of the upper (eastern) lake, climb the left (south) side of the obvious bowl. At 11,100 feet, trend to the right and climb a final wide couloir to a small bowl. Continue up to the major saddle (12,300 feet) between the lower East Summit and the East Main Summit. Take the wide East Ridge ½ mile northwest to the East Main Summit. Descend your ascent route, or drop into the bowl from a point a few hundred yards down the ridge from the summit.

Start: Dinkle Lake Divide, 8,640 feet

Summit: 12,953 feet

Vertical gain: 4,313 feet

Round trip distance and time: 12 miles, 10 hours

Ascent: Intermediate

Glisse: Advanced

Maps: USGS 7.5 minute, Mount Sopris, Basalt

Skiing on Mount Sopris. *Louis Dawson*

Guidebook: *Colorado High Routes,* Louis Dawson
First ascent: Dr. Albert Peale and other Hayden Survey workers, 1873
Weather: As with most Colorado mountains, skiing on Sopris is best in spring after the snow has compacted and the access road opens up, usually after late April. For weather reports, use the NOAA weather radio broadcast from Grand Junction, Colorado.
Red Tape: The upper reaches of Mount Sopris lie in legal wilderness, with the boundary following the southern shore of lower Thomas Lake (marked on the USGS Mount Sopris quadrangle map)

Mount Elbert—Box Creek Cirque

The highest peak in Colorado happens to be one of the best glisse peaks in Colorado. Mount Elbert (14,433 feet, the second highest peak in contiguous U.S.) is a wide peak with skiable terrain on every flank. The west side of the peak offers several 3,000-vertical-foot chutes, while the east side yields a variety of gentle terrain mixed with a few steep drops, and provides the classic descent covered here.

Mount Elbert's first recorded ski descent was made in 1941 via the east side, by John Ambler, Whitney Borland and friends. Ambler's crew had stopped in Leadville for dinner. Upon leaving the restaurant, the group noticed the full moon lighting a tempting path up the peak. Forthwith, they made a night climb and ski. "The ascent was beautiful," wrote Ambler in *Trail and Timberline*, "as the moonlight, in addition to providing almost perfect visibility, added an unearthly charm. After about

Mount Elbert from the northeast. Box Creek Cirque directly below summit. *Louis Dawson*

seven hours of climbing ... we reached the summit just as the sun was rising over the Mosquito Range. It seemed as if we were in another world, completely remote from anything familiar. The valleys on all sides remained dark, while the mountain tops appeared glowing as if aflame. In the west, where the moon was setting, we could see the shadow of Mount Elbert in the sky. A flying descent on skis, through powder snow on a firm base, down a 4,000-foot drop, marked the finale of this perfect trip."

The following is the easiest and hence most popular way to ski Mount Elbert. Other fine routes exist, and are detailed in regional guidebooks. Drive Colorado Highway 82 to the small town of Twin Lakes. Drive east from Twin Lakes on Highway 82, and at 2.4 miles turn left (north) onto County Road 24. Continue on Road 24 to Lakeview Campground. Follow signs in the campground for the Mount Elbert Trailhead at the northwest end of the campground.

From parking at the trailhead, hike the Colorado Trail (marked with small white triangles) as it follows a Jeep trail. At 2 miles the road becomes a foot trail, crosses a creek, then follows an easy grade ⅛ mile to a fork with good signs. Take the indicated Mount Elbert Trail up Elbert's broad eastern flanks. At snowline use your map to stay on the summer trail. Glisse your ascent route, with logical variations such as the steeper Box Creek Cirque north of the ascent ridge.

Start: 9,600 feet
Summit: 14,433 feet
Vertical gain: 4,833 feet
Round trip distance and time: 10 hours, 11¼ miles
Ascent: Intermediate
Glisse: Intermediate, Box Creek Cirque is Advanced
Maps: USGS 7.5 minute, Mount Elbert, Leadville South
Guidebook: *Dawson's Guide to Colorado's Fourteeners, Volume 1*, Louis Dawson
First ascent: Prospectors, mid 1800s
First ski descent of peak and route: John Ambler, Whitney Borland and several others, 1941
Weather: Use NOAA weather radio, and local news media for weather reports
Red Tape: None

Humboldt Peak—Southeast Flank

Steep, dry, remote—extraordinary in their beauty. These words do scant justice to the Sangre de Cristo Mountains. Spanish missionaries, so the story goes, saw alpenglow ignite the summits and named the range for the "Blood of Christ." First seen by explorers in the late 1600s, the Sangres were the first mountains of Colorado known to the Europeans.

Bivouacking at 14,433 feet, the summit of Colorado's highpoint, Mount Elbert. Looking south at the summits of the Sawatch Range. *Louis Dawson*

As a mountain range, the Sangres form a clean 120-mile spine snaking south from Salida, Colorado, to the foothills above Santa Fe, New Mexico. The Colorado section of the range is the highest, and contains the state's most southerly fourteeners. Bordered on the east by the irrigated ranch lands of the Wet Mountain Valley, and on the west by the vast San Luis Valley (including the huge sand mountains of the Great Sand Dunes National Monument), the Sangre fourteeners are divided into two subgroups: the Sierra Blanca to the south and the Crestones to the north. The jagged summits of Crestone Peak and Crestone Needle have awed mountaineers for years. In contrast to the easy skiing and climbing on the "humps" of Colorado's Front Range and Sawatch Mountains, climbers in the Crestones find they must occasionally do enjoyable hand-and-foot climbing on the range's steep and mostly solid rock. For the same reasons that the climbing is good, the skiing is limited. The exception is the classic Southeast Flank of 14,064 foot Humboldt Peak, used by Howie and Mike Fitz, and Bob Pfeiffer, for the first descent in 1983.

In 1978 Pfeiffer and the Fitzes skied their first fourteener, Mount Massive. They decided to make a try for them all, and nailed several every spring for nine years. In 1987, with their count up to 45, the group ran out of steam. Pfeiffer, a father of three—and then six after triplets—was less than enthusiastic about skiing peaks such as Pyramid (they'd left the most dangerous for last),

Fourteener ski pioneers Bob Pfeiffer, Mike Fitz, Howie Fitz (L to R), sitting below the south side of Humboldt Peak. They skied 45 of the 54 fourteeners, and pioneered many new routes. *Louis Dawson*

and Howie Fitz's knees were shot from a lifetime of turns. Mike Fitz could have gone on and finished the project, but he'd made a vow to ski the peaks with his crew. Before their effort fizzled Pfeiffer and the Fitzes made several notable first descents. One fourteener, Kit Carson Mountain in the Sangre de Cristo, appeared to have no ski-able line. The crew hired an airplane for a bird's view and discovered a unique hidden couloir, which in 1987 they skied from the summit. As for Humboldt Peak, the obvious stripe of snow on the Southeast Flank lured the trio like thoughts of gold lured the Spanish conquistadors. In 1983, they climbed the route in a "constant 60-mph wind," then "skied off the slope on perfect snow … 2,800 feet at a constant pitch."

Drive Highway 96 or 69 to the small town of Westcliffe outside of Humboldt Peak. From the main street take the well-signed turn south onto Highway 69. Drive 69 for 4½ miles to the well signed Colfax Lane (County 119). Turn onto Colfax and drive 6 miles south on Colfax to a T intersection. This is the snowplow turn-around in the winter. In spring and summer, take a right (west) on to the well signed South Colony Lakes Road (County 120). All but the lowest-slung cars can make it up about 3 miles to two-wheel-drive parking (9,600 feet). From this point, any short-wheel-base 4x4, driven well, can handle the track.

In mid May, snow closure is around 9,500 feet, or somewhat higher after a light winter (inquire locally). The road is well used by snowmobiles in the winter, as well as by a snowcat that travels the road once a month to measure the snowpack water content. In the winter, it's common for climbers to get a pull from local snowmobilers.

Depending on snow coverage, walk, drive, or ski to 10,880 feet on the South Colony Road (section introduction), head north through dense timber, working up then gradually east to intersect a drainage with an intermittent stream. Follow the snow-filled stream course, then obvious slopes, to the summit. Descend your ascent route.

Start: 9,600 feet

Summit: 14,064 feet

Vertical gain: 4,464 feet

Round trip distance and time: 8 hours, 11 miles

Ascent: Intermediate

Glisse: Advanced

Maps: USGS 7.5 minute, Crestone, Beck Mountain

Guidebook: *Dawson's Guide to Colorado's Fourteeners, Volume II,* Louis Dawson

First ascent of peak: Government surveyor Momsen, 1883

First ski descent of peak and route: Howie and Mike Fitz and Bob Pfeiffer, 1983

Weather: The Sangres are dry, and far enough south to have a noticeably higher timberline and earlier spring than central and northern Colorado. As early as March, snow climbers and skiers may find a firm melt-freeze snowpack on all but northern exposures. Useful weather reports for the Sangres are hard to get. Use general weather maps and air-mass reports from weather television, and draw your own conclusions.

Red Tape: None

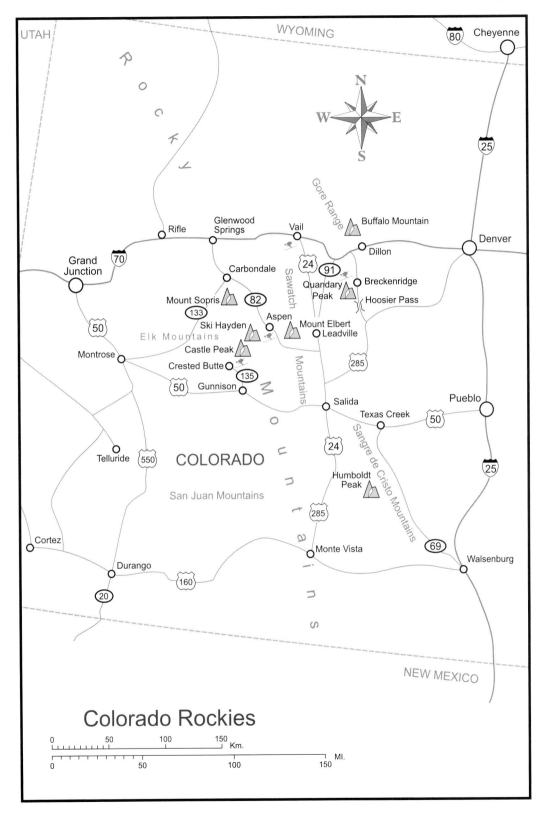

Colorado Rockies

CLASSIC BY DEFINITION:
MOUNTAINS OF THE NORTHEAST

Classic by Definition:
Mountains of the Northeast

The pioneer European ski mountaineers were a group of Norwegians and Englishmen who in 1884 tackled the Brocken in Germany's Harz Mountains. North American ski alpinism developed behind Europe; but it was hardly as backward as common wisdom holds. About two decades after the Brocken got skied, the first North American ski alpinists tackled the mountains of the northeastern United States.

Where are these Northeastern peaks? New England locals bounce odd alpine names around like a hockey puck, but the widespread Northeastern mountain ranges can thoroughly confuse an outsider. The mountain ranges of the region are all parts of the great Appalachian range, which runs more than 1,600 miles south from Quebec to Alabama. Somewhat attached to the Appalachians, but by some definitions part of the Laurentian Mountains, are the Adirondacks. The true Appalachians are east of the Adirondacks, and hold such favorite subranges as the White, Blue and Green Mountains, and the Taconic Range. Farther north in the Appalachians, Katahdin is another magnet for the backcountry crowd.

Irving Langmuir was the first of the ski pioneers to explore these Northeastern mountains. As a teenager Langmuir spent time in Europe and fell in love with the mountains. He then did his graduate studies in Germany, where he began a lifelong devotion to skiing; and where he no doubt learned his glisse from the source—the masters of arlberg technique.

After school in Europe, he moved to Schenectady, New York, to work for General Electric as a chemist (he would later win a Nobel Prize for chemistry). By the winter of 1906–7, nostalgic for the alpine reaches of Europe, Langmuir was visiting every Northeastern mountain he could. In February of 1907 he skied Wittenberg Mountain in the Catskill Mountains of New York State; this was probably the first intentional mountain descent on the continent. The next winter he skied Mount Greylock in the Taconic Range of Massachusetts, another first on a classic mountain.

Langmuir out-skied and out-climbed most people he partnered with, until in 1910 he met outdoorsman John Apperson. With a few tips from Langmuir, Apperson took to skiing like a moose to water. At least as hardy as Langmuir, Apperson may have actually surpassed him in devotion to mountaineering. The pair attacked the Northeastern highlands with seldom-equaled verve and enthusiasm. In 1911, John Apperson, Jean Canivet and another man headed for the Adirondacks, and did the probable first ski of Mount Marcy. In 1920, Apperson made the first ski descent of nearby Haystack with Langmuir and another local legend named Jackrabbit Johannsen. Seven years later, Apperson was the first skier on Basin and Saddleback Mountains. No doubt Apperson would have been credited with scores of other firsts if he'd bothered to record his trips, but he disliked publicity.

In 1904, while Apperson and Langmuir were just starting their lives as Northeastern outdoorsman, an Adirondack mountain

◄ Mount Washington, Tuckerman Ravine. Note the skiers dwarfed by the bowl's immensity. *Bradford Washburn*

resort known as the Lake Placid Club stayed open for its first winter season. The club promoted sports such as sledding and ice skating—and imported 40 pairs of Norwegian skis. This was the first true ski resort in North America. Moreover, most of the skiing done out of the Lake Placid Club was accomplished in fine backcountry style: the skiers climbed for their vertical, and enjoyed wilderness travel as much as socializing around the club fireplace.

Soon, fraternal skiers were frequenting the Lake Placid Club. A group from the influential Appalachian Mountain Club (AMC) visited in 1908 and regularly after that. A few years later, a flock of enthusiasts formed a ski club called the Sno-Birds. Hundreds participated. In 1915, a Norwegian by the name of Herman Smith Johannsen joined up, and New England skiing would never be the same.

Herman "Jackrabbit" Johannsen was born in 1875 in Norway. He emigrated to the U.S. in 1899, and made skiing wild snow the focus of his life in North America. From 1915 to 1928 Jackrabbit lived in the Lake Placid area and skied the region more than anyone else at the time. During his first winter there he skied several routes on Mount Marcy, and enjoyed many ski trips on Whiteface Mountain. The master skier loved carrying a light pack and covering

Skiing with fur coat at the Lake Placid Club, 1933.
Appalachian Mountain Club

distance, often bivouacking with little more than a fire. By traveling with such efficiency he made many long traverses, and was the first to ski many remote mountains. Most importantly, Jackrabbit's skill as a skier and his commitment to outdoorsmanship gave Lake Placid locals the impetus to explore higher and farther on their planks.

In 1920, the inevitable happened when Irving Langmuir and John Apperson teamed up with Jackrabbit for a ski assault on Haystack Mountain (4,960 feet) in the Adirondacks. Though Haystack is now graced with ski lifts, getting up the mountain in the 1920s was an expedition. Donning crampons for the last few hundred feet, Jackrabbit and Apperson left their companions and reached the summit as the moon rose over Giant, a nearby high Adirondack peak.

Jackrabbit aged well and ski toured into his 100th year. As an octogenarian, he'd ski in front of the thousands of racers crowded at the starting gates of the famed Birkebeiner—presumably to tout the life enhancing effects the participants would soon endure. Throughout the 1960s and early 1970s, Jackrabbit's renown was also furthered by his eponymous ski wax, which came about as close to a universal formulation as anyone has ever achieved. As Jackrabbit explained to writer Sally Moore:

> Skiing is a means of getting health and happiness if it's used the right way. Learn to live in the wilderness. Use the canoe in summer and skis in winter. Travel way back in the bush—the wilderness—on trails made by the animals. Make a campsite every night and build a fire. Have embers for cooking in the morning. Take a snow bath in front of the fire, and set out for another campsite. That's the way to live!

Besides the Lake Placid skiers, several other clubs cemented the foundation of Northeastern backcountry skiing. The first was formed in 1882 in Berlin, New Hamp-

Northeast legend Jackrabbit Johannsen lived to 111 years old, and enjoyed backcountry skiing for a century.
Whyte Museum of the Canadian Rockies

shire (at the heart of the White Mountains), eventually taking the name "Nansen Ski Club" after the famed Norwegian skier and explorer (see History chapter). The Nansen group were ski jumpers, membership was initially limited to "Scandinavians," and they did little mountain skiing. Interestingly, in 1912, a few years before Jackrabbit Johannsen started his legendary skiing, Nansen visited Lake Placid (perhaps having a ski club named after him made the visit mandatory). He taught technique to the locals and skied Whiteface Mountain with his daughter; if not the first ski of Whiteface, this certainly was one of the earliest.

By 1896, students at Dartmouth College in New Hampshire had began to wonder why they spent winters in their "stuffy" rooms playing cards, while a white wonderland waited outside their doors. The air must have indeed been foul, because "general sluggishness" continued to rule for the next decade at Dartmouth—until freshman Fred Harris showed up with his skis in 1907.

Harris had become a refined skier by practicing near his home in Vermont. He was also an innovator. Not content with skis of the day, he considered ideas such as fat skis in his diary, and acted on such problems as boot-sole edges dragging during

turns: "Today I cut my shoes because my feet project out over the sides."

During his first two years at Dartmouth, Harris skied by himself. Those must have been lonely times for the young man, since he regarded skiing as a social sport. By 1909 Harris was fed up with solitude and wrote a letter to the school newspaper proposing a club for "out-of-door winter sports." Thus, through the vision of Fred Harris the Dartmouth Outing Club (DOC) was born.

The DOC began with 60 members, and is still a major and influential New England outdoors institution. Mountain skiing came naturally to the young adventurous men of the club—their trips ranged from frigid epics on Mount Washington to fun antics on the lower hills of the New England ranges.

The Dartmouth Outing Club's debut in pioneer ski mountaineering happened in 1913, when Fred Harris (as a graduate) led 16 DOC members to the top of Mount Washington. While most of the climbers hiked to the top, Harris and two others kept their boards on their feet, thus becoming the first people to ski to the summit. No doubt they skied most, if not all the way down, and thus made the first ski descent as well. Other firsts were ski ascents and descents of Moosilauke Peak and Mount Monadnock in the White Mountains by DOC president Carl Shumway and companions. In 1914, Mount Mansfield in the Green Mountains (a hulking timber-covered ridge and Vermont's highpoint) saw it's debut ski descent, also done by a DOC member.

Throughout his days with the DOC Fred Harris was a tireless promoter of skiing. Traveling on snowshoes was then and continues to be popular in the Northeast, and there was no small amount of rivalry between the 'shoe crowd and the skiers. Harris would say "if snowshoeing be the prose, then skiing is the poetry of winter."

As far as skis were concerned, in 1927 the snowshoe versus ski debate reached its darkest hour. Two groups climbed Haystack: one on snowshoes and the other on planks. The snowshoe crowd beat the skiers back to camp by almost six hours! Apparently, even though Irving Langmuir and John Apperson ramrodded the skiers, their long boards were defeated by dense timber and difficult snow. On subsequent trips snowshoes continued to rule. Indeed, a definitive guidebook of the time stated "snowshoes are still the only practical means of travel where trails are steep and narrow."

The tide turned somewhat when, in 1930, a group using snowshoes and skis climbed Mount Marcy via a gradual route. The skiers aced the 'shoers by several hours. A year later, skis proved their mettle again when famed mountaineer Fritz Wiessner and German alpinist Milana Jank made a winter ski traverse of the northern Presidential Range, including mounts: Washington, Clay, Jefferson, Adams, and Mount Madison. Jank had recently completed a 146-day ski traverse of the Alps, ending on the summit of Mount Blanc, but she took the smaller New England challenge seriously, "for the mountains are very destructive, … there were days with devastating winter storms. Impenetrable was the blowing, drifting snow."

Even with the examples set by the likes of such as Milana Jank, Fritz Wiessner, and Fred Harris, from the 1930s to the late 1960s skis took second fiddle to snowshoes for Northeastern mountaineering. The ski gear and technique of the day only worked for exceptional athletes, while snowshoes worked for everyone. The important part of all this was that mountain sports such as skiing, snowshoeing and even "bare booting" all became entrenched in Northeastern culture. Thousands of people now enjoyed wild snow, and the scene was primed for resort skiing, and eventually backcountry glisse, to take off.

At first, without mechanized uphill travel, backcountry skiing and "downhill" skiing at Northeastern "ski areas" blended almost seamlessly. As they did elsewhere on the continent, skiers would climb for just a few runs each day, but what runs they were. Even then, for many skiers the thrill of a downhill run was their *raison d'être*. In the AMC *Bulletin* of 1930, an introduction to a lengthy list of ski trails stated: "For the benefit of the ever-increasing number of ski enthusiasts … who have conquered nearby golf links and yearn for real hill or mountain skiing, the following has been compiled."

They wanted vertical, and they'd get it any way they could. In a mutation somewhat unique to the Northeast, since they didn't have many natural open areas such as those of the high Rocky Mountains, New England skiers took to cutting steep narrow trails that plunged like Olympic luge runs down the region's timbered hills. This was the time of the Great Depression, and by 1933 the Civilian Conservation Core (CCC) was employing millions of jobless depression victims in "conservation" related projects such as trail building, reforestation—and cutting Northeastern ski trails. The harder trails, often designed by the best skiers of the day, plunged and twisted like organic couloirs, with room to turn sometimes measured in inches. Still other hand-hewn runs were easier to ski, and quite beautiful. Known as "walk-up" trails, all these runs were designed to be climbed up and skied down. Dozens of trails were completed. In the Adirondack Mountains, for example, the 1937 Adirondack Mountain Club bulletin included a map and detailed descriptions to a number of beautiful trails on mountains such as Marcy, Nye and Jo. Presently, many of the best trails have grown in (a process that only takes about 25 years), but both formal and informal efforts are made to cut brush from the more popular runs. If such limited maintenance can stay ahead of nature remains to be seen.

Mount Mansfield was perhaps the area most shaped by the 1930s trail cutters. Indeed, local guidebook author David Goodman suggests that "much of the history of skiing … in New England can be found in the history of the [Mount Mansfield] ski trails." Mansfield trail hacking started in 1933, when a crowd of CCC workers led by State Forester Perry Merrill cut the famed Bruce Trail, an intense drop of 2,600 vertical feet on the southeast side of the mountain. Soon, skiers in love with the Bruce Trail were designing and cutting more runs on the mountain, such as Nose Dive and Teardrop.

Another impetus in Mansfield trail cutting was a lumberman and skier named Craig Burt, who's known as the father of Stowe, the large Northeastern ski resort now located on Mount Mansfield. Burt enjoyed scrounging around the woods on his planks, often using the excuse of going hunting, but usually coming home with an empty bag. After completing his logging operations on Mansfield, Burt would have his workers do extra cutting to create better skiing. Much of the improved terrain from the 1930s was incorporated into the present day Stowe ski area and several ski touring centers (including the Trapp Family Lodge, famed for its *Sound of Music* ambiance).

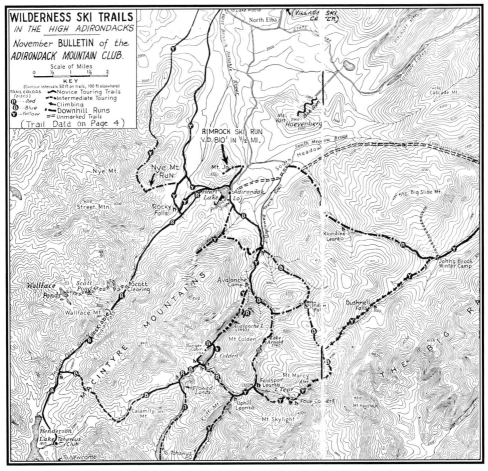

An amazing array of ski trails were hacked through the Northeast bramble. This 1937 map details many (notice Mount Marcy near bottom.). *Adirondack Mountain Club*

One place with plentiful natural ski terrain, (yet still receiving trail improvements from the CCC crews), was Tuckerman Ravine. A huge glacial cirque on the southeast side of New Hampshire's Mount Washington, Tuckerman (also known as Tuckerman's, but usually written without the possessive) is known for its deep snow and steep walls. Dropping more than 1,000 feet, the pitch reaches more than 50 degrees at the lip of the famous Headwall, a steep transition in the upper part of the cirque.

By today's standards of liability and safety paranoia, an amazing thing happened in Tuckerman Ravine for several years in the late 1930s: there was a ski race. Known as the Inferno, this contest epitomized the tough, crazed, aggressive skiing of the era—a raw athleticism that makes today's media-hyped "extreme" snow sports look like family dining. Nothing less than the first extreme skiing competition in history, the Inferno had no gates and allowed competitors to pick their own route down the precipitous headwall. "We just started the clock when they left the summit [of the mountain] and stopped it when they showed up at the swinging bridge," says organizer Joe Dodge in his biography. Dodge, a legendary curmudgeon who managed the AMC

A 1931 Northeastern stylist. *Appalachian Mountain Club*

hut system for many years, recalls many stories of the wildmen who ran the Inferno, from a drunken racer who passed out before he finished the course, to honed speedsters bent on going supersonic. Toni Matt was one of the latter.

During the last of the Inferno races, on a windy day in 1939, Toni Matt stood atop Mount Washington, poled over the lip of the headwall, then dropped into the Inferno. The next thing he knew he was skipping the turns, and broke 80 mph on a run now legendary in North American skiing. He won the race of, course—by 6½ minutes. In Matt's words:

> I ran as straight as I could, trying to get into Tuckerman Ravine. … I figured I'm gonna make three or four turns over the lip itself and on into Tuckerman Ravine. And before I knew it, I dropped over the lip and there wasn't any *sense* in turning; it wouldn't slow me down anyway! I decided it's much safer to go straight than to go by turning on this kind of pitch and I was stupid enough and strong enough to be able to stand up. … It wasn't completely an accident because I planned to make turns. I just forgot how—really! …Going over the lip is a terrifying experience, especially for the first time. It's like jumping into a 600-foot-deep hole from a speeding car. … I figure I hit 85 miles per hour.

Aside from the tradition of skiing Tuckerman, which persisted after the last Inferno, Northeastern ski mountaineering was somewhat dormant throughout the war years and into the early 1960s. Snowshoes continued to be the eastern alpinist's choice tool, and mechanized skiing became a ubiquitous distraction for would-be ski mountaineers. Indeed, during part of this era the AMC's publication *Appalachia* even devoted pages to describing the latest ski resort developments—hardly the style of a wilderness lover's almanac!

Archly termed the "second coming of the ski" by historians Guy and Laura Waterman, a huge increase in Northeastern back-country skiing occurred in the late 1960s and early 1970s. As was happening in the rest of North America, this was caused mostly by a change in values. Overall inter-est in backcountry recreation was growing, and with it the desire to adventure ski. In the Northeast, improved gear and (perhaps more importantly) improved technique allowed these new adventure skiers to take their skis into tight trees and brush: previ-ously the province of a select few. What's more, highly motivated outdoors people who'd been enjoying "cross-lot" Nordic skiing began to experiment with downhill skiing on their free-heel gear. Soon these adventurers were able to combine fiberglass skis and improved technique in a blend which allowed them to climb and ski the New England peaks without ski lifts. While this new generation of eastern skiers had mostly rediscovered the wonders enjoyed by Langmuir, Harris and Jackrabbit, they also had a fresh vision. The Appalachian moun-tains were the stage for their dream.

At first, even with their strong motiva-tion and practiced technique, the Northeast's "second coming" skiers did better going up than coming down, especially those experi-menting with Nordic skis. They spent a lot of time side-stepping, snowplowing, and just plain "survival skiing" on (or "in") the brush-choked down-mountain trails of their ances-tors. Indeed, if powder snow defines western skiing, vegetation defines that of the North-eastern mountains. Back in 1928, Terris Moore skied the region and suggested tying ropes around your skis instead of using climb-ing skins because "upon the final steep grades, a roped ski will catch and hold branches." When David Goodman authored the area's definitive backcountry ski guide 60 years later, his sage advice included the warning that "eye protection for skiing through trees or on hiking trails … is essential."

Yet despite, or because of, the desper-ate brush, the new breed quickly improved their skills. Many learned to ski downhill on lightweight Nordic gear, while others were content to haul alpine equipment. Whatever their choice in tools, by the early 1980s Northeastern backcountry skiers were descending terrain formerly considered impossible. They nailed all the skiable slopes in the Adirondack Mountains, and whipped Mount Washington into submis-sion by skiing virtually every line on its massive bulk. On Katahdin, in the Maine Appalachians, ski instructors and outdoors-men Mike Perry, Rick Poulin, Larry Smith and Eric Wright made the expedition style approach to Chimney Pond in 1980 and repeated Arthur Comey's descent of Baxter Peak (see Katahdin section). During the same trip, they were the first to ski several steeper couloirs rising from Chimney Pond to the saddle north of Baxter's summit.

As in the early days of Appalachian wild snow, many skiers of the 1980s era were also accomplished mountaineers. Climber Geoff Smith was at the forefront of a group who called themselves the Ski-to-Die Club, coining that famous phrase in the process. Expert climber-cum-skiers such as Michael Hartrich, John Imbrie, and seasoned climber Andy Tuthill led the charge in the White Mountains.

Present day snowboarding and skiing in the Northeastern backcountry is a popular and accessible sport. In 1986, Dick Hall, Winslow Ayer, Gary Faucher, Roger Simmerman and Dean Mendell skied one of the region's finest extreme lines when they nailed Katahdin's Chimney Couloir (a riven slot dropping between Baxter and Pamola Peak). The region got a fine guidebook in 1989 when David Goodman's *Classic Back-country Skiing* was published. On Mount Washington, Tuckerman Ravine continues to be an amazing spring carnival. Aspirants from all over the region attack peaks such as Greylock, and steeper couloirs such as those on Katahdin are seeing exciting glisse.

The Northeastern mountains are accessible, possess great natural beauty, and they have snow. What more does a glisse alpinist need? "These hills of the Northeast have been and will be unfailingly interesting," write Guy and Laura Waterman in *Forest and Crag*, their definitive history of the region. "Certainly they are small— absurdly small to be called mountains in comparisons with the world's great ranges. But that smallness gives them the intimate connection to people ... the hills of the Northeast ... are available to all who respond to the natural world."

Katahdin—Baxter Peak

Katahdin means "great mountain" in indigenous tongue (so the word is used here without "Peak" or "Mountain"). At 5,267 feet Katahdin is the highest point in Maine and the seventh highest in New England. The mountain lives up to its name, and belies the common notion of small Northeastern peaks. In full majesty worthy of any great alp, Katahdin rises 4,500 feet above its southern foot. The top stretches along a four-mile wind-beaten ridge topped with highpoints: the North Summits (two), Hamlin Peak, Baxter Peak, South Peak, Pamola Peak, and Chimney Peak. Baxter Peak is the highest and thus Katahdin's true summit.

Katahdin was first climbed in 1804 by a survey party. Winter climbs were uneventful, the first probably done in 1887. The mountain had an active logging operation at the time, which helped keep the roads opened, thus making the ascent somewhat a stroll compared to other New England winter struggles. When the lumber camps closed in the 1920s Katahdin became a winter

objective with challenge equal to its size. It became necessary to launch a mini-expedition just to approach the peak, and only a few alpinists succeeded in winter. A man named Arthur Comey was one of these elite.

In 1923, an AMC splinter group spent a raucous week climbing and skiing at Crawford Notch in lodging known as the "Bemis Place." Hence known as the Bemis Crew, the group would meet every winter for a major outing—usually covering an amazing amount of ground. During one week long adventure, several group members climbed 20,000 vertical feet! Organized like a ship's crew, with shouts of "breakers ahead," they'd switch leaders in deep snow and jam ahead through everything the Appalachians could throw at them.

The Bemis was a tight crew. One member drove a repair truck to the outings with everything needed to fix the somewhat flimsy gear of the day. Both sexes participated. The women included Irving Langmuir's niece Ruth Langmuir, pioneer rock climber Marjorie Hurd, and Florence Luscomb, a "perennial champion of feminist causes and all other causes." The male contingent was equally forceful, with famed alpinists, guidebook writers and all-round endurance athletes contributing an enthusiasm for alpinism that's been seldom equaled and never surpassed. Yet even among these enthusiasts Arthur Comey was an exception.

By profession an urban planner and by avocation a consummate ski mountaineer, Arthur Comey was "one of the most tireless and innovative Northeastern climbers of the 1920s," write Guy and Laura Waterman. Comey organized numerous AMC ski trips, and even co-authored one of North America's first backcountry ski how-to books. He also promoted lightweight travel, extolling the virtues of a 10 pound pack—a lighter load than most people would carry today, using modern gear 70 years later. Comey

Hardman Arthur Comey atop Baxter Peak, ready to launch the first ski descent of Katahdin in 1927. *Appalachian Mountain Club*

Looking north from the summit of Katahdin during the second ski descent in 1928. *Appalachian Mountain Club*

was also the Bemis Crew bad boy. In his writings he mentioned skiing dressed only in his boots and beret. No matter what people thought of skiing naked in the 1920s, admitting to it in writing was certainly risqué! Possessed of a legendary temper, Comey would "almost literally bare his teeth," when he blew his top. "Get him at a party … he might throw the watermelon," remembered one Bemis alumni.

Because of his harsh personality Comey was "black listed" from many Bemis outings; no doubt this became fuel for his already raging fire. He spent almost every winter weekend mountaineering. During one three-year stint when he kept records, Comey logged 1,115 miles on his planks! He tirelessly promoted skiing through the AMC, and led numerous ski trips that no doubt contributed to the sport's popularity. Comey's tough workmanlike skiing was legendary. Guy and Laura Waterman wrote that the hardman skied "through krummholz, over rocky ridges—even up fire ladders."

By 1926 Katahdin had become an attractive winter haunt for tougher New England skiers, and Arthur Comey was the upstart who cut the biggest piece of the Great Mountain. That year Katahdin veteran and Bemis Crew charter member Willard Helburn organized yet another Katahdin trip. This time, aside from the usual Bemis Crew epic of massive vertical "at lightning speed in a cloud of snow," Robert Underhill and Comey decided to ski to the top of Baxter Peak, Katahdin's highest summit (apparently the Bemis blacklist was suspended at the time). Underhill switched to crampons just before the summit, but Comey used his skis for the whole climb, then most probably skied down, thus making the first ski of Katahdin.

The next year, Comey invited AMC members on another Katahdin trip with an understated blurb in the AMC *Bulletin*: "This trip adapted to anyone with some experience skiing up and down … and with reasonable endurance." A year later, in 1929, he published an article about Katahdin in *Appalachia*: "Long diagonal traverses linked by slow but sharp Christiania turns permit slow running, particularly when the ground is a bit bumpy. The Saddle gained, if the snow on the steep slide is not too hard the greatest thrill comes when one dips the ski-points over the rim … and then, if the runner is a bit tired and not particularly expert, he will probably use the "Sitz-Telemark" turn, said to have been invented by Professor Sitz for just such occasions."

Skiing on Katahdin is still an expedition. Your first goal is Baxter State Park. In northern Maine, drive to Baxter Park by taking Interstate 95 and exiting at Medway. Continue west on Highway 157 to the city of Millinocket. From Millinocket, follow obvious signs to Baxter State Park and drive 14 miles from Millinocket to parking on Golden Road near River and Compass Ponds.

From parking, make a flat 10-mile slog approach along the snow-covered Roaring Brook Road to basecamp at Roaring Brook Campground (1,500 feet). This can usually be done in one day, but allow for slow going in case the snow is bad. From Roaring Brook Campground, climb west 3 miles and 1,400 vertical feet to the famed Chimney Pond

Mount Katahdin. Baxter Peak is highpoint, with Chimney Pond below. *David Hiser*

(2,914 feet), a small lake at the base of numerous steep couloirs. Comey's ski route (about 2 miles) goes from the Pond up west through the Great Basin, crests a huge saddle, then continues south to the Baxter Peak. Wind-scoured areas may prevent a complete ski ascent and descent. You'll find steeper and possibly more reliable descents in the couloirs rising from Chimney Pond and South Basin. With good snow-cover, some couloirs may connect from near the summit. Return to civilization via your approach route.

Start: Golden Road, 530 feet

Summit: 5,267 feet

Vertical gain: 4,737 feet

Round trip distance and time: 30 miles, multiday

Ascent: Advanced

Glisse: Advanced

Maps: Appalachian Mountain Club, Baxter State Park

Guidebook: *Classic Backcountry Skiing*, David Goodman

First ski descent of peak and route: Arthur Comey, 1926

Weather: Winter weather on Katahdin may be slightly milder than the legendary wind on Mount Washington. Even so, be prepared for arctic conditions. The best time for ski-ing on Katahdin is late winter to early spring, depending on the snow accumulation.

Red Tape: Baxter State Park has an entrenched bureaucracy, and you must register for backcountry recreation in the park. Do so well in advance (at least a month), by contacting Baxter State Park (see Directory).

Mount Washington—
Tuckerman Ravine

First climbed in a remarkable effort by Darby Field and several Indian guides in 1642, in "terrible freesing weather [sic]," Mount Washington has garnered a cloak of legend unlike any other mountain in North America. First ascensionist Field was probably looking for riches, perhaps of the mineral variety. He didn't reap but a few mica crystals. Yet since Field's day, Mount Washington has provided virtually infinite recreational treasure. Starting in 1803, what was probably the first mountain guiding in the United States was practiced on Mount Washington. Inaugurating a tradition of Appalachian hard-bodies which continues to this day, one guide and mountain man was described as "capable of lifting 500 pounds, wrestling bears, and carrying tourists up the last part of the trail."

At 6,288 feet, Mount Washington is the highest peak in the Northeast, and the third highest mountain in eastern North America. A carriage road was built to the summit in 1861, later replaced by an auto road. Though it's closed to cars in winter, the road provided an easy route for Mount Washington's first skiers in 1913: Fred Harris and 16 other Dartmouth Outing Club skiers. Harris and two others kept their skis on for the whole trip up and back.

Weather is Mount Washington's bane—winter on the peak can be as harsh as anywhere on the planet. Killer gales screech like howling banshees across the frozen summit tundra. But such winds are a plus for skiers. The gales scour the broad summit cone, and dump much of that snow into the vast glacial cirque of Tuckerman Ravine. Even during "dry" years, by springtime Tuckerman will boast a snowpack at least 60-feet deep.

While Mount Washington is laced with dozens of excellent ski routes, Tuckerman Ravine is the most popular. Tuckerman was first skied by hut manager Joe Dodge and his friends in 1926. Word soon spread about the Ravine's phenomenal spring skiing. By 1930, with a plowed road now providing access to the lower trailheads, the Appalachian Mountain Club was organizing ski trips to Tuckerman, and in 1931 two

Early skiing on Mount Clay, circa 1940, looking at the Mount Washington summit cone. *Winston Pote*

On skis near Mount Washington's summit, circa 1940. *Appalachian Mountain Club*

Dartmouth skiers became the first to ski the complete run, including the steep headwall. In the early days a harsh bushwhack into the cirque kept all but the most committed skiers away. Then, in 1932 a hiking trail was cut from Pinkham Notch to the cirque, and more skiers came. A few years later the Sherburne Trail was built. This connected more directly to Pinkham Notch, thus providing a continuous easy trail to Tuckerman Ravine, and a sometimes skiable drop of up to 4,250 vertical feet. Ski trains brought thousands of skiers to the Appalachian high country that same year, and many made Tuckerman their goal. During this period the famous Inferno races were held (described p. 216), and the more obvious lines in the cirque were skied.

In the winter 1931, photographer Winston Pote, Joe Dodge and several others spent a few weeks living at Mount Washington's summit. They did a small amount of pioneer skiing, but harsh weather and other priorities limited their time on skis. Based on the group's experience, Dodge made a proposal to the New Hampshire Academy of Science to establish and man a weather observatory on the summit. The plan was approved, and a group of men spent the winter of 1932–33 living on the apex making scientific observations. One of the scientists, Bob Monahan, spent time skiing much of the terrain around the summit. The observatory has remained an active project and has contributed much to weather research over the years. On April 12, 1934, the highest land-based wind measurement ever recorded was made at the Mount Washington summit observatory: 231 miles per hour!

Over the next few years, Winston Pote and his friends, often based at the summit observatory, did much skiing on Mount Washington and in the surrounding Presidential peaks. In 1940 Pote organized a trip with "four top skiers ready to take advantage of the excellent snowcover—a dream come true," as he wrote in his book *Mount Washington in Winter*. To prepare, Pote left supplies at the Mount Washington summit and at the base of Mount Adams. The trip went well, and Pote published the resulting photographs in his book. The vast terrain in the pictures, viewed from such lofty stances as Mount Adams and Mount Jefferson, appears as a skier's paradise. The subsequent popularity of skiing on Mount Washington, at least in spring, owes its beginnings to Pote and his friends.

Possibly the man who pioneered the greatest number of extreme routes in Tuckerman was Joe Dodge's son Brooks, a fabulous skier who raced at both the 1952 and 1956 Olympic Games. Brooks skied at least 10 radical routes in the cirque, including the Lion's Head gullies and the Icefall, a route descending the center of the Headwall, and which guidebook author David Goodman suggests "has apparently been skied one other time," (though more descents may have recently been made).

Presently, spring glisse in Tuckerman Ravine is nothing less than a backcountry carnival. Thousands of people visit, with spring weekends resembling a stadium

A modern crowd below Tuckerman Ravine at the Caretaker's Shelter. *Dick Hall/NATO*

concert rather than a mountaineering experience. Many snowboarders and skiers tackle the Headwall. Some spend their stay sun bathing—others partying. Still others frolic with innertubes or sleds. It's wild, raucous, and crowded. Not a peaceful venue, but as one local explains, "the Tucks experience without the people wouldn't be the Tucks experience. It's a mountain festival. It's people enjoying themselves, indulging themselves in springtime in the mountains: a wilderness extravaganza ski trip."

For Mount Washington, drive Highway 16 in New Hampshire to Pinkham Notch Camp. From parking, take the Tuckerman Ravine Trail 2½ miles to the base of the cirque at the Hermit Lake shelters. The route up the headwall is obvious. Spring weekends are crowded; winter weekdays are quiet.

Start: Pinkham Notch Camp, 2,000 feet
Summit: 6,288 feet
Vertical gain: 4,288 feet
Round trip distance and time: About 5 miles for Tuckerman Ravine, several more miles for summit. Plan a full day for summit; the Ravine is often skied without summiting.
Ascent: Advanced
Glisse: Advanced to Extreme, depending on exact route and snow conditions
Map: Appalachian Mountain Club, Mount Washington
Guidebook: *Classic Backcountry Skiing*, David Goodman
First ski descent of route: John Carleton and Charlie Proctor, 1931
First ski descent of peak: Fred Harris and two companions, 1913
Weather: Be prepared for some of the worst weather in the world. Reports are available through local television (weather forecasts are broadcast from the summit) and radio.
Red Tape: Hermit Lake shelters are limited and require reservations. You're better off staying in a motel or roadside campground.

Mount Marcy—Adirondack Loj

The Adirondack Mountains are the Northeast's most wild range. The State Park south of here is the largest in the lower forty-eight. The area's highest peak, Mount Marcy (5,344 feet), was first climbed more than a century after the peaks in other ranges were seeing regular visitors. Mount Washington, for example, was climbed a full 195 years before the first known ascent of Mount Marcy.

Winter sports followed the same pattern. Other Northeast ranges had better access and more lodges, and winter climbing was not the recreation of the masses. The first winter ascent of Marcy was done in 1893, with subsequent ascents few and far between for the next decade. Many of the other Northeastern peaks saw plentiful winter activity well before that year.

Marcy was first skied in 1911 by hard-core John Apperson (see this chapter's beginning), Jean Canivet and one other mountaineer. The skiers used an old trail built 30 years before by the legendary mountain man Henry Van Hoevenberg (who also built the Adirondack Loj at the base of the peak).

Change came in the winter of 1945, with the opening of the Lake Placid Club for winter sports (see chapter introduction). The Appalachian Mountain Club first visited the Lake Placid Club in the winter of 1908, climbed Marcy, and subsequently brought hundreds of winter recreationists to the Adirondacks. As skiing gained favor, many of the climbers eschewed the more common snowshoes for footwear of the sliding variety.

As an indicator of how popular skiing on Mount Marcy became, starting in 1927 an outdoorswoman named Fay Loope led numerous YMCA ski ascents of the mountain. The skiers wanted to share their fun, so their club newsletter advertised guided ski

The Mount Marcy summit cone. *Dick Hall/NATO*

Marcy is just high enough to get you above the Northeastern vegetables. *Dick Hall/NATO*

trips on Marcy—perhaps the first guided ski mountaineering in North America.

In 1932, ski fever hit Lake Placid when the area hosted the United States' first winter Olympics. Having the best skiers in the world show up on their doorsteps was no doubt an exciting event for Lake Placid's local sliders. One such citizen, the famed Jackrabbit Johannsen (see "Classic by Definition" Introduction), deigned to guide the visitors on a favorite tour. For starters, he took the world-class athletes on a one-day ski that normally took four days. As they skied by Mount Marcy on the last leg of their anaerobic jaunt, the local legend suggested they ski to the summit—more than 2,000 vertical feet up the Van Hoevenberg Trail. The gauntlet was down. Could these famous athletes return home and admit they'd not risen to the local's challenge—especially when the local was twice their age? No way. The crew reached the summit at dusk, then made a moonlight ski descent of Marcy down to Adirondack Loj.

For Mount Marcy, drive to Lake Placid, located on Highway 86 in northern New York. From Lake Placid, drive Route 73 and Heart Lake Road to parking at Adirondack Loj. From the lodge, follow the trail to the summit snowdome. Several small headwalls and bowls provide interesting glisse near the summit, while plentiful low-angled terrain yields a mellow route back down to treeline and the long trail back to the Adirondack Loj.

Start: Adirondack Loj, 1,844 feet
Summit: 5,344 feet
Vertical gain: 3,500 feet
Round trip distance and time: 15 miles, 8 hours

Ascent: Novice

Glisse: Intermediate with good snow, Advanced with ice

Map: Trails of the Adirondack High Peak Region, Adirondack Mountain Club (see Directory)

Guidebook: *Northern Adirondack Ski Tours*, Tony Goodwin

First ski descent of route and peak: John Apperson, Jean Canivet and another, 1911

Weather: Mid to late winter and spring are the best times to ski or snowboard on Mount Marcy. In winter, be prepared for arctic conditions. Use local television and radio for weather reports.

Red Tape: A parking fee may be required

Mount Greylock—The Thunderbolt

The huge wooded hump of Mount Greylock (3,487 feet) is the highest peak in Massachusetts. It was climbed in the early days by such notables as Henry David Thoreau, who was warned by R. W. Emerson of a "serious mountain." Until this time mountains were still regarded more as painful obstacles than objects of beauty or recreation. If any event signifies the change in thinking to our modern view of mountains, it's Thoreau's 1844 climb of Greylock. He ended up bivouacking under an old door from a shack, but rather than blaming the peak for an uncomfortable or even dangerous experience, he found inspiration while observing a sublime dawn from his summit bivvy.

Greylock still shows the creativity and vision of local outdoors people and the Civilian Conservation Corps (CCC) trail cutters. From the early days, the peak had several roads gracing its flanks. In 1830 a group of Williams College students cut the "Hopper Trail" from a road terminus to the summit. They started a trend. By the 1930s the CCC had cut several beautiful ski trails on Greylock—perhaps the most sublime being the Thunderbolt.

Ski fanatic Charlie Parker designed the Thunderbolt as a "Class A ski racing trail." Which in plain English meant the route had to be steep and long. Racing on

The summit of Greylock is quite civilized, but the amenities are closed in winter. *S/Z Marketing* the Thunderbolt was a backcountry venture. The snow was not groomed (though the racers did what they could to improve the surface), and you walked to the top. Then you turned around and schussed 2,500 vertical feet; if you were "class A" you did it in three minutes! Today's backcountry skiers might take it a little slower, but the criteria for cutting ski trails in the 1930s makes for a fine ski trail no matter how fast you slide. As Goodman wrote in *Classic Backcountry Skiing*: "It is an exhilarating steep run that will keep you swooping through turns throughout its entire length."

Drive Route 8 in northwestern Massachusetts to the town of Adams to reach Mount Greylock. From the center of Adams, drive west on Maple Street then take a left on West Road. After .4 mile on West Road, turn right on unmarked Gould Road, which heads toward Greylock and an abandoned ski area. Turn right off Gould Road onto Thiel Road, and park at snow closure. Head up snow-covered Thiel Road for ¾ mile, then swing left, cross a meadow, and take a vague trail through timber to the start of the Thunderbolt proper. Ascend the steep Thunderbolt to intersect the Appalachian Trail (AT) at 3,100 feet on Greylock's North Ridge. Follow the AT to the summit and descend your ascent route. The racers of old started from the top of the peak—for the classic run do the same.

Start: Thiel Road, 1,200 feet
Summit: 3,487 feet
Vertical gain: 2,287 feet
Round trip distance and time: 2 miles, 4 hours
Ascent: Novice
Glisse: Advanced
Map: New England Cartographics, Mount Greylock
Guidebook: *Classic Backcountry Skiing*, David Goodman
First ski descent of peak: Irving Langmuir, 1908
First ski descent of route: Racers of the 1930s
Weather: Skiing on lower New England peaks such as Greylock may vary from non-existent to sublime, all based on the winter's snowfall. Thus, according to locals the season for skiing Greylock is "any time it has enough snow to ski!" That's usually from January to April. Use local television and radio for weather reports.
Red Tape: None

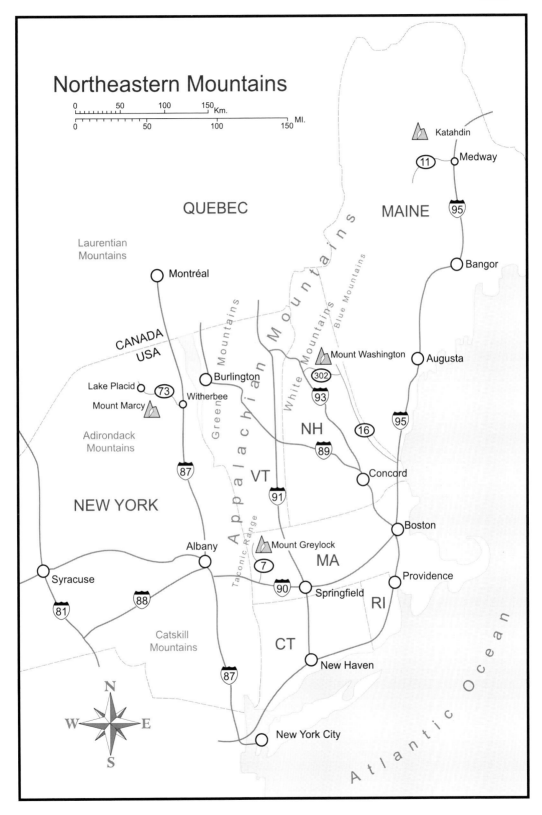

Northeastern Mountains

Katahdin

Medway

11

95

QUEBEC

MAINE

Laurentian
Mountains

Montréal

Bangor

CANADA
USA

Mount Washington

Augusta

Lake Placid

Burlington

73

Witherbee

302

93

Mount Marcy

16

95

Adirondack
Mountains

NH

89

87

VT

Concord

91

NEW YORK

Boston

Albany

Mount Greylock

Syracuse

7

MA

Providence

88

90

Springfield

81

RI

Catskill
Mountains

CT

New Haven

87

Atlantic Ocean

N
W   E
S

New York City

Greenen Mountains

Green Mountains

White Mountains

Blue Mountains

Appalachian Mountains

Taconic Range

0   50   100   150 Km.
0   50   100   150 MI.

APPENDIX

Appendix: Directory

Alaska

Chugach National Forest, Glacier District: 907-783-3242

Talkeetna Ranger Station, Denali National Park: 907-733-2231

Public Lands Information Center (maps and information): 907-271-2738

Anchorage Convention and Visitors Bureau: 907-276-4118

Anchorage Nordic Club: 907-561-0949

Hatcher Pass snowcats: 907-373-3118

Canada

Alpine Club of Canada: 403-678-3200

Banff weather: 403-762-2088

Canadian Map Office: 615 Booth St., Ottawa, Ontario, Canada, K1A 0E9

Yoho National Park: 604-343-6324

Mount Robson Provincial Park: 604-566-4325

Glacier National Park: 604-837-6274

Garibaldi Provincial Park: 604-898-3678

Berg Lake helicopter transport: 604-566-4700

Cascades

Mount St. Helens National Volcanic Monument: 360-750-3961

Mount Baker National Forest: 206-220-7450

Mount Baker Ski Area: 360-734-6771

Mount Rainier—Paradise Ranger Station: 360-569-2211

Mount Adams—Trout Lake Ranger Station: 509-395-3400

Mount Hood National Forest: 503-667-0511

Timberline Lodge: 503-272-3311

Colorado

10th Mountain Hut Association: 970-925-5775

Colorado Mountain Club: 303-477-6343

Mount Logan

Kluane National Park: 403-634-7250

Mount Shasta

Fifth Season ski shop: 916-926-3606

Fifth Season 24-hour report: 916-926-5555

Mount Shasta Ranger District: 916-926-4511

Local information: Wonderland Association, 916-243-2643

Tahoe Sierra

Alpine Meadows ski conditions: 916-581-8374

Tahoe National Forest: 916-573-2674

Tahoe area road information: 800-427-7623

High Sierra

Inyo National Forest, Mount Whitney Ranger District: 619-876-6200

San Gabriel and San Bernardino Mountains

San Antonio Hut, Los Angeles Sierra Club: 213-387-4287

New England

Baxter State Park: 207-723-5140

Appalachian Mountain Club (AMC): 617-523-0636

New England Cartographics: 413-549-4124

North American Telemark Organization (NATO): 802-496-4387

Mount Washington Observatory: 603-356-8345

Tetons

Weather phone: 307-733-1731

Grand Teton National Park: 307-733-2880

Grand Targhee National Forest: 208-624-3151

Exum Guides: 307-733-2297

Signal Mountain Lodge Marina: 307-543-2831

AAC Grand Teton Climbers Ranch: 307-733-7271

Utah

Wasatch-Cache National Forest: 801-524-5030

Wasatch avalanche information: 801-364-1581

General

Trails Illustrated Maps: 1-800-962-1643

Selected Bibliography

Barnett, Steve. The Best Ski Touring in America. Sierra Club Books, 1987 (out of print).

Beck, David. Ski Touring In California. Pika Press, 1980 (out of print).

Beckey, Fred. Cascade Alpine Guide. Volumes 1 and 2. Mountaineers Books, 1987.

Beckey, Fred. Challenge of the North Cascades. Mountaineers Books, 1969.

Bernbaum, Edwin. Sacred Mountains of the World. Sierra Club Books, 1990.

Bueler, William. Roof of the Rockies. Pruett Publishing, 1974.

Burhenne, H.J. Sierra Spring Ski Touring. Mountain Press, 1971 (out of print).

Burton, Hal. The Ski Troops. Simon and Schuster, 1971 (out of print).

Cliff, Peter. Ski Mountaineering. Pacific Search Press, 1987.

Corcoran, Thom. Mount St. Helens. KC Publications, 1985.

Dawson, Louis. Colorado 10th Mountain Trails. WHO Press, 1991.

Dawson, Louis. Colorado High Routes. Mountaineers Books, 1987 (out of print).

Dawson, Louis. Dawson's Guide to Colorado's Fourteeners: Volume 1, The Northern Peaks. Blue Clover Press, 1995.

Dawson, Louis. Dawson's Guide to Colorado's Fourteeners: Volume 2, The Southern Peaks. Blue Clover Press, 1996.

Dyer, John Lewis. The Snow-Shoe Itinerant. Cranston and Stowe, 1891.

Farquhar, Francis. History of the Sierra Nevada. University of California Press, 1966.

Fay, Abbott. Ski Tracks in the Rockies. Cordillera Press, 1984.

Goodwin, Tony. Classic Adirondack Ski Tours. Adirondack Mountain Club, 1994.

Hart, John L. Jerome. Fourteen Thousand Feet. Colorado Mountain Club, 1971 (out of print).

Jay, John. Ski Down the Years. Award House, 1966 (out of print).

Johannsen, Alice E. The Legendary Jackrabbit Johannsen. McGill-Queens University Press, 1993.

Kelner, Alexis. Skiing in Utah: A History. Author published, 1980.

Kelsey, Michael. Climbing and Exploring Mount Timpanogos. Kelsey Publishing, 1989.

LaChapelle, Dolores. Deep Powder Snow. Kivaki Press, 1993.

LaChapelle, Edward R. The ABC's of Avalanche Safety. Second Edition. Mountaineers Books, 1985.

Lavender, David Sievert. One Man's West. Doubleday, 1956.

Leigh N. Ortenburger and Reynold G. Jackson. A Climber's Guide To The Teton Range. Third Edition. Mountaineers Books, 1996.

Lev, Peter (with Ed LaChapelle and Liam Fitzgerald). Snow Avalanche Atlas, Little Cottonwood Canyon U-210. Utah Department of Transportation, 1987.

◄ A ski alpinist ponders the future. *Louis Dawson*

Litz, Brian and Kurt Lankford. Skiing Colorado's Backcountry. Fulcrum Press, 1989.

Lund, Morten, ed. The Ski Book. Arbor House, 1982.

Lund, Morten and Bob Laurie. Skier's Paradise. G.P. Putnam's Sons, 1967 (out of print).

Lunn, Arnold. The Mountains of Youth. Eyre and Spottiswoode, 1925 (out of print).

Miura, Yuichiro and Perlman, Eric. The Man Who Skied Down Everest. Harper and Row, 1978 (out of print).

Molenaar, Dee. The Challenge of Rainier. Mountaineers Books, 1979.

Moynier, John. Backcountry Skiing in the High Sierra. Chockstone Press, 1992.

Munday, Don. The Unknown Mountain. Mountaineers Books, 1975.

Nansen, Fridtjof. Farthest North. Volumes 1 & 2. Harper, 1897 (out of print).

Nelson and Potterfield. Selected Climbs in the Cascades. Mountaineers Books, 1993.

Pennington, Janice. Husband, Lover, Spy. St. Martin's Press, 1994.

Perla, Ronald and M. Martinelli. Avalanche Handbook. U.S. Department of Agriculture #489, 1976.

Peters, Ed, ed. Mountaineering: The Freedom of the Hills. Mountaineers Books, 1991.

Pote, Winston. Mount Washington in Winter. Down East Books, 1985 (out of print).

Putnam, William Lowell. Joe Dodge. Phoenix Publishing, 1986.

Richards, Rick. Ski Pioneers: The Making of Taos Ski Valley. Dry Gulch Publishing, 1992.

Roper, Steve and Allen Steck. Fifty Classic Climbs. Sierra Club Books, 1996.

Schniebs, Otto. American Skiing. E. P. Dutton, 1939 (out of print).

Scofield, Bruce. High Peaks of the Northeast. New England Cartographics, 1993.

Secor, R.J.. The High Sierra: Peaks, Passes and Trails. Mountaineers Books, 1992.

Selters, Andy and Michael Zanger. The Mount Shasta Book. Wilderness Press, 1995.

Sinclair, Pete. We Aspired: The Last Innocent Americans. Utah State University Press, 1993.

Smith, Carolyn, ed. Alaska Almanac. Alaska Northwest Books, 1994.

Tejada-Flores, Lito. Backcountry Skiing. Sierra Club Books, 1981.

Turiano, Thomas. Teton Skiing: A History and Guide. Homestead Publishing, 1995.

Tweed, William. Shorty Lovelace, Kings Canyon Fur Trapper. Sequoia Natural History Association, 1980 (out of print).

Vielbig, Klindt. Cross-Country Ski Routes of Oregon's Cascades. Mountaineers Books, 1985.

Waterman, Guy and Laura. Forest and Crag. Appalachian Mountain Club, 1989.

Waterman, Jonathan. High Alaska: A Historical Guide to Denali, Foraker and Hunter. American Alpine Club Press, 1996.

Waterman, Jonathan. In the Shadow of Denali. Doubleday, 1993.

Waterman, Jonathan. Surviving Denali: A Study of Accidents on Mount McKinley 1903-1990. American Alpine Club Press, 1996.

Watters, Ron. Ski Camping. Solstice Press/Chronicle Books, 1979.

Weamer, Howard. The Perfect Art: The Ostrander Hut & Ski Touring in Yosemite. Author published, 1995.

Williams, Knox and Betsy Armstrong. The Avalanche Book. Fulcrum Press, 1986.

Williams, Knox and Betsy Armstrong. The Snowy Torrents: Avalanche Accidents in the United States. Teton Bookshop Publishing, 1984.

Michael Kennedy

Index

Adams, Mount, New Hampshire, 224
Adams, Mount, Cascades, Southwest Chute,
    route description, 69
Adirondack Loj, 225, 226
Adirondack Mountains, 211
Advanced-rated climb, defined, XXX
Advanced-rated glisse route, defined, XXXII
Aemmer Couloir, Mount Temple, 131
Aesthetics, importance of, XXVIII
aircraft, XXVIII, 72, 88, 91, 103, 106, 118,
    121, 208
    photo, 104
Alaska, map, 123
Alaska and Yukon, chapter, 101
Alaska Range, XXVIII, 102, 109, 120
chapter section, 104
Alaskan Railroad, 116
Alaskana, 116
Albizi, Marquis, 126
Alf Engen Ski School, Utah, 168
Alfred Braun Huts, 13, 184, 190
Aloña, Miguel, 181
Alpine Club of Canada (ACC), 6, 10, 85,
    95, 125, 126, 140
Alpine Meadows ski area, California, 33,
    34, 36
alpine touring bindings, 16
Alta ski school, Utah, 165
Alta, Utah
    Dick Durrance invents single dipsy turn,
        165
    Dolores LaChapelle there, 167
    double dipsy turn invented, 165
    early skiing without lifts, 163
    first ski lifts, 164
    first Utah skier avalanche death, 165
    history of ski resort, 164
    invention of modern powder skiing, 165
    mining camps, early skiing, 163
    Mount Superior, 173
    photo, Dick Durrance skiing Alta, 162
    Ski School, 165, 168
    The Alta Start, 166

    The Snakepit, 165
    WWII soldiers train there, 165
Alturas Snow-Shoe Club, 25, 26
Alyeska Ski Resort, Alaska, 101, 103
Alyeska, Mount, Alaska, 112
Ambler, John, 205
American Alpine Club, 147, 148
American Skiing, book, 183
Anchorage Nordic Club, Alaska, 117
Anchorage, Alaska 101, 102, 103, 109, 111,
    112, 113, 114, 116, 117, 120
Andromeda, Mount, Skyladder route, 131
Apocalypse Couloir, Prospectors Mountain,
    154
Appalachian Mountain Club, 13, 26, 212,
    221, 222, 224, 225
Appalachian Mountains. See Northeast
    Mountains chapter
Apperson, John, 225
Apperson, Orr, 81
Arctic Ocean, 112
Argenta Chute, Utah, 170
Argentiere glacier, 8
arlberg technique, 4, 6, 10, 16, 50, 69, 163,
    165, 211
Armadillos, 29, 31
Armstrong, John, 181
Arthur, Paul, 29, 38, 41, 47, 49
Ascent ratings, defined, XXX
Aspen, Colorado, 10, 185
    Bill Briggs in, 149
    skis during mining days, 181
Aspen Mountain ski area, 198
Assiniboine, Mount, Canada, 126
Athabasca Glacier, Alberta, 134, 135, 136,
    137, 138
Athabasca, Mount, 131, 134
Atwell, Mount, British Columbia, 90
Authors Note, XIX
Avalanche Gulch, Mount Shasta, route
    description, 78
avalanches
    at Rogers Pass, British Columbia, 141

Enos Mills story, 182
in Wasatch Mountains, 165
most deadly, 142

backcountry glisse, defined, XXVI
backcountry ski renaissance, Utah, 168
Backcountry Skiing the High Sierra,
guidebook, 21
Backcountry Skiing Washington's Cascades,
guidebook, 63
Baffin Island, 16
Baker, Jim, 181
Baker, Mount, Easton Glacier, Cascades,
route, 61
Baldwin, John, 96
Baldwin, John, guidebook author, 89
Baldy. *See* San Antonio Peak, California
Baldy Chutes, Alta, 166
Balfour Hut, Canada, 15, 127, 138
Ballinger, Wally, 38
Banff, Alberta, 125, 127, 140, 141
Bard, Allan, 25, 32, 47
Barnett, Steve, 18, 59
Bartholomew, Orland, 5, 26, 30, 47
Bates, Bob, 148
Baxter Peak, Katahdin
first descent, 217
first ski descent, 220
photo, 221
route, 218
Baxter State Park, Maine, 220
Beartooth Mountains, XXIX
Beck, Dave, 28, 33
Becker, Brian, 187
Beckey, Fred, 58, 68, 70, 71, 74, 88
Beghin, Pierre, 21, 109
Beloit Wisconsin, 2
Bemis Crew, 218, 220
Bemis Place, 218
Benedict, Fritz 9, 183, 193
Bengston, Kermit, 65
Bennet, Tom, 154
Bennett, Russell H., 135
Berg Lake, Mount Resplendent, 133
Berlin, New Hampshire, 212
Bernard Gouvy, XXVI
Bernese Oberland, Switzerland, 4
Bierstad, Mount, Colorado, 183
Bilgeri, Georg, 4

bindings, 2, 4, 169
cable, 6, 8, 10, 11, 16
first step-in, 10
first safety, 8
Bishop, Barry, 110
Bishop, California, 31, 33, 46, 47
Blackcomb Mountain ski resort, 88
Blanc, Mount , France, first ski descent,
10
Blaurock, Carl, 5, 182, 183
Bloody Mountain, Bloody Couloir,
California, route description, 44
Boivin, Jean-Marc, 19, 152
Bolton, John, 150
Bonneville, Captain Louis, 147
Borkovec, Rick, 184
Borland, Whitney, 205
boundaries, ski resort, 192
Bounous, Junior, 166
Bow Hut, Canada, 127, 139, 140
route desciption, 138
Bradley, Tyson, 21, 106
Bradly Packer Grader, photo, 14
Braun Huts. *See* Alfred Braun Huts
Braun, Alfred, 13, 184, 190
Breckenridge, Colorado, 181, 196
Brennan, Mount, British Columbia, route
description, 143
Brewer, William, 196
Brewster, Norman, 140, 141
Briggs, Bill, 1, 15
first traverse of Bugaboo Mountains,
Canada, 11, 127
on Mount Rainier, 59, 66
profile, 148
first descent of Grand Teton, 150, 151,
187
first descent, Mount Moran, 157
first descent, Middle Teton, 158
photo, 13
Brighton, Utah, 164, 168, 170, 175
British Columbia Mountaineering Club
(BCMC), 88
Brocken Mountain, Germany, 211
Brooks Range, Alaska, 16
Brooks, Samuel, 69
Brower, David, XXI, 26-28
Brown, Roger, 66
Bryce, Mount, photo, 136

Bubble Fun Couloir, Tetons, 154
Buck Mountain, Tetons, 11
    route description, 159
Buffalo Mountain, Colorado, 193
    Silver Couloir, route description, 193
Bugaboo mountains, Canada, 11
    first traverse, 127
Bunny Flat, Mount Shasta, 81
Burgdorfer, Rainer, 63, 68, 70
Burgdorfer, Rainer, guidebook author. *See*
    Cascade route descriptions
Burhenne, H.J., 33
Buzzell, Doug, 184

caches, use for ski traverses, 29, 120, 189
California, chapter, 25
California fourteeners, 31, 33
Camp Hale, Colorado, 8, 183
    photo, 9
Camp Muir, Mount Rainier, Cascades, 67
Canadian Alpine Journal (CAJ), 126
Canadian Coast Mountains
    weather, 92
Canadian Pacific Railroad, 125
Canadian Rocky Mountains
    map, 145
    chapter, 125
Canadian transcontinental railroad, 125
Canivet, Jean, 225
Capitol Peak, Colorado, 186, 191, 192
Carbondale, Colorado, 202
Cardiac Ridge, Utah, 170
Cariboo Mountains, Canada, 86
Carleton, John, 224
Carmichael, Bob, 151
Carpathian Peak, Alaska, 112
Carr, Tom and Jim, 187
Carson Pass, 32
Carter Notch Hut, New Hampshire, 13
Carter, Tom, 32, 47
Cascade Mountains, XXX
    chapter, 57
    weather, 63
Cascade Mountains, map, 83
Castle Peak, California, 31
    photo, 37
Castle Peak, Colorado, 183
Castle Peak, Mountezuma Basin, Colorado,
    route description, 196

Castle Peak, Central Couloir, California,
    route description, 36
CCC, see Civlian Conservation Core
chair lift
    first in Colorado, 183
    world's first at Sun Valley, 7
Chamonix France, 5
Chamonix, France, 152
Chimney Pond, 217, 220, 221
Cho Oyu, Tibet, 185
christiania (christie) turn, 2
Chrzanowski, Peter 89, 131, 132
Chugach Mountains, Alaska, 101-103, 111,
    115, 117
Civilian Conservation Core (CCC), 214,
    215, 216, 227
Clair Tappaan Lodge, 27
Clark, Lewis, 26
Clark, Mount, 28
Clarke, John, 88
classic, definition, XXVII
Classic Backcountry Skiing, guidebook,
    XXIX, 217, 221, 224, 228
cliff jumping, 19
climbing skins, first described, 2
clubs, role in development of ski
    mountaineering, 57
Clyde's Gully, California, 33
Coalpit Gulch, Utah, 175
Coast Mountains of British Columbia
    birth of ski alpinism in, 88
    chapter, 85
    Don and Phyllis Munday, 85
    geography, 85
    map, 99
Coast Ranges, Alaska, defined, 101
Cochetopa Pass, Colorado, 181
Cole's Couloir, Kit Carson Mountain, 192
Coleman, Arthur, 134
Coleman, Edmund, 63
Coleman, Edmund T., 61, 63
Collie, Norman, 134
Colón, Jorge, 154, 160
Colorado map, 209
Colorado fourteeners (14,000 foot peaks).
    See fourteeners
Colorado Grand Tour, 189
Colorado High Routes, guidebook, *see*
    Colorado chapter

Colorado Mountain Club (CMC), 18, 182
Colorado Mountain Club newsletter, 18
Colorado Rockies chapter, 181
Columbia Crest, highest point of Mount
    Rainier, 65
Columbia Icefield, 6, 131, 134, 135, 137,
    138
Columbia, Mount, Alberta, 134, 135
Comey, Arthur, 217, 218, 219, 220, 221
Comici, Emilio, XXVII
commercial alpinism, 132
conservatism, Northwest attitude, 58
Coombs, Doug, 19
    photo, 20
Corbet, Barry, 127, 128, 148, 159, 160
corn snow, XXIX, 21, 25, 36, 53, 148, 176,
    191, 193
Corridor Glacier, Mount Munday, 91
Couloir Magazine, 154, 189
Cowlitz Glacier, Mount Rainier, Cascades, 68
Cox, Chris, 32
crampons, need for, XXX
Crawford Notch, 218
Crested Butte, Colorado, 149, 181, 183,
    189, 190, 198
Crestone Needle, Colorado, 207
Crestone Peak, Colorado, 192, 207
Crestone Peaks, Colorado, 207
Cross Couloir, Mount of the Holy Cross, 187
Cross Country Downhill, book, 18
cross-lot Nordic skiing, 217
Crosson, Mount, Alaska, 109
Cubco bindings, 10
culture, alpine, 126

Dalby, Greg, 184
Dartmouth College, 4, 127, 148, 149, 213,
    222, 223
Dartmouth Outing Club, 148
Davos Switzerland, 167, 200
Dawson, Lou, XXI, XXIV
    photo, 16, 191
    On Colorado Fourteeners, 19, 192
Dawson's Guide to Colorado's Fourteeners,
    guidebook, *see* Colorado chapter
Deadly Bells, Colorado, 187
death
    Boomer McClure on Matterhorn, 151
    cliff jumping, 21

first North American extreme skier, 21
first North American skiers by avalanche,
    181
first U.S. skier to die in avalanche, 181
in definition of extreme skiing, 189
Jackrabbit Johannsen, 21
Koven & Carpe on Denali, 105
race with an avalanche, 165
ski racers, 65
Trevor Petersen in Europe, 90
Vallencant and Boivin, 21
valley of, XXVIII
yearly avalanche, 165
Denali, Alaska, 101
    aircraft on, 103
    as only one of many peaks, 101
    best season for glisse, 110
    Chris Landry fall, 108
    circumnavigation on skis, 16
    coldest temperature recorded, 105
    Erling Strom on, 6
    first ascent, 102
    first complete ski descent, 15
    first ski descent, 106
    first skiers on, 103
    Koven & Carpé on, XXVII, 105
    location, 102
    Messner Couloir, 109
    movies, 105
    Muldrow Glacier, 103
    name origin, XIX
    photos, 104,110
    repeat of Strom trip, 106
    skis out of favor, 106
    style of ski descent, XXVII
    Sylvain Saudan on, 109
    West Buttress route, 104
    West Buttress route description, 109
    West Rib, 108
    Wickersham Wall, 106
    Wickersham Wall descent, 21
    see also Mount McKinley
Denver, Colorado, 9, 15, 190, 193, 204
development
    10th Mountain Division veterans role in, 9
    European glisse alpinism, 19
    in Utah, 170
    lured backcountry skiers, 27
    Mineral King, California, 28

of ski resorts, 27
role of war in, 8
skiers employed by, 27
Devils Cleaver, California, photo, 24
Diamond Peak, Chugach Mountains, 101
Dicky, William, XIX
Diller Canyon, Mount Shasta, 80
Disney, Walt, 28
Dodge, Brooks, 224
Dodge, Joe, 216, 222, 223, 224
dog sledding, 3, 102, 103, 118
used for Glacier Circle Cabin, 141
Donner Pass, 33
Donner Skiway, 27
Donner Summit, California, 26, 27, 54
Douglas, David, 134
Dryer, Thomas, 72, 74
Dunaway, Bil, 66, 183, 186, 187, 204
first descent of Mount Blanc, France, 10
photo, 12
Durrance, Dick, 162, 165
Dyer, Father John, 2, 3, 181
Dylan, Bob, 149

Easter, Dick, 59
Easton Glacier, Mount Baker, Cascades, 61
Eaton, Earl, 193
87th Mountain Regiment, 8
El Capitan, ski descent. *See* Rick Sylvester
El Diente Peak, Colorado, 192
Elbert, Mount, Box Creek Cirque, Colorado,
route, 205
Elderberry Canyon, Mount Tom, 29
route description, 46
Eldorado Peak, Cascades, 58, 60
Elk Mountains, Colorado, 182-196, 200, 202
Emerson, R. W., 227
Emmons Glacier, Mount Rainier, Cascades,
65, 67
route description, 63
Engen, Alf and Sverre, 165, 166, 168
environmental movement, 28
environmentalism, 167, 28
equipment fetishism, 17
Ericsson, Leif, 2, 125
Erikson, Stein, 148
Ervin, William, 5, 182
ethics, XXV, 125
Europa ski, 16

Europe, XXVI, 2, 3, 4,
ethics of skiing there, XXVI
first extreme skiing, 8
golden age of climbing, 2
guides from, 126
Irving Langmuir brings skiing from, 4
mountaineering ski races, 65
powder skiing learned from Utah skiers,
166
powder skiing there, 163
skiers come U. S. to develop ski industry,
27
start of modern exreme skiing, 11
powder skiing learned from Utah skiers,
166
Evans, Mount, Colorado, 183
Everest, Mount, XXV, 47
ski descents, 21
expedition skiing, 15
extreme, word overused, 19
extreme climb, defined, XXX
extreme skiing
first, 8
first paid in North America, 152
championships, 101
media coverage of, 19
Extreme-rated glisse route, defined, XXXII
Exum Guides, Wyoming, 64, 127, 147, 149

Fairy Meadow Hut, Canada, 15, 127
fall
Briggs on Grand Teton, 151
Chris Landry on Denali, 189
recorded on film, 15
Stammberger on North Maroon Peak, 187
Steve Shea in Tetons, 152
see also death
Fall Line, ski movie, 152
Farney, Dave, XXIV
Fessenden, Bruce, 31
Field, Darby, 222
Field, Mount, 140, 141
figle, XIX, 49
first descent, defined, XXVI
first North American ski alpinists, 211
Fisk, Billy, 200
Fitz, Howie and Mike, 207, 208
Flattop Mountain, Alaska, 102, 112, 113
route description, 113

Flynn, Tom, 200
Foraker, Mount, Alaska, XXVIII, 21
    first ski descent, 109
    Sultana Ridge ski descent, photo, XXIX
Ford Couloir, Grand Teton, 154
    used for first descent, 151
Forest and Crag, book, 218
Fort Lewis, Washington, 8
Forty-niners, 2, 25
fourteeners (14,000-foot peaks)
    all in Colorado climbed, 182
    all in Colorado skied, 191
    California, 31
    Colorado early history, 181
    early extreme descents in Colorado, 187
    easiest to climb and ski in Colorado, 195
    goal of climbing all 54 in Colorado, 182
    in Colorado climbed by Hayden Survey,
        198
    in Colorado Sangre de Cristo, 207
    last in Colorado climbed in winter, 186
    last one skied in Colorado, 192
    many other Colorado peaks, 192
    objective for ski alpinists, 182
free-heel skiing, XIX, 4, 19, 151
"free your heel—free your mind" 17
French, Roberts 11, 65, 66, 68, 127, 149
Friends Hut, Colorado, 190
Fuhrer Finger Couloir, Mount Rainier, 60

Gannet, Henry, 198
Gannet Peak, Wyoming, photo, 148
Gardner, Don, 15, 129
Garibaldi Névé, 94
Garibaldi Provincial Park, 88, 92, 93
Garibaldi, Mount
    origin of name, 93
Garibaldi, Mount, Névé Traverse, route
        description, 93
Garnet Canyon, XXIII, 1, 158
Garrett, Robbie, 150
Gaspe Peninsula XXIX
gear
    Improvements after WWII, 10
    obsession with, 17, 154
Genoe, California, 3
George, Hans, 29, 44, 45, 47
Gibson, Rex, 132, 133
Giese, Hans-Otto, 69

Gifford Pinchot National Forest, 70
Gillette, Ned, 15
Glacier Circle Cabin, 141
Glacier House Lodge, Canada, 125
Glacier National Park, 13, 125, 126, 142
glacier travel confuses ratings, XXXII
glaciers, number and coverage in Alaska, 101
Glade skiing, Utah, photo, 172
Glick, Loren, 170
glissade
    early on Mount Shasta, 79
    Middle Teton, 158
    via tin plate, Mount Adams, 69
    via trash bag, Mount Logan, 121
glisse, defined, XIX
glisse ratings, defined, XXX
Gmoser, Hans, 11, 12, 106, 129, 138
God, 69, 79
gold rush, Alaska, 102
Goodman, David, XXIX, 215, 217, 221,
        224, 228
Gordon, Mount, Alberta, history & route, 138
Gore Range, Colorado, 185
Goss, Elliot, 160
Gothic Peak, Colorado, 184
Gottschalk, Victor, 7
Grage, Hans, 69
Grand Teton National Park, 157, 158
Grand Teton, Wyoming, 1, 15, 19, 160
    filming on, 152
    first ascent, 147
    first descent, 150-153
    Hossack-MacGowen route, 154
    photo, 146
    skied by Rick Wyatt on lightweight
        Nordic gear, 168
    Teton Glacier, 154
Grandview, Alaska, 116
Granite Chief Wilderness, California, 34
Great Cairn Hut, Canada, 127
Great Depression, The, 164, 214
Great Divide Traverse, Canada, 129, 130
Great Sand Dunes National Monument,
        Colorado, 207
Green Mountains, Northeast, 211
Greenland, 3, 125, 127
Greylock, XXVII, 211, 218, 227, 228
Greylock, Mount
    early history, 227

see also Thunderbolt

Grizzly Peak, Colorado, XII, 185

groom, XXIX, 12, 46, 228

Gross Ventre Mountains, 1

Grouse Mountain , British Columbia, 86

guide service, first modern for backcountry
    skiing, 168

guidebooks, need to use, XXXII
    also see all route descriptions in text

guiding, mountain, first in U.S., 222

Gustofsen, Carl, 31

Haakonson, King, Norway, 1

Hackett, Bill, 110

Haemmerle, Florian, 7

Hagen, Grant, 148

Haldemeir, George, 174

Half Dome, California, 31

Hamlin Peak, Katahdin, 218

Hanscom, David, 169, 170

Harlin, John, 189

Harper Glacier, Denali, 105

Harriman, Averell, 6, 10, 200

Harris, Fred, 213, 214, 222, 224

Harz Mountains, Germany, 211

Hatch Peak, Alaska, route description, 110

Hatcher Pass, Alaska, 110

Hayden massif, Colorado, 200

Hayden Peak and Ski Hayden Peak
    panorama, 202

Hayden Survey, 181

Hayden Survey, on Mount Sopris, 204

Head, Howard, 10, 127

Head skis
    invention of, 10
    photo, 13
    sponsorship of Wickersham attempt, 106
    used for Bugaboo ski traverse, 127

Hearst, Randolph, 81

helicopter skiing, 58, 87
    accident on Mt. Robson, 131
    ethics, XXV-XXVII
    first commercial, 12
    in Valdez, Alaska, 101
    in Wasatch, 170
    Mt. Waddington
    Saudan on Mt. Hood, 75

Hennig, Andy, 7, 9, 10, 33

Hermit Hut, Canada, 13

High Rustler, Alta, 166

High Sierra, California, chapter section, 41

Highland Bavarian Corporation, 200

Hildebrand, Joel, 26, 36

Himalayan mountaineering, XXV

Himalayas, Fritz Stammberger in, 187

hippies, 151

History, importance of, XXVIII

Hoevenberg, Henry Van, 225

Holbrook, Mark, 170

Holecek, Phil, 80

Holy Cross, Mount of the, 187

Holzer, Heini, 11

Hood, Mount, Oregon, XXIV, 5, 57, 75, 77,
    78
    photo, skiing northwest side, 56
    route description, 74

Hossack-MacGowen route, Grand Teton, 154

Hotlum Glacier, 80

how-to book, early by Arthur Comey, 219

Hoyt, Fletcher 80, 81

Humboldt Peak, Southeast Flank, Colorado,
    route, 206

Hunter Mountain ski area, 149

hunting, 3, 28, 104, 215

Hutchinson, James, 41

huts
    10th Mountain Division, Colorado, 190
    allow access to backcountry, 13
    difference between Europe and North
      America, 190
    Canada, 126
    in Colorado, allow access to terrain, 190

Hvam, Hjalmar, 5, 8, 75

hydrographic apex, North America, 134

ice ax, XXX, 62, 78, 87, 105, 174

Icefall route, Tuckerman Ravine, 224

Icefields Parkway, Canada, 12, 127, 137, 138
    photo, 11

"If you fall, you die" origin of phrase, 189

Illecillewaet Glacier & Icefield, Canada,
    126, 129, 141

Independence Mine State Historical Park,
    Alaska, 111

Intermediate rated snow route, defined, XXX

Isaacs, John, 16

Jackson Lake, Wyoming, 150, 156, 157

Jackson, Wyoming, 147
Japanese television, ski alpinism covered by, 106
Jasper, Alberta, Chapter Section, 132
Jasper to Lake Louise traverse, Canada, 126
Jasper, Canada, 11, 15, 126, 127, 129, 132, 133, 134, 135, 136
Jefferson, Mount, New Hampshire, 224
Johannsen, Jackrabbit, 6, 21, 211, 213, 226
Juneau, Alaska, 101
Jungen, Troy, 21, 132

Kahiltna Glacier, Denali, 106, 108, 109
Kain, Conrad, 86, 125
Kammerlander, Hans, 21
Kamp, William, 164
Katahdin, Main, 217
    Baxter peak, true summit, 218
    bureaucracy, 221
    Chimney Couloir, 217
    first ascent, 218
    Great Basin, 221
    list of summits, 218
    location, 211
    logging on, 218
    modern skiing on, 217
    origin of name, 218
    photo, 221
    route, 218
Kautz, Lieutenant A. V., 63
Kazarinoff, Koli, 184
Kehrlein, Oliver, 81
Keller Peak Hut, California, 52
Kelley, Pam, 32
Kelner, Alexis, 169, 170
Kenai Mountains, Alaska, 102, 113, 114, 116
    Grandview ski train, 116
    chapter section, 114
Kennedy, Michael, 188
Kerouac, Jack, 41
Ketchum, Idaho, 7
Kieler, Jens, 58
King, Clarence, 41
Kit Carson Mountain, Colorado, 192
    first descent, 208
Kitchener, Mount, 134
Klinaklini Glacier, British Columbia, 89
Kluane National Park, Yukon, 122
Knife Ridge, Capitol Peak, 192

Koch, Stephen, 154
Kochs Couloir, Tetons, 152
Koedt, Peter, 157

La Porte, California, 25, 26
LaChapelle, Dolores, 165, 167, 170
LaChapelle, Ed, 167
LaFarge, Ann, 160
Lake Crowley, California, 46
Lake Louise, Alberta, 15, 126, 129, 137, 141
    chapter section, 140
Lake Magog, Canada, 126
Lake Placid Club, 212, 225
Lake Placid Olympic Games, 226
Lake Tahoe, California, 25, 33, 34, 37, 38
Landry, Chris 18, 31, 59, 66, 108, 187
    photos, 18, 189
Landry, Jean, 65
Lange, Bob, 10
Lange, Gunther, 200
Langmuir, Irving, 211
Langmuir, Ruth, 218
Laughlin, James, 164
Laughlin, Jay, 166
Leadville, Colorado, 181, 183, 205, 206
Lev, Peter, 168, 169, 174
Liberty Ridge, Mount Rainer, Cascades, 59, 66, 67
Lindley, Alfred, 104
Lion's Head gullies, Tuckerman Ravine, 224
Liske, Neil, 15, 129
Little Bear Peak, Colorado, 192
Little Cottonwood Canyon, Utah, 169, 174, 175, 176
Litz, Brian, 194
location and access, in defining classic route, XXVIII
Locke, Charlie, 15, 129
Lodgepole, California, 27
Logan, Mount, 101, 105, 120, 121
Logan, Mount, Yukon, 120
    route description, 121
    first ski descent, 121
logging roads, 88, 96, 144
Lone Peak Wilderness, Utah, 176
Lone Peak, Utah, 168
    route description, 176
Lone Pine, California, 49
Loness, Ed, 61, 63

longboards, 2
Longs Peak, Colorado, 181, 189
Loope, Fay, 225
Los Alamos Ranch School, 201
Lovelace, Shorty, 28
    photo, 29
Lowe, Alex, 170
Lund, Morten, 9
Lunn, Sir Arnold, 5
Luscomb, Florence, 218
Lyell, Mount, 28
Lynx Mountain, 86

MacCarthy, Captain A.H., 120
machinery, XXV, XXVI
Mammoth Lakes, California, 44, 45
Mammoth Mountain, California, 29, 44, 45
Man Who Skied Down Everest, The, 15
Manual of Ski Mountaineering, book XXI,
    28
Map
    Adirondack Mountains, antique, 215
    Alaska & Yukon, 123
    California Sierra, 55
    Canadian Rocky Mountains, 145
    Cascade Mountains, 83
    Coast Mountains, British Columbia, 99
    Colorado Rocky Mountains, 209
    Hayden Massif, Colorado, oblique
        drawing, 201, 202
    Northeastern U.S., 229
    North America, XVI, XVII
    Teton Mountains, 161
    Utah Wasatch Mountains, 179
Marcy military expedition, 181
Marcy, Mount
    early history, 225
    early ski guiding on, 226
    first winter ascent, 225
    route description, 226
Marjorie of the Wasatch, movie, 165
Maroon Bells, Colorado, 173, 198
    Fritz Stammberger first descent, 186-187
Matanuska valley, Alaska, 102
Matier, Mount , Anniversary Glacier, route,
    92
Matt, Toni, XXVII, 216
Matterhorn Peak, California, 28, 43, 44
    photo, 42

route description, 41
Matterhorn, Switzerland, 19, 151
Mattsson, Peter, 89, 90
Mazamas Mountain Club, 57, 75
McCoubrey, Alexander (A.A.), 6, 125, 140,
    141
    photo, 124
McCoy, Carl (Peanut), 15, 45
McCoy, Davey, 33
McGee, Mount, East Gully, California,
    route description, 45
McGowan, Graeme, 5, 182
McKinley, Mount
    name changed to Denali, XIX
McLean, Andrew 169
McNamara Hut, Colorado, 190
media extreme skiers, 19
Mendel Couloir, California, 31
Mendel, Mount, 31
Merriam, Florence, 163
Merry, Wayne, 15
Messner Couloir, Denali, XXVIII
Messner, Reinhold, XXV
Middle Teton, Southwest Couloir, route
    description, 158
Milana Jank, 214
Miller, Jack, 15
Mills, Enos, 181, 182
Mineral King, California, 7, 27, 28
mining, 26, 149, 163, 164, 181, 183, 204
Misery Hill, Mount Shasta, 81
Miura, Yuichorio, 15
    photo, 14
Monahan, Bob, 223
Montecucco, John, 21, 106
Montezuma Basin, Colorado, 198, 199
Moore, Dean, 154
Moore, Terris, 117, 118, 120, 217
Moore, Terris & Katrina, 117
Moran, Mount, Tetons, 11, 147, 154, 156,
    157, 158, 159, 160
    first descent, 150
Mosauer, Walter, 6, 26, 50, 51, 53, 69, 70
Mosquito Pass, Colorado, 2, 3, 181
Mount Baker Ski Area, 61
Mount McKinley National Park, *See* Denali
Mount Olympus Couloir, 170
Mountain Club of Alaska (MCA), 103, 112
mountain regions, defined, XXX

Mountaineers, The, mountaineering club, 49, 57
movies, 15
Moynier, John 33, 44, 45, 46, 47
Muir Snowfield, Mount Rainier, 64
Muir Trail, Sierra
    first ski, 26
    first repeat, 15
    traverse, long version, 32
    speed traverse, 17
Muir, John, 2, 26, 41, 49, 78, 182
Muldrow Glacier, Denali. *See* Denali
Munday, Don and Phyllis, 85, 87, 88, 90, 91, 92, 93
Munday, Mount, British Columbia
    first ascent, 88
    named, 90
    route description, 90
mushing, *see* dog sledding
Mystery Mountain, 87
    see also Mount Waddington

naked skiing, 220
Nansen Ski Club, 213
Nansen, Fridtjof, 3, 14, 22, 127
natural snow, 2, 18, 165
Neal, Sterling, 127
Nebo, Mount, Utah, 163, 168
Neffs Canyon, Utah, 171
Neil, Sterling, 11
Nelson, British Columbia, 143
New Hampshire Academy of Science, 223
Newcomb, Mark, 154
Niagara Falls, ski descent, 19
Nice, Trish, 15
Nicolai, Bill, 32, 59
Nordic descents, 17
Nordic downhill. *See* telemark and free-heel
Nordic ski equipment, 16
Norheim, Sondre, 2
North Maroon Peak, Colorado, XXVII, 15, 187
    first descent, 15
    photo, skiing north face, XXXI
North Pole, 3
North Star Mountain, Cascades, 8, 58
Northeast U.S.
    chapter, 211
    geography, 211

map, 229
Norwegian Civil War, 1
Norwegian Snowshoes (early name for skis), 163, 181
Norwegian Soldier, photo, 1
Novice-rated routes, defined, XXX

ore cars, 181
Ogilvey, David, 61, 63
Olympic Games, 5, 8, 226
On Ski over the Mountains, book, 50
one-upmanship, 19, 108, 152, 186
Olympus, Mount, Utah, Route Description, 170
Ontario Peak, California, 50
Orient Express, Denali, 108
Ostrander Hut, California, 28
Otis Couloir, Utah, 170
Ouray, Colorado, 181

Palmer chair lift, Mount Hood, 77
Pamola Peak, Katahdin, 217, 218
Paradise region, Mount Rainier, 64
Park City, Utah, 173
Parsons, Pete, 6, 133
Paul Petzoldt, XXIV, 9, 183
Paulke, Wilhelm, 4
Peak 10,420, Utah, route description, 173
Peale, Dr. Albert, 204
Pearl Pass, Colorado, 198, 199
Peck, Brad, 154
peddle turn, 165
Pehota, Eric, 89
Pelion Mountain–North Glacier, route description, 95
Pemberton, British Columbia, 92
Pennington, Janice, 187
Pepper, Fred, 141
Perfect Art, The, book, 28
Perlman, Eric, 31, 80, 132
Person, Dick, 157
Peter Grubb Hut, California, 36
Petersen, Trevor, 89
Petzoldt, Paul, XXIII, XXIV
Pfeiefferhorn, Northwest Col , Utah, 170
Pfeiffer, Bob, 207, 208
Philips Exeter Academy, 148
Pikers Peak, Mount Adams, Cascades, 70
Pikes Peak, Colorado, 5, 165, 182, 187

Pinnochio Couloir, Middle Teton, 152
Pioneer Lodge, 7
Placerville, California, 3
Plake, Glen, 19, 33
Pokress, Michael, photo, XXXI
politics, 170, 186
Pomona college, California, 50
Portland, Oregon, 74
postwar renaissance, 10
Pote, Winston, 223
Povolny, Brian, 60, 69
Powder Magazine, 18, 19
powder skiing, invention of. *See* Utah
    Wasatch chapter
Presley, Elvis, 187
Proctor, Charlie, 224
Prospectors Mountain, Tetons, 154
Ptarmigan Peak, Alaska, 102
Ptarmigan Trailhead. Mount St. Helens, 73
Ptarmigan Traverse, Cascades, 59
Pyramid Peak, Alaska, 112
Pyramid Peak, Colorado, XXI, 18, 19, 186,
    207
    East Face, 187
    East Face photo, 188

Quadra, Mount, North Face ski descent, 131
Quandary Peak, East Ridge, Colorado, route
    description, 195
Quebec, Canada, 6, 211

Racing the Sun Couloir, Raynolds West, 156
Railroad Couloir, Pikes Peak, 187
Rainier Mountaineering Guide Service, 64
Rainier, Mount
    Briggs's early descent, 66
    early access & first ascent, 63
    Emmons Glacier route, 63
    exact summit, 65
    first ski descent, 65
    first winter ascent, 64
    focus of Northwest alpinism, 64
    glaciers on, 63
    size, 57
    snowfall on, 63
    steam caves, 64
    weather, 68
Randall, Glenn, 192
rappell, XXVI

ratings, defined, XXX
Raymer, Tom, 160
Razorback Mountain, British Columbia, 90
Red Banks, Mount Shasta, 81
Red Lady Mountain, Colorado, 184
Redcloud Peak, Colorado, 187
Redline Traverse, California, 32
Reese, Rick, 168
Resplendent, Mount, Alberta
    climbed by Mundays, 86
    history of skiing, 132
    route description, 133
Rhoads, Jeff, 154
Richards, Rick, 198
Roaring Twenties, 26
Roberts, Dave, 65
Robinson, Doug, 15, 29, 47, 66
Robson, Mount, Canada, 86, 133
    attempts at descent, 131
    first ski descent, 132
    North Face, 21
    photo, 22
Roch, Andre, 5, 6, 8, 27, 75, 198, 200, 202
    photo, 7
rock climbing, rating, XXXII
Rocky Mountains, Colorado, chapter, 181
Rogers Pass, Canada, 10, 21, 125, 127, 131,
    chapter section, 141
Roloff, Louise, 112
rope, need for, XXX
rope tow, first in North America, 125
Roper, Steve, XXI
Roosevelt, Franklin D., President, 75
Rosicrucians, 79
Rough Neck Ski Club, Utah, 4, 164
Rowell, Galen, 31, 49
Ruff, Paul, 21
Ruth Glacier, Alaska, 109
Ruth Mountain, Cascades, 58
Ryan, Ted, 200

safety, XXVII
Saint-Exupery, Antoine, XXVI
Salida, Colorado, 207
Salt Lake City, Utah, 4, 163, 164, 170, 171,
    173, 174, 175, 177
San Antonio Hut, California, 7, 51, 52, 53
San Antonio Peak (Baldy), 50
    route description, 50

San Bernardino Mountains, California, 33
San Gabriel Mountains, California
   chapter, 25
   climate, 53
   chapter Section, 50
   location, 33
San Gorgonio, Mount, California, 47, 50
San Jacinto, Mount, California, 51
San Juan Mountains, Colorado, 182, 187
San Luis Valley, Colorado, 207
Sanford, Mount, Alaska, Sheep Glacier
   history of ski descent, 117
   route description, 120
Santa Fe, New Mexico, 207
Saskatchewan Glacier, Alberta, 135
Saudan, Sylvain, 11, 15, 59, 75, 78, 89, 109
Sawatch mountains, Colorado, 185
Sawtooth Mountains, XXIX, 7
Sawyer, Mike, 131
Schaffgotsh, Count Felix, 6
Schmeidtke, Cliff, 65
Schmidt, Scott, 19, 33
Schmidtz, Kim, 31
Schneider, Hannes, 1, 4, 183
Schniebs, Otto, XXIII, 183
Scott, Chic, 15, 21, 129, 133, 134, 138, 140,
   141, 143, 144
Seibert, Pete, 193
Selkirk Mountains, Canada, 125
Sequoia National Park, 27
Seven Steps of Paradise, Youngs Peak, 142
Seymour, Mount, British Columbia, 88
Seymour, Mount, Southwest Side, route
   description, 98
Shasta Indians, 79
Shasta, Mount, California, 57, 78, 79, 82
   early glissade, 79
   first descent, 80
   Kehrlein's Schuss, 81
   Lemuria, 79
   Old Ski Bowl, 81
   route description, Avalanche Gulch, 78
   weather, 81
Shea, Steve, 18, 152, 153
Sheep Glacier, *See* Sanford, Mount
Sherman Crater, Mount Baker, Cascades,
   62
Shuksan, Mount, North Face, Cascades, 58,
   60

Siberian Express, Mount Atwell, British
   Columbia, 90
Sibley, Paul, 185
Sierra Blanca, Colorado, 207
Sierra cement, 36
Sierra Club, 27, 49, 51, 81
   against development of Mineral King, 28
   Angeles chapter, 53
   Bulletin, 26
   founded by John Muir, 26
   more about founding, 41
   Mount Shasta hostel, 80
   Peter Grubb Hut, 36
   San Antonio Hut, 51
   ski hostels, 26
   Southern California Section, 50
   winter sports committee, 26
Sierra High Route, The, California, 32, 40
Sierra Mountains, California, chapter, 25
Sierra Spring Ski Touring, guidebook, 33
Silver Skis races, Mount Rainier, 65
Silver Star Mountain, Cascades, 58
Silverthrone, Mount, British Columbia, 89
Silvretta binding, 16
Sineau, Jacques, 184
single dipsy turn, 165
Singler, Gerhart, 21
Sir Sandford, Mount, 127
Ski boots, 1, 6, 8, 10, 11, 16, 17, 168
Ski Hayden Peak
   photos, first descent, 201
   route description, 200
ski instructors, 7, 9, 10, 45, 151, 217
ski lifts, 27, 212, 217
   used by early backcountry skiers in
     Alaska, 112
   built during postwar resort boom, 9
   early ones part of backcountry, 12
   first in Wasatch, Utah, 163, 165
   in Tetons, 148
   role in backcountry skiing, XXV
   used to practice telemark, 183
ski mountaineers, first in Europe, 211
ski patrol, 8, 21, 36, 174, 184
ski races, first in Colorado, 181
ski resorts, seduction, 27
Ski to Die, 19
ski train, North America's first, 164
Skiing Magazine, 80

Skillet Glacier, Mount Moran, Wyoming, 11, 150,
   route description, 156
   photos, XV, 156
skis
   composite, 10
   first use in Colorado, 181
   as a tool of alpinism, 19
   oldest, 1
Skoog, Lowell & Carl, 58, 59, 60
Snake Couloir, Mount Sneffels, 187
Snakepit, the, Utah, 165
Sneffels, Mount, Colorado, 187
Snow Dome, Alberta
   history, 134
   route description, 137
   first ski descent, 135
Snow King ski area, Wyoming, 148, 150, 154
snowboard
   as tool of glisse alpinism, XIX
   use by Steven Koch, 154
Snowcrest Lodge, California, 53
Snowmass Lake, Colorado, photo, XXXIII
snowmobile, XXV, XXVI, 62, 70, 111, 157, 170, 204, 208
snowplow, 4, 208, 217
snowshoe, XIX, 25, 102, 105, 106, 181, 213, 214, 225
Snowshoe Thompson, 3, 181
Snowy Range, 202
"soft, succulent people," John Muir said, 49
Solitude Ski Area, Utah, 173
Sopris, Mount, photo, 203
Sopris, Mount, Thomas Lakes Bowl, Colorado, route, 202
Sopris, Richard, 202, 204
Sormer, George, 168
sourdoughs, on Denali first ascent, 102
Southern Columbia Mountains, British Columbia, chapter section, 143
Southwest Couloir, Middle Teton, route description, 158
southwest couloir, Mount Moran, 154
Sovereign Mountain, Alaska, 102
Spalding Peak, Tetons, 155
Spanish missionaries, 206
Spearhead Traverse, British Columbia, 88
Sperlin, Robert, 61

Speyer, Fred, 165
Sphinx Glacier, Mount Garibaldi, 94
spiritual, 132
spirituality, 19, 41
Split Mountain, California, 33
Sports Illustrated, 18, 189
Spricenieks, Ptor, 21, 132
Squamish, British Columbia, 94
Squaw Valley, California, 31, 34
St. Elias Mountains, 16
   chapter section, 120
St. Elias, Mount, 101, 122
St. Helens, Mount, avalanches caused by eruption, 67
St. Helens, Mount, Cascades
   first ascent, 72
   skiing after eruption, 72
   volcanic eruption, 71
   route description, 71
St. Nicholas, Mount, Alberta, 139
Stage, Dan, 59
Stammberger, Fritz, XXVII, 11, 15, 185, 187
Star Peak, Colorado, 198
Starr King, Mount, 28
Static Peak—Southeast Face, Tetons, route description, 160
Steamboat Prow, Mount Rainier, 58
Steiner, Beat, 89, 90
Steiner, Otto, 7, 27, 28
stemming, 4
Stettner Couloir, Grand Teton, 151, 152
stick riding, 4
Stoneman, Darwon, 174
Stoney, Charles, 163
Strom, Erling, 6, 103, 104, 126
style, XXVII
Sullivan, Brian, 59
Summit Magazine, first published, 33
Summits & Icefields, guidebook, 21
Sun Valley Ski Guide, guidebook, 33
Sun Valley, Idaho, 6, 7, 8, 10, 33, 148, 164, 200
Sundance Ski Resort, 178
Superior, Mount, Utah
   early descents, 174
   route description, 173
survival skiing, 170, 217
Sweden, 1
Swiss guides, 13

Sylvester, Rick, 18, 31

Taconic Range, Northeast, 211
Tagert Hut, Colorado, 10, 197, 198
Tahoe Sierra, 3, 26, 33
Talkeetna Mountains, location in Alaska, 102
    chapter section, 110
Tallac, Mount, Northeast Face, California
    route description, 38
    photo of snowboarding on, 39
Taoism, 31
Taos, New Mexico, 21
Tardivel, Pierre, 21
Tejada-Flores, Lito, 18
Telegraph Peak, California, 50
Telemark County, Norway, 2
telemark turn
    origin, 2
    revival in Colorado, 183
    debate, 18
Telluride Film Festival, 19
Telluride, Colorado, 19, 181
Tent, The, Mount Garibaldi, 94
10th Mountain Division, 8, 10, 165, 168,
    183, 193
10th Mountain Hut Association, 190
Teocali Mountain, Colorado, 184
Terray, Lionel, 10
Teton Glacier, Grand Teton, 152, 154
Teton Mountains, Wyoming
    Bill Briggs in, 148
    chapter, 147
    early extreme skiing, 152
    early mountain men, 147
    early skiers, 147
    geography, 156
    map, 161
    recent extreme skiing, 154
    weather, 158
Teton Pass, Wyoming, 21, 147, 148
Teton Skiing, guidebook, 156
Thomas Lakes, Colorado, 204
Thomas, Gorden, 80
Thompson, David, 32
Thompson, Snowshoe, 25, 26
Thoreau, Henry David, 227
Thousand Dollar Run, Hatch Peak, Alaska
    110
Three Sisters, Oregon, photo, 59

Thunder Ridge, Utah, 175
Thunderbolt Trail, Mount Greylock
    early history, 227
    route description, 228
Timberline Lodge, Oregon, XXIV, 75, 76,
    77, 78
Timpanogos, Mount, Utah, 168, 177
    Summer Ski Classic race, 177
    Timp Glacier, 177
    Timp Hike, 177
    route description, 177
Timpanogotzis Indians, 177
tin plate descent, Mount Adams, 69
Tincan Ridge, Alaska, route description, 114
Tinniswood, Mount, 89
Tirich Mir, Pakistan, 187
toe iron bindings, 4
Tolcat Couloir, Mount Olympus, Utah 170,
    171
Tom, Mount, California, 25, 29, 31
    route description, 46
Tournier, Andre. See
Trail and Timberline, CMC journal, 182
Trail Glacier, Alaska, 117
tramway on Hayden Peak, Colorado, 200
trap-crust, 28, 57, 157, 169
Tuckerman Ravine, Mount Washington,
    XXI, XXVII, 149, 150, 217, 222, 223
    photo, 210
    Inferno race & schuss of the Headwall,
    216
    route description, 224
Turiano, Thomas 154, 157, 160
Turnagain Arm, Alaska, 102, 114
Turnagain Pass, Alaska, 114
Twin Peaks, California
    photo, 35
    route description, 34
Twin Peaks, Utah, 168

Udall, Brad, 17
Udall, Mark, 16
Udall, Randall, 16, 17
Ueki, Tsuyoshi, 15, 106, 110
Underhill, Robert, 220
U-Notch Couloir, California, 31, 32
Utah Department of Transportation (DOT),
    169, 170
Utah Wasatch Mountains, map, 179

Vadasz, Bela, XXII

Vail ski resort, Colorado, 193

Valdez, Alaska, 101

Vallencant, Patrick, XXVI, 19,
    attempt on Wickersham Wall, Denali, 106

Vancouver, British Columbia, 85, 86, 87,
        88, 91, 92, 93, 94, 95, 96, 98

Varsity Outdoor Club (VOC), 88

vegetation, in Northeastern mountains, 217

V-Notch Couloir, California, 3, 32

volcanoes, XXIX, 57, 63, 69, 74

Waddington, Mount, British Columbia
    first ski descent, 89
    photos, 84, 90, 91
    ski traverse from, 88

Wapta Icefield, Alberta
    history of, 138
    route description, 138
    chapter section, 138

Ward, Jim, 15

Warren, Tom, XXIII

Wasatch Mountain Club, 8, 163, 164, 165

Wasatch Mountains, 4

Wasatch Mountains, Utah
    chapter, 163
    chute skiing, 170
    Dolores LaChapelle in, 167
    early huts, 10
    early ski huts, 164
    early skiing, 164
    first skier avalanche death, 165
    geography & weather, 163
    guidebook, 169
    in Summit Magazine, 168
    invention of powder skiing in, 165
    map, 179
    politics, 170
    training of military skiers in, 165

Wasatch Tours, guidebook, 169, 171, 173,
    175, 176

Washburn, Bradford, 110, 120, 118

Washington, Mount, 150, 221, 217
    carriage road, 222
    Dartmouth College skiers, 223
    first ascent, 222
    first skiers on, 222
    Joe Dodge on, 222

record wind speed, 223
severe weather, 222
weather observatory, 223
Toni Matt on, 216
see also Tuckerman Ravine

Waterman, Guy and Laura, 216, 218, 219,
    220

Waterman, Jonathan, 23, 101, 103, 106

Watson, George, 164

Weamer, Howard, 28

Weber, Sepp, 121

wedlin, 10

Weiss, Joe, 5, 132, 133, 135, 138

Welsh, Charles E., 65

West Buttress, Denali, Alaska, route
        description, 109

Westcliffe, Colorado, 192, 208

Wetterhorn, 2

Whedon, John, 170

Wheeler Survey, 181

Wheeler, A.O., 126

Whetstone Mountain, Colorado, 184

Whirlpool River, Alberta, 129

Whistler, British Columbia, 21, 60, 88, 89,
    90

White Mountain Peak, California, 31

White Mountains, California, 31, 213, 217

White, Clifford, 135, 138

Whitmer, Gordon 186

Whitney Portal, California, 32, 49

Whitney, Mount, 2, 25, 26, 27, 29, 33,
    direct ski descent, 47

Whitney, Mount, Mountaineers Route,
    California
    John Muir first ascent, 2, 49
    first descent of route, 49
    route description, 47

Whittaker, Jim & Lou, 66

Whymper, Edward, 2

Wickersham Wall, Denali
    photo, 100
    ski descent, 21, 100, 106, 107, 108

Wiessner, Fritz , 214

Wild Men From Heaven, Utah, 165

wilderness
    Alaska & Yukon as, 101
    in Utah, 170

Williams College, 227

Williamson, Jed, 15

Williamson, Mount, California, 31, 47
Wilson, Ted, 168
Wind River mountains, Wyoming, ski
    traverse, 16
Wintun Glacier, 80
Wister, Mount, 154
Wolley, Hermann, 134
Wolling, Mark, 154
Woodstock, Vermont, 127
Woolsey, Elizabeth, 148, 174
Works Progress Administration (WPA), 164
World War I, 26, 86
World War II, 8, 10, 27, 165, 183, 198, 200,
    201
Wrangell Mountains, Alaska, 102, 117, 120
  chapter section, 117
Wyatt, Rick 17, 168
Wyoming, *see* Teton chapter

Y Couloir, Utah, route description, 175
Yaekle, Leonard, 80
Yoho district, Alberta, 140
Yosemite Valley, XXI, 18, 29
Youngs Peak, British Columbia, route
    description, 142
Yout, Larry, 47, 49
Yukon map, 123
Yukon and Alaska, chapter, 101

Zdarsky, Mathias, 3
Zenophon, historian, 1
Zwickey, Dr. F., 47

Louis Dawson ▶